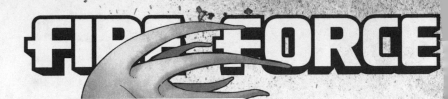

FIRE FORCE

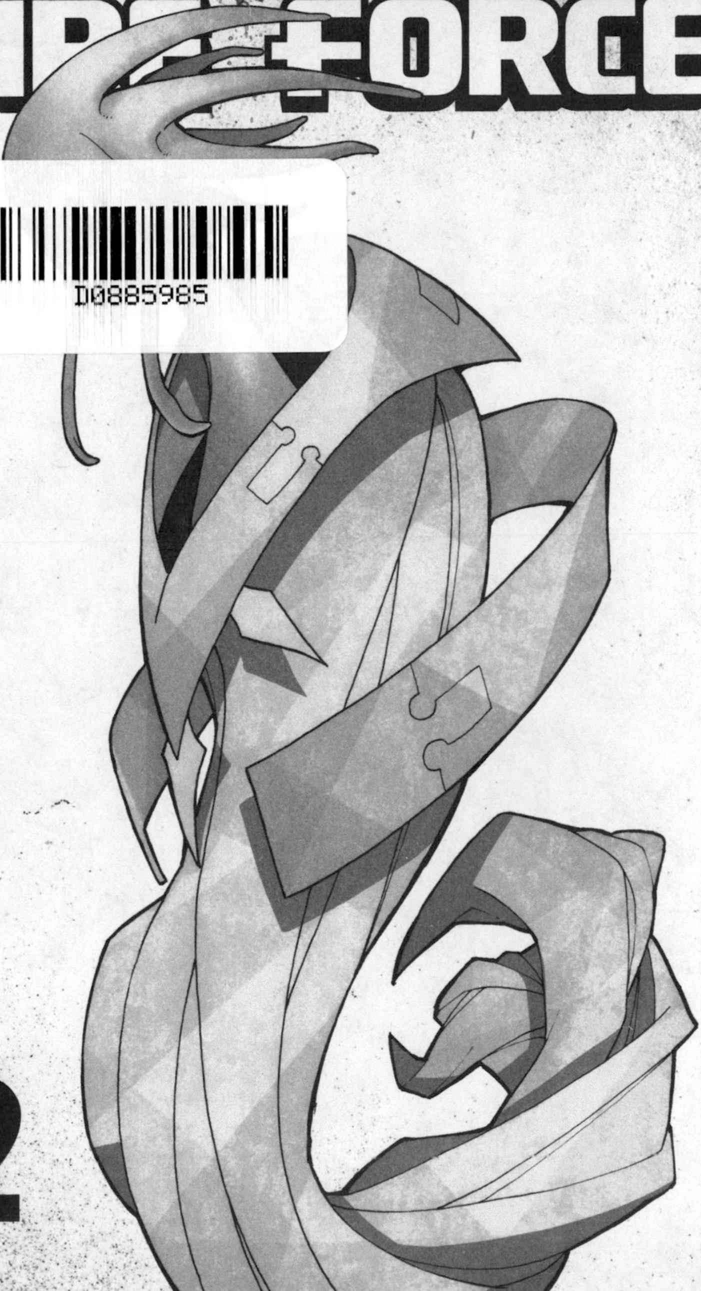

22

ATSUSHI
OHKUBO

battle 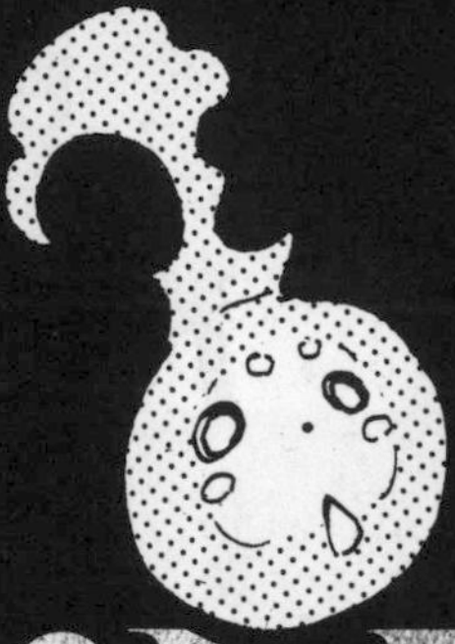 the child.

VOL. 22

ATSUSHI OHKUBO

Spare the
and
spoil

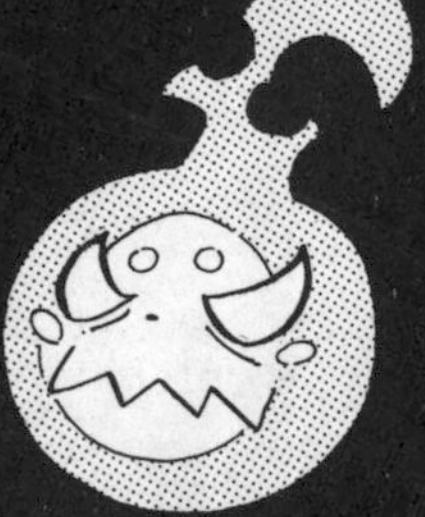

FIRE FOR

SPECIAL FIRE FORCE COMPANY 8

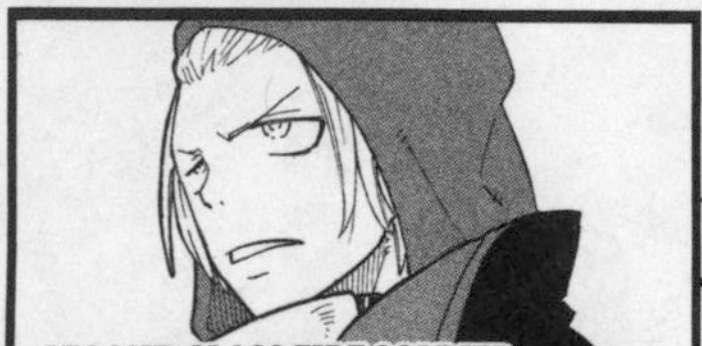

SECOND CLASS FIRE SOLDIER (THIRD GENERATION PYROKINETIC)

ARTHUR BOYLE

Trained at the academy with Shinra. He follows his own personal code of chivalry as the self-proclaimed Knight King. He's a blockhead who is bad at mental exercise. But girls love him. He creates a fire sword with a blade that can cut through most anything. He's a weirdo who grows stronger the more delusional he gets. He now confronts the Destroyer Dragon...

CAPTAIN (NON-POWERED)

AKITARU ŌBI

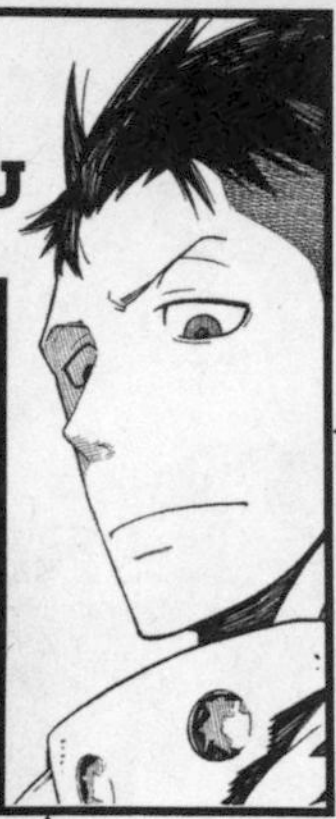

The caring leader of the newly established Company 8. His goal is to investigate the other companies and uncover the truth about spontaneous human combustion. He has no powers, but uses his finely honed muscles as a weapon in a battle style that proves his worth as Captain. Currently he is being detained by the military.

WATCHES OUT FOR

TRUSTS

IDIOT!!

WATCHES OUT FOR

TRUSTS

STRONG BOND

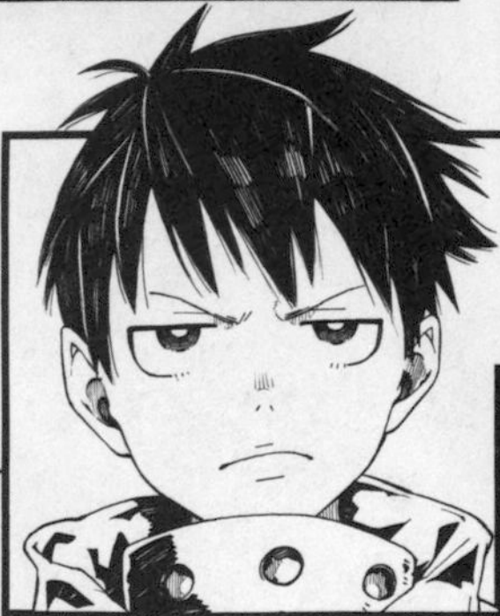

SECOND CLASS FIRE SOLDIER (THIRD GENERATION PYROKINETIC)

SHINRA KUSAKABE

The bizarre smile that shows on his face when he gets nervous has earned him the derisive nickname of "devil," but he dreams of becoming a hero who saves people from spontaneous combustion! His weapon is a fiery kick. He wields a special flame called the Adolla Burst. In Asakusa, he mastered the hysterical strength of the fight-or-flight response. He is currently fighting Burns at Fuchū.

A NICE GIRL

LOOKS AWESOME ON THE JOB

A TOUGH BUT WEIRD LADY

HANG IN THERE, ROOKIE!

TERRIFIED

STRICT DISCIPLINARIAN

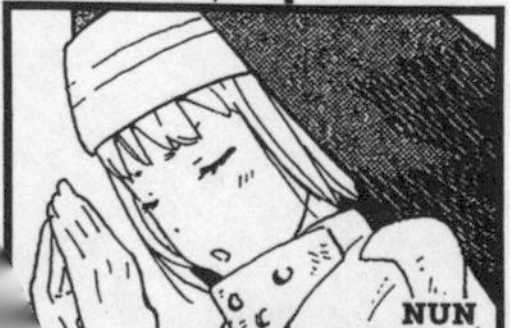

NUN (NON-POWERED)

IRIS

...r of the Holy Sol Temple, her ...are an indispensable part of ...shing Infernals. Personality- ...'s no less than an angel. ...are big. Very big. She ...d incredible resilience ...Infernal hordes. She is ...8's sunflower. Except

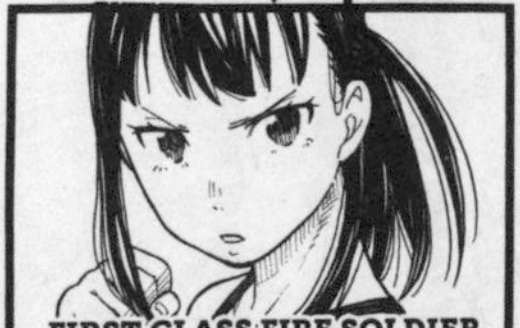

FIRST CLASS FIRE SOLDIER (SECOND GENERATION PYROKINETIC)

MAKI OZE

A former member of the military, she is an excellent fighter who controls fire. She's a cool lady, but is mad about love stories, and her beauty is overshadowed by her "head full of flowers and wedding bells." She's friendly, but goes berserk when anyone comments on her muscles. She temporarily returned to the Imperial Army, but she is now back in Company 8 and has been promoted to unit leader.

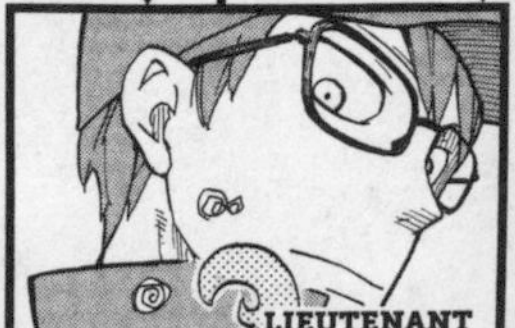

LIEUTENANT (SECOND GENERATION PYROKINETIC)

TAKEHISA HINAWA

A dry, unemotional ex-military man, whose stern discipline is feared among the new recruits. He helped Ōbi to found Company 8. He never allows the soldiers to play with fire. The gun he uses is a cherished memento from his friend who became an Infernal.

THE GIRLS' CLUB

RESPECTS

SPECIAL FIRE FORCE COMPANY 1

HOLY SOL TEMPLE + "EVANGELIST"

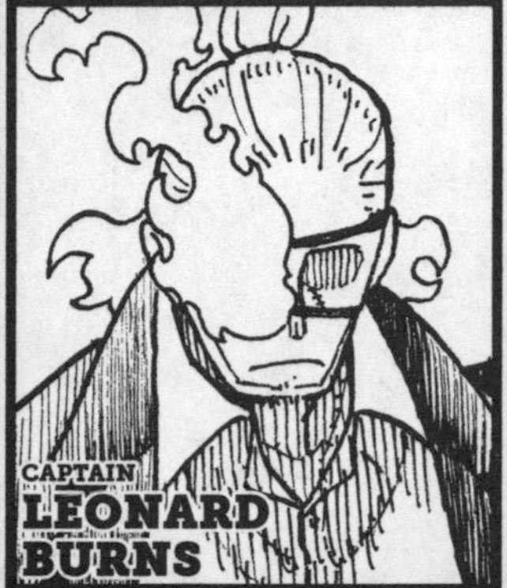

CAPTAIN
LEONARD BURNS

Has the Stigma of one who has experienced an Adolla Link. As a devout priest of the Holy Sol Temple, he decides to turn against Company 8, falling in with the White Clad soldiers who claim to be doing the will of the Great Sun God.

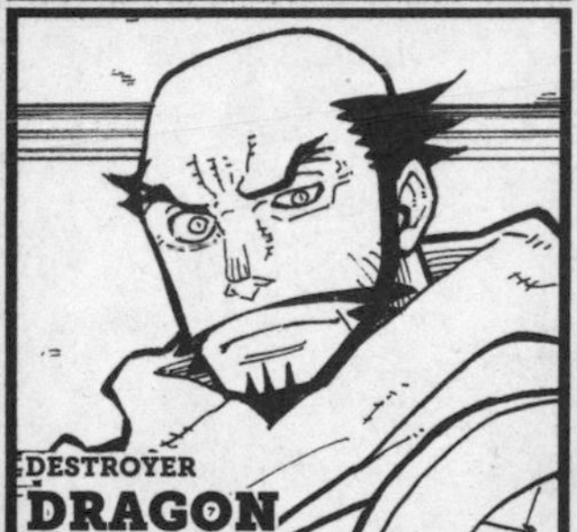

DESTROYER
DRAGON

An overpowering presence, breath that burns with a single exhale, adamantine scales...with powers equal to his name, the dragon stands before the self-proclaimed Knight King Arthur.

TRAITORS TO THE EMPIRE

VS.

CAPTORS OF THE CAPTAIN

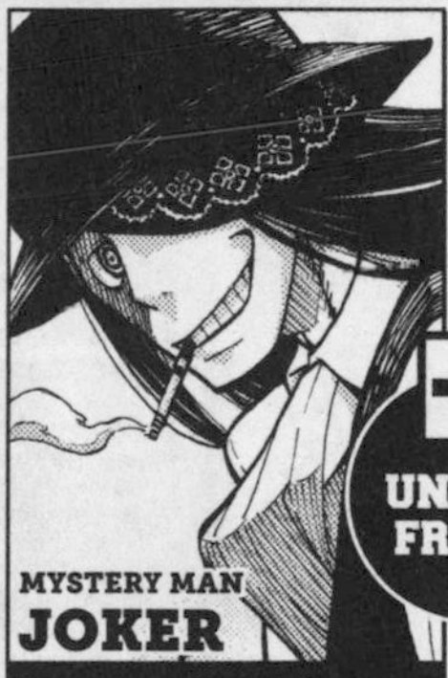

MYSTERY MAN
JOKER

A man who appears out of nowhere, who has turned against the Tokyo Empire in his search for the world's truth. He was raised as a member of the Holy Sol Temple's secret death squad, the Holy Sol's Shadow, but has left the organization.

+ UNITED FRONT

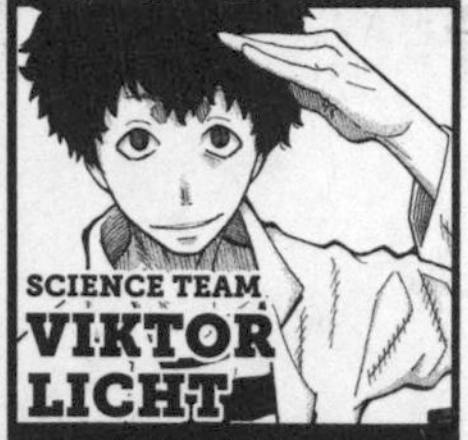

SCIENCE TEAM
VIKTOR LICHT

A suspicious genius deployed from Haijima Industries to fill the vacancy in Company 8's science department. Has confessed to being a Haijima spy.

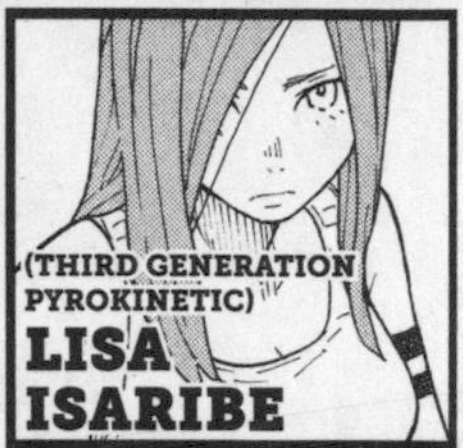

(THIRD GENERATION PYROKINETIC)
LISA ISARIBE

A former Knight of the Ashen Flame sent by Dr. Giovanni to spy on Vulcan, she has now joined Company 8 as she recovers from her trauma. She controls tentacles of flame.

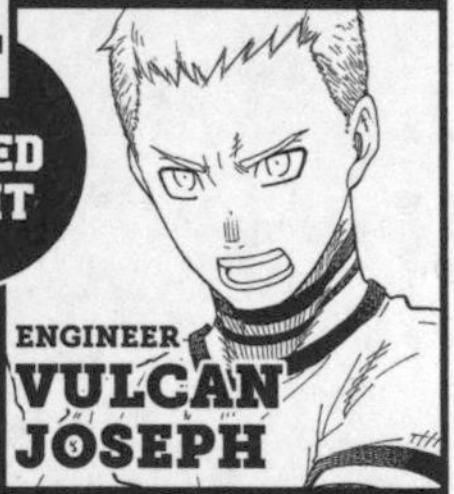

ENGINEER
VULCAN JOSEPH

The greatest engineer of the day, renowned as the God of Fire and the Forge. The weapons he created have increased Company 8's powers immensely.

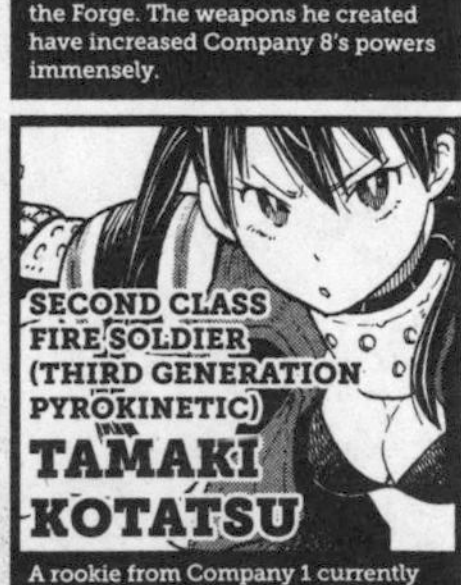

SECOND CLASS FIRE SOLDIER (THIRD GENERATION PYROKINETIC)
TAMAKI KOTATSU

HAS HIM ON HER MIND

A rookie from Company 1 currently in Company 8's care. Although she has a "lucky lecher lure" condition, she nevertheless has a pure heart. She controls nekomata-like flames. While training in Asakusa, she shed her bad habits.

SUMMARY

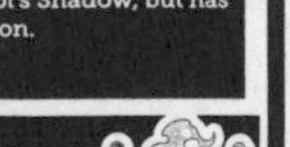
SPUTT
SPUTT

The Holy Sol Temple has joined forces with the Evangelist. To rescue Captain Ōbi from their clutches, Company 8 teams up with Joker, the man from the shadows, and together they storm Fuchū Grand Penitentiary. Shinra and Joker are first on the scene, where they are met by Company 1 Captain Burns. Unconvinced of Burns's new allegiance, Shinra engages him in battle. Meanwhile, the rest of the Company is ambushed by the Destroyers, a team of experts who specialize in fighting pyrokinetics. They have defeated Gold and Stream, and the next Destroyer, Dragon, now stands before Arthur....

FIRE FORCE 22
CONTENTS

YOU
ALWAYS DO
THIS.

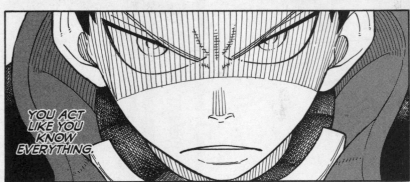

YOU ACT
LIKE YOU
KNOW
EVERYTHING.

BUT YOU
WON'T SAY
ANYTHING.

YOU ALWAYS
BELIEVE THAT
YOUR OWN
CONCLUSIONS
ARE CORRECT.

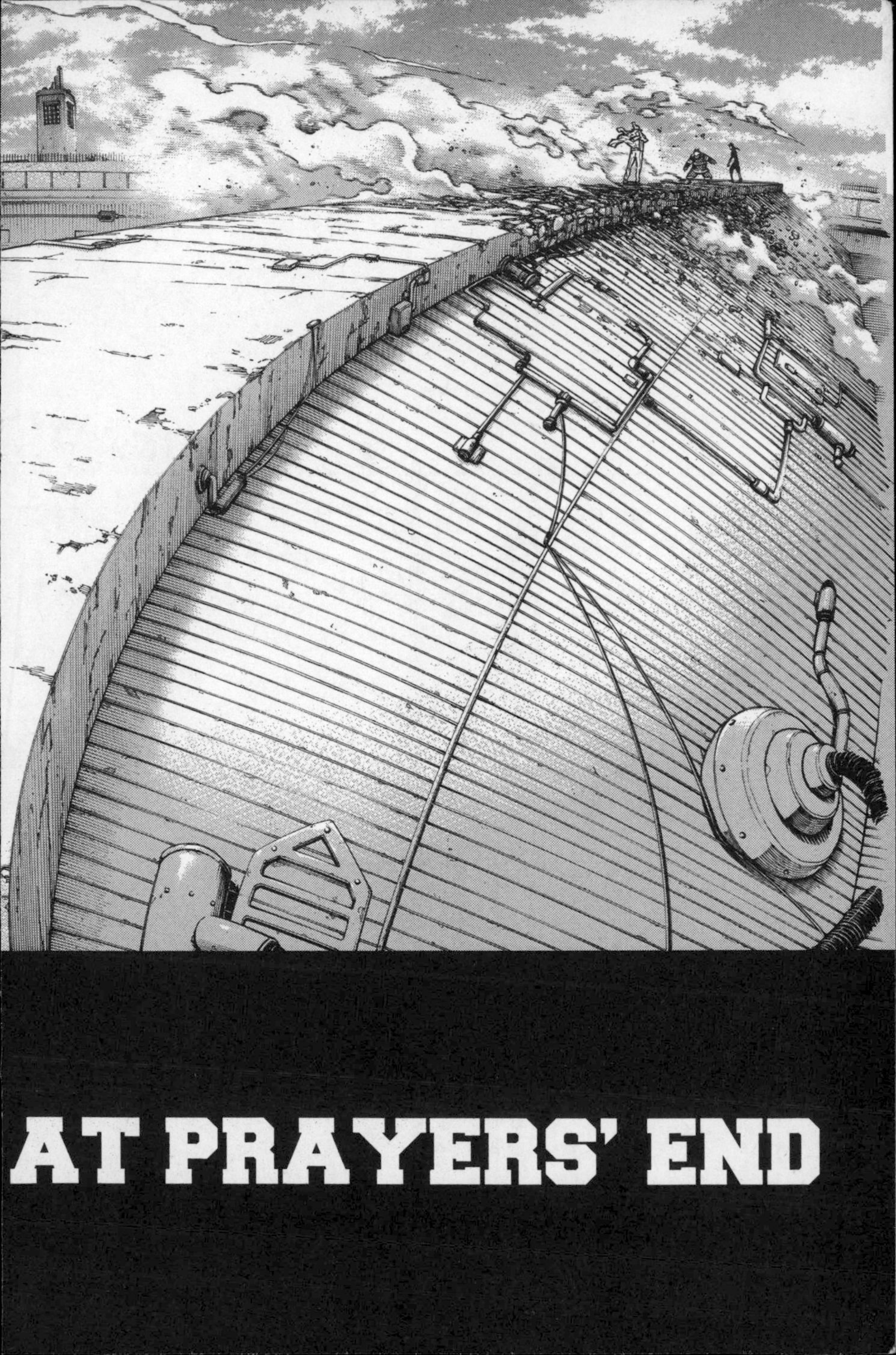

AT PRAYERS' END

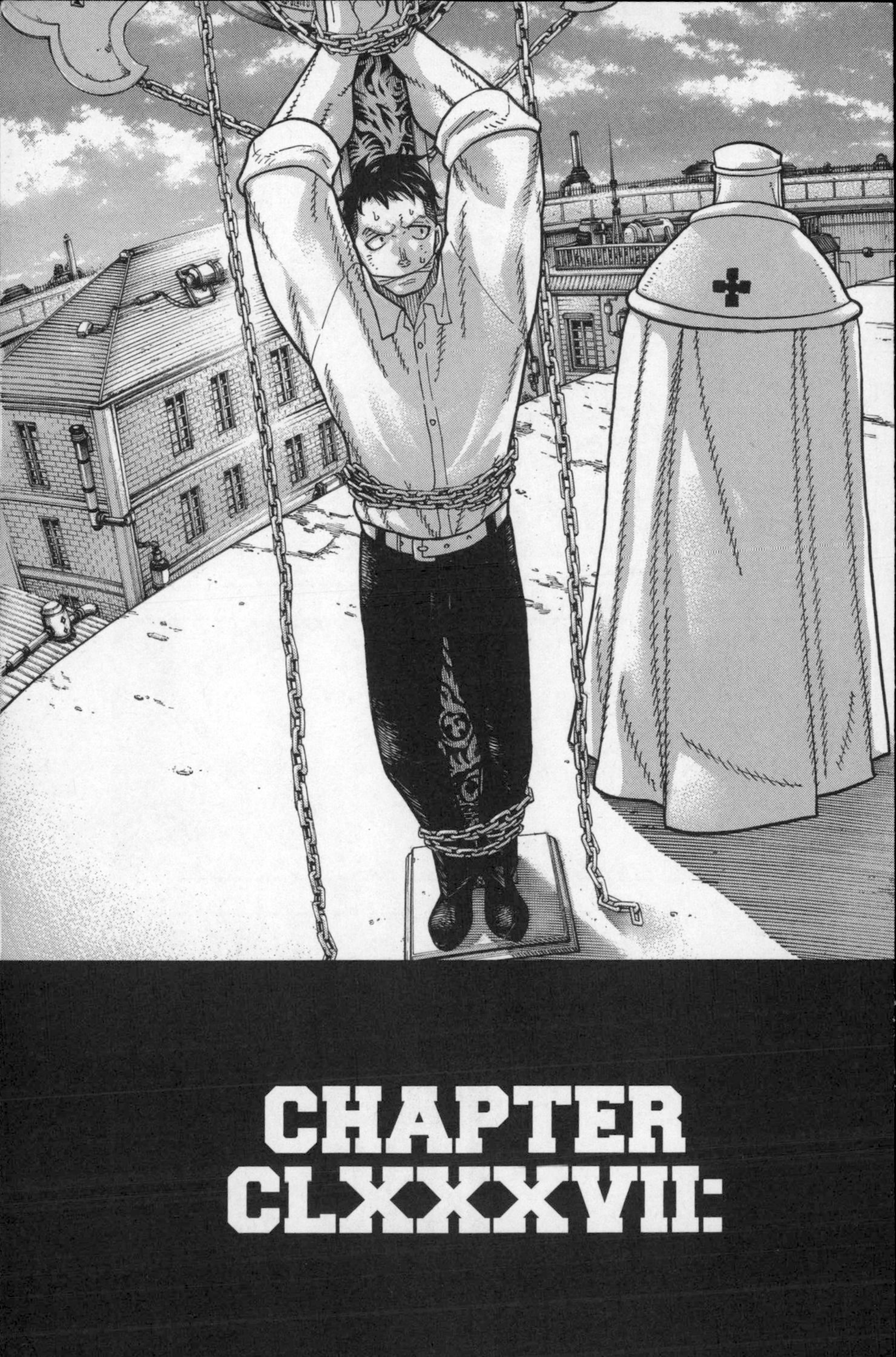

CHAPTER CLXXXVII:

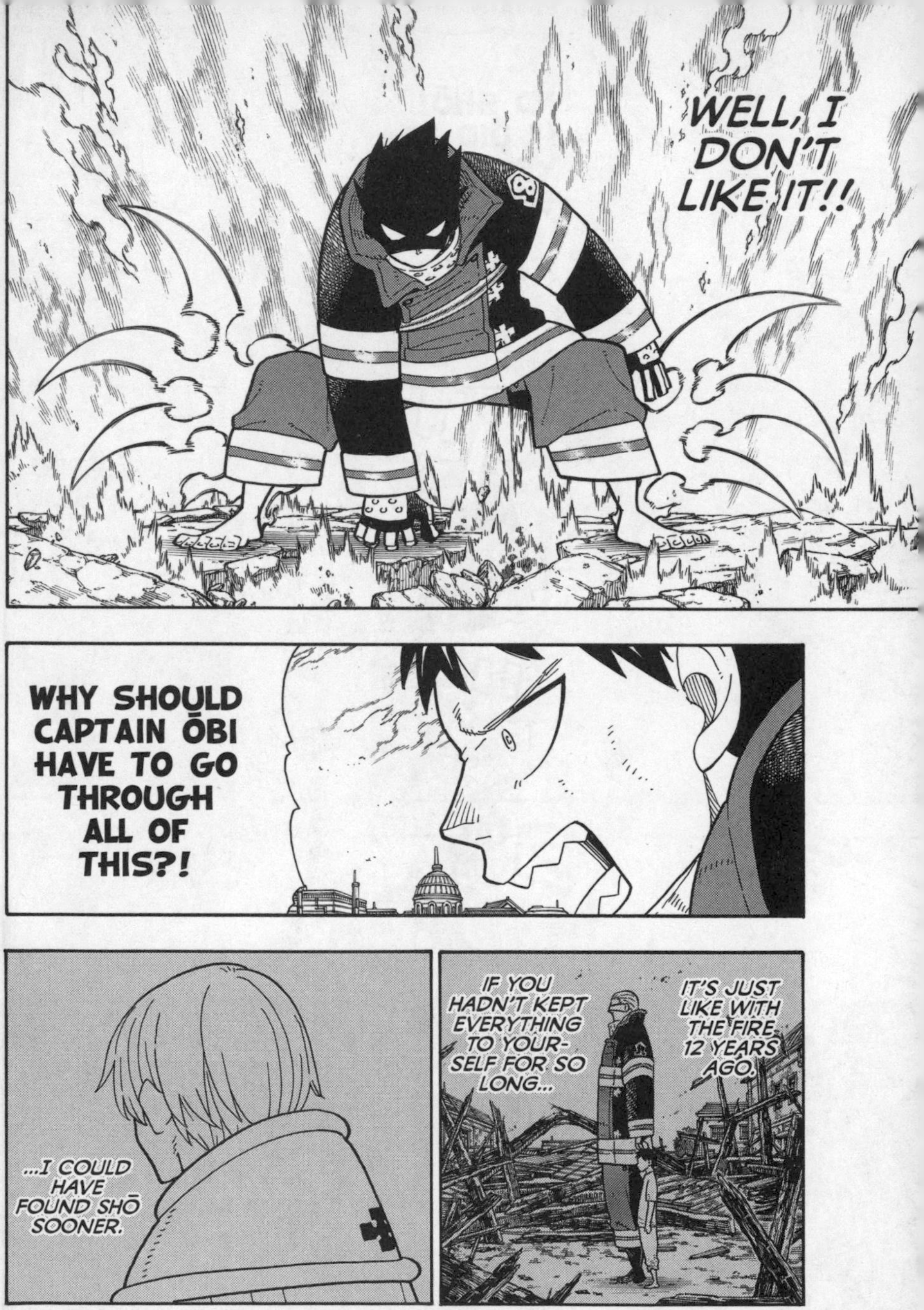
WELL, I DON'T LIKE IT!!
WHY SHOULD CAPTAIN ŌBI HAVE TO GO THROUGH ALL OF THIS?!
IT'S JUST LIKE WITH THE FIRE 12 YEARS AGO.
IF YOU HADN'T KEPT EVERYTHING TO YOUR-SELF FOR SO LONG...
...I COULD HAVE FOUND SHŌ SOONER.

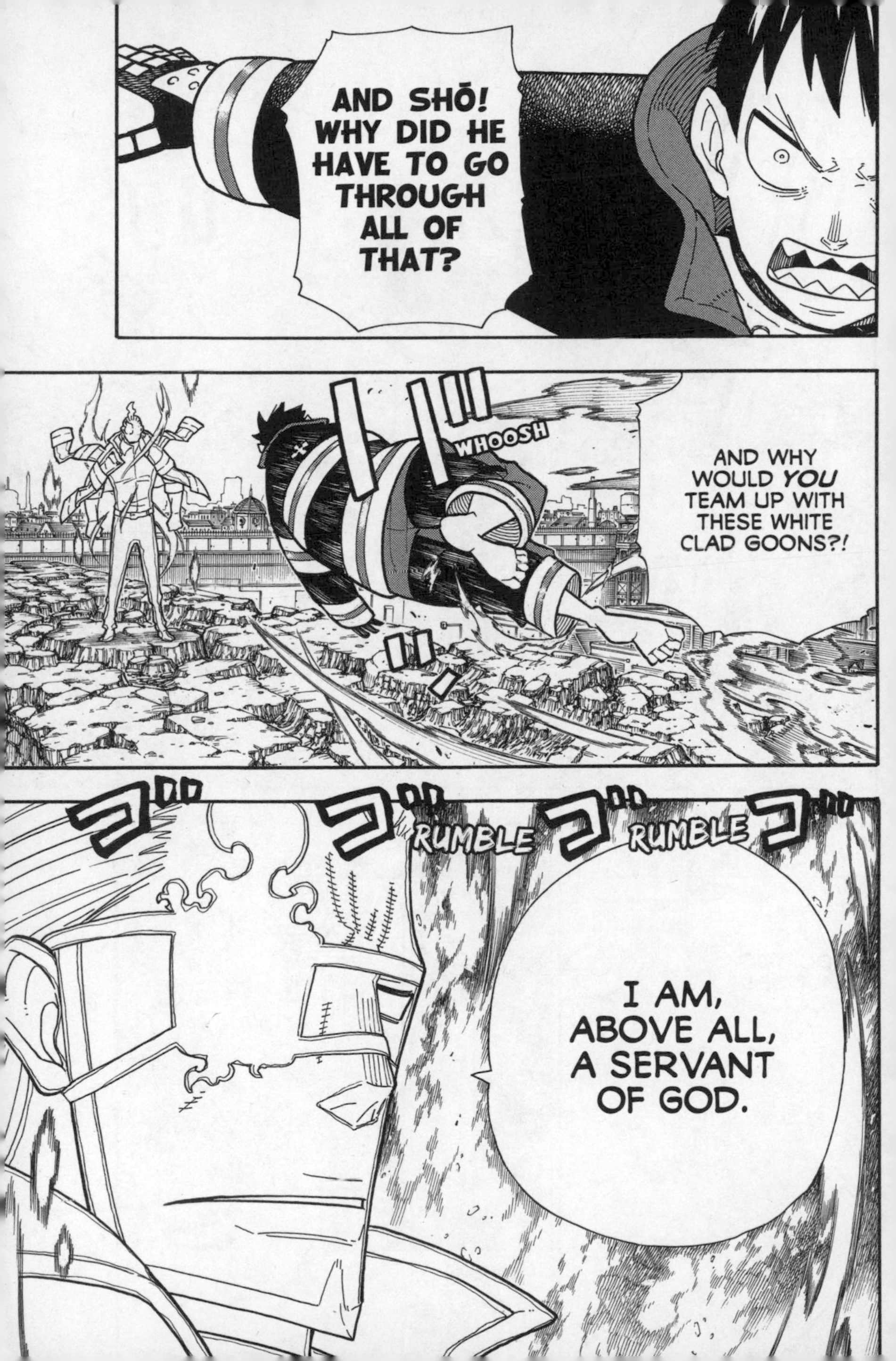
AND SHŌ! WHY DID HE HAVE TO GO THROUGH ALL OF THAT?
AND WHY WOULD *YOU* TEAM UP WITH THESE WHITE CLAD GOONS?!
WHOOSH
RUMBLE
RUMBLE
I AM, ABOVE ALL, A SERVANT OF GOD.

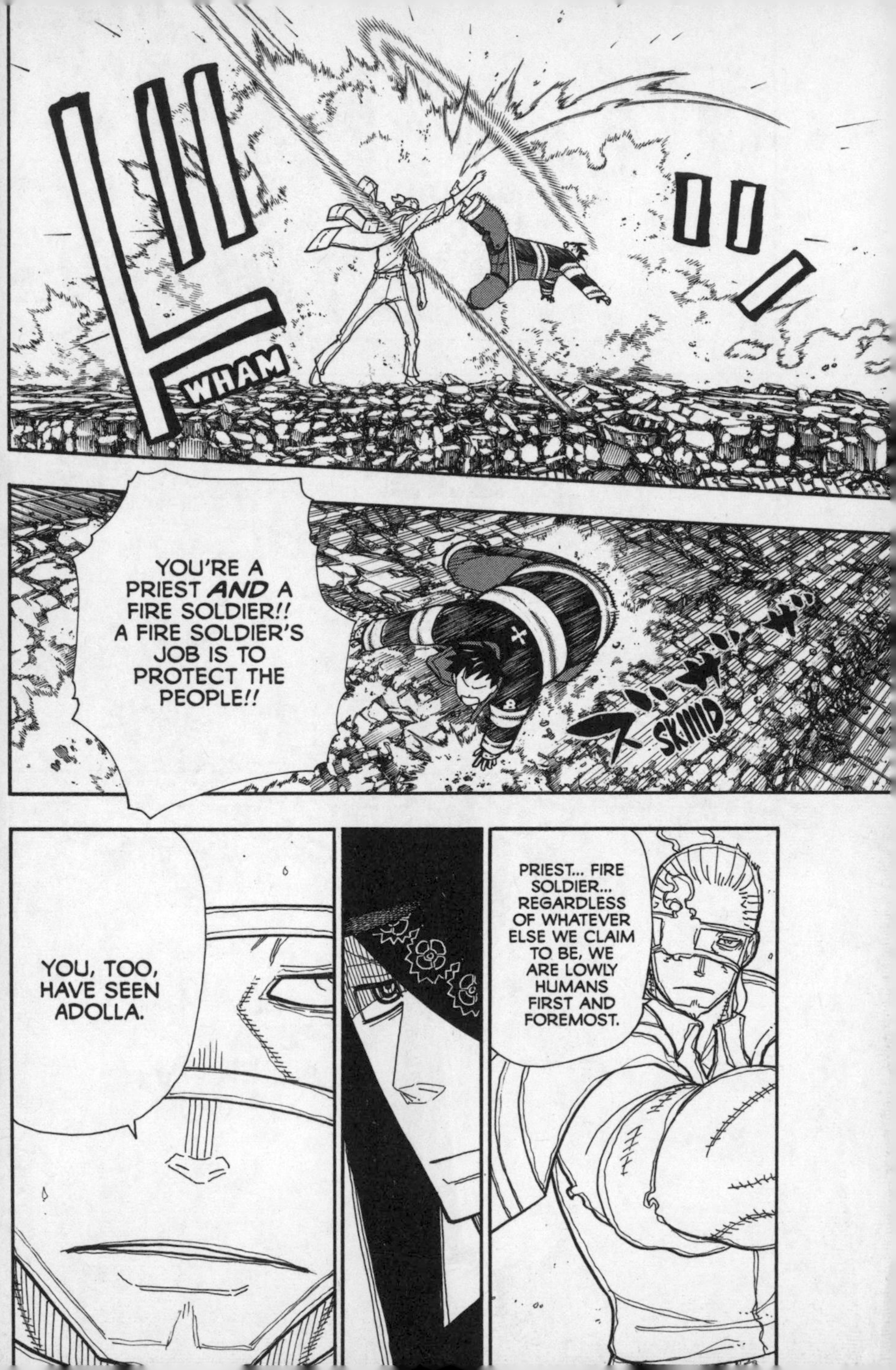
WHAM
SKIIID
YOU'RE A PRIEST *AND* A FIRE SOLDIER!! A FIRE SOLDIER'S JOB IS TO PROTECT THE PEOPLE!!
PRIEST... FIRE SOLDIER... REGARDLESS OF WHATEVER ELSE WE CLAIM TO BE, WE ARE LOWLY HUMANS FIRST AND FOREMOST.
YOU, TOO, HAVE SEEN ADOLLA.

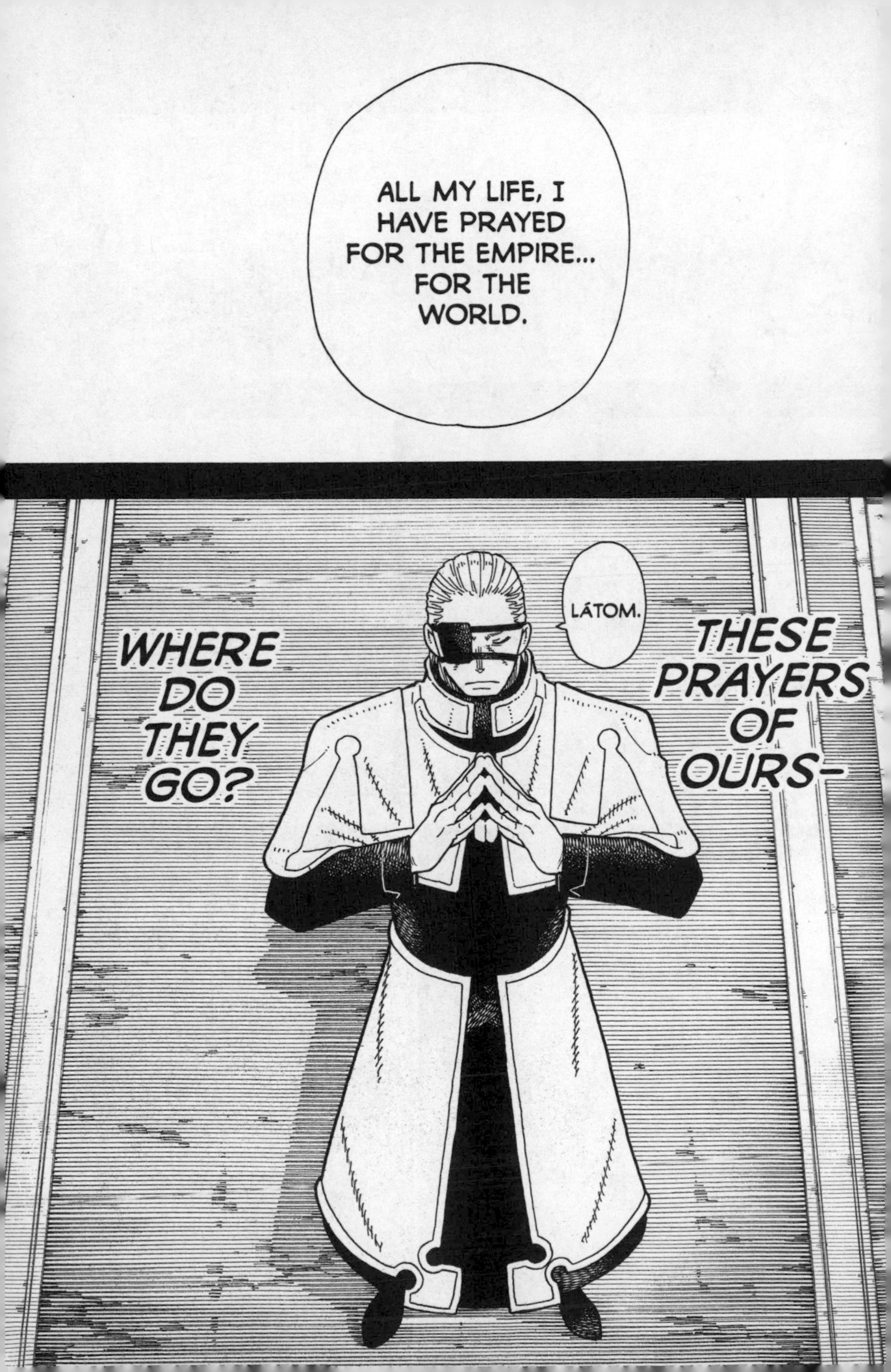
ALL MY LIFE, I HAVE PRAYED FOR THE EMPIRE... FOR THE WORLD.
THESE PRAYERS OF OURS-
LÁTOM.
WHERE DO THEY GO?

AH HA HA! HA

AH HA HA! HA

I'M IN AWE OF THAT BOY'S CONCENTRATION WHILE PRAYING.

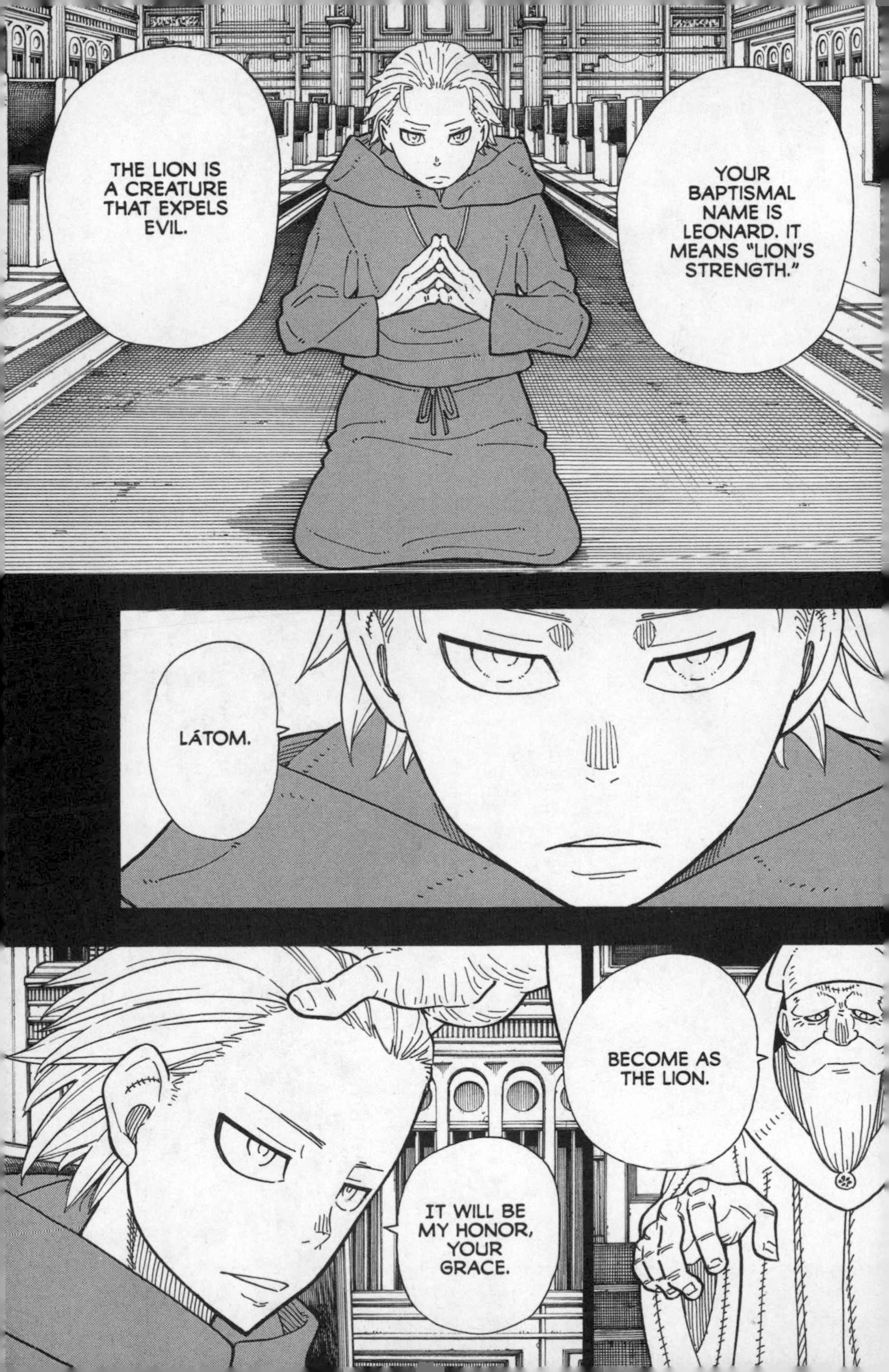
YOUR BAPTISMAL NAME IS LEONARD. IT MEANS "LION'S STRENGTH."
THE LION IS A CREATURE THAT EXPELS EVIL.
LÁTOM.
BECOME AS THE LION.
IT WILL BE MY HONOR, YOUR GRACE.

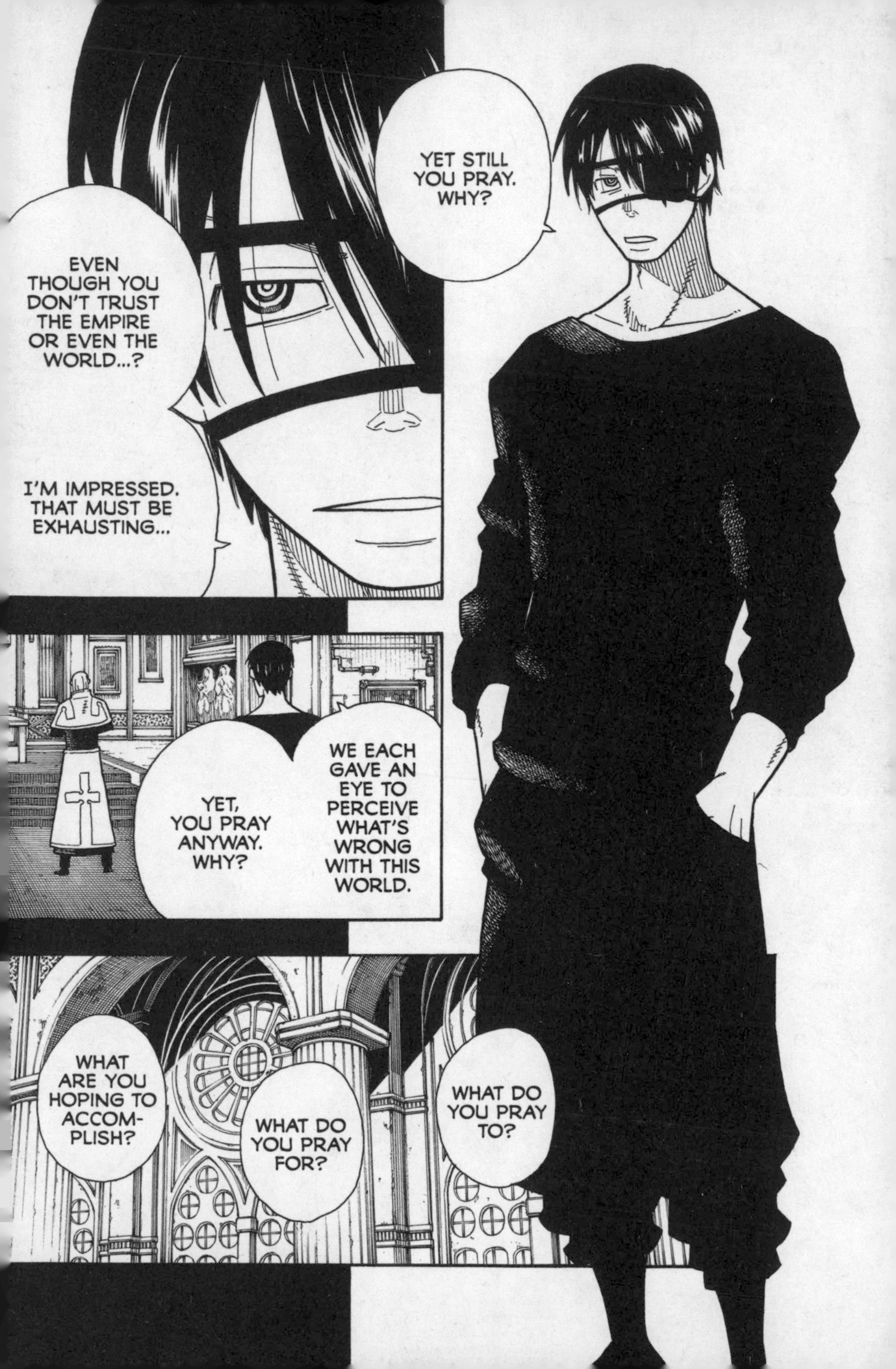
YET STILL YOU PRAY. WHY?
EVEN THOUGH YOU DON'T TRUST THE EMPIRE OR EVEN THE WORLD...?
I'M IMPRESSED. THAT MUST BE EXHAUSTING...
WE EACH GAVE AN EYE TO PERCEIVE WHAT'S WRONG WITH THIS WORLD.
YET, YOU PRAY ANYWAY. WHY?
WHAT DO YOU PRAY TO?
WHAT DO YOU PRAY FOR?
WHAT ARE YOU HOPING TO ACCOMPLISH?

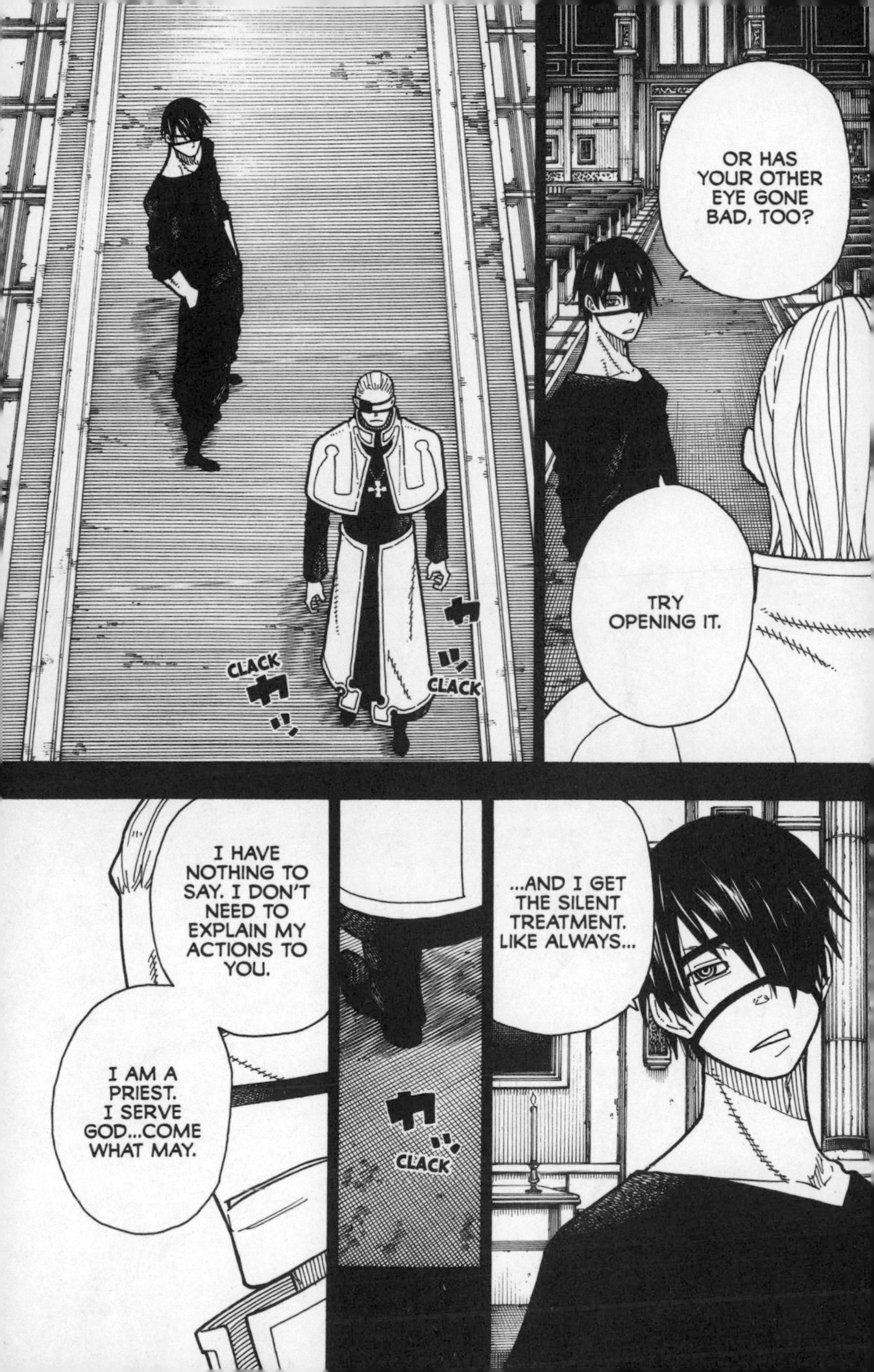
OR HAS YOUR OTHER EYE GONE BAD, TOO?
TRY OPENING IT.
CLACK
CLACK
...AND I GET THE SILENT TREATMENT. LIKE ALWAYS...
CLACK
I HAVE NOTHING TO SAY. I DON'T NEED TO EXPLAIN MY ACTIONS TO YOU.
I AM A PRIEST. I SERVE GOD...COME WHAT MAY.

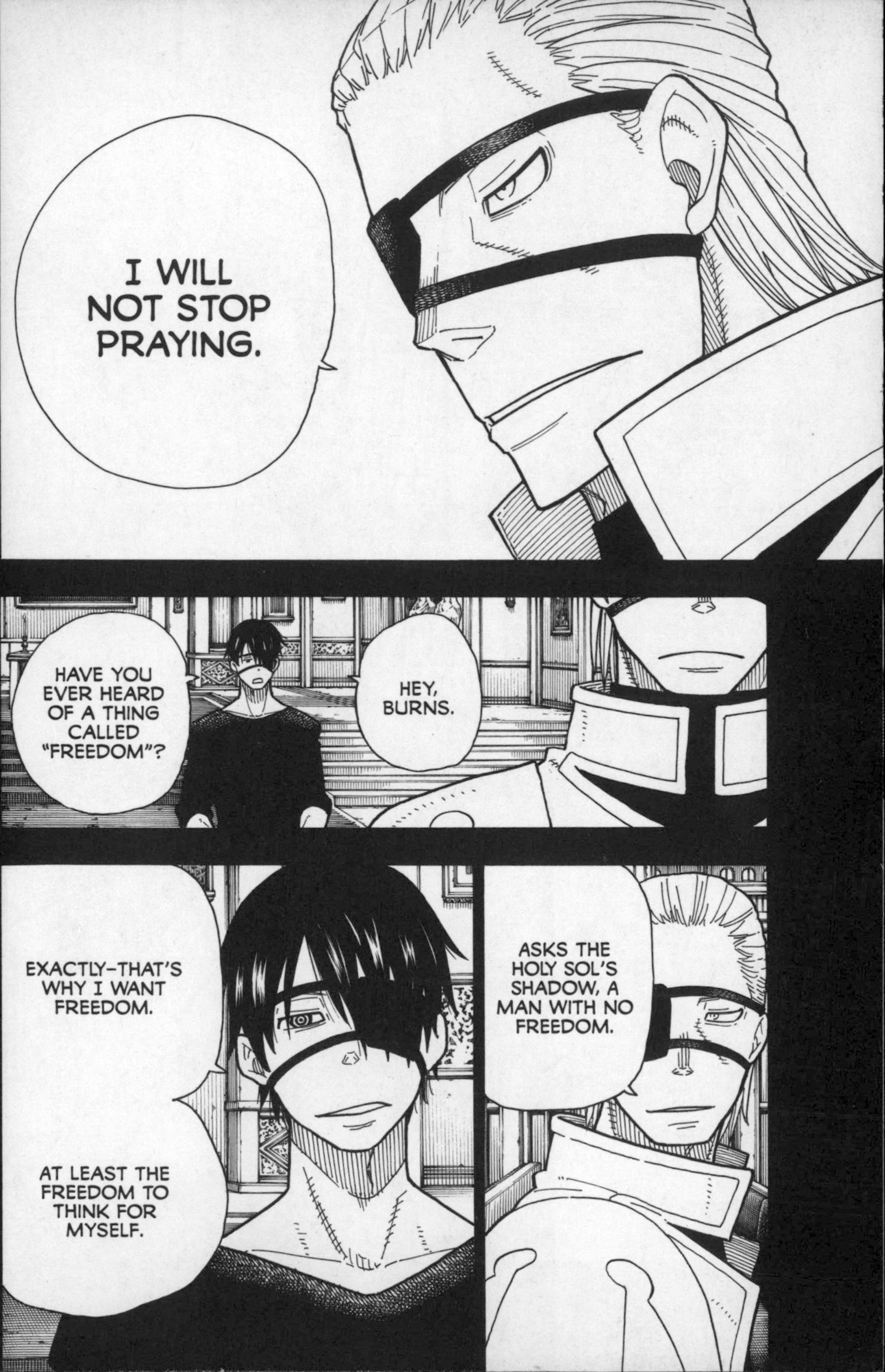
I WILL NOT STOP PRAYING.
HEY, BURNS.
HAVE YOU EVER HEARD OF A THING CALLED "FREEDOM"?
ASKS THE HOLY SOL'S SHADOW, A MAN WITH NO FREEDOM.
EXACTLY–THAT'S WHY I WANT FREEDOM.
AT LEAST THE FREEDOM TO THINK FOR MYSELF.

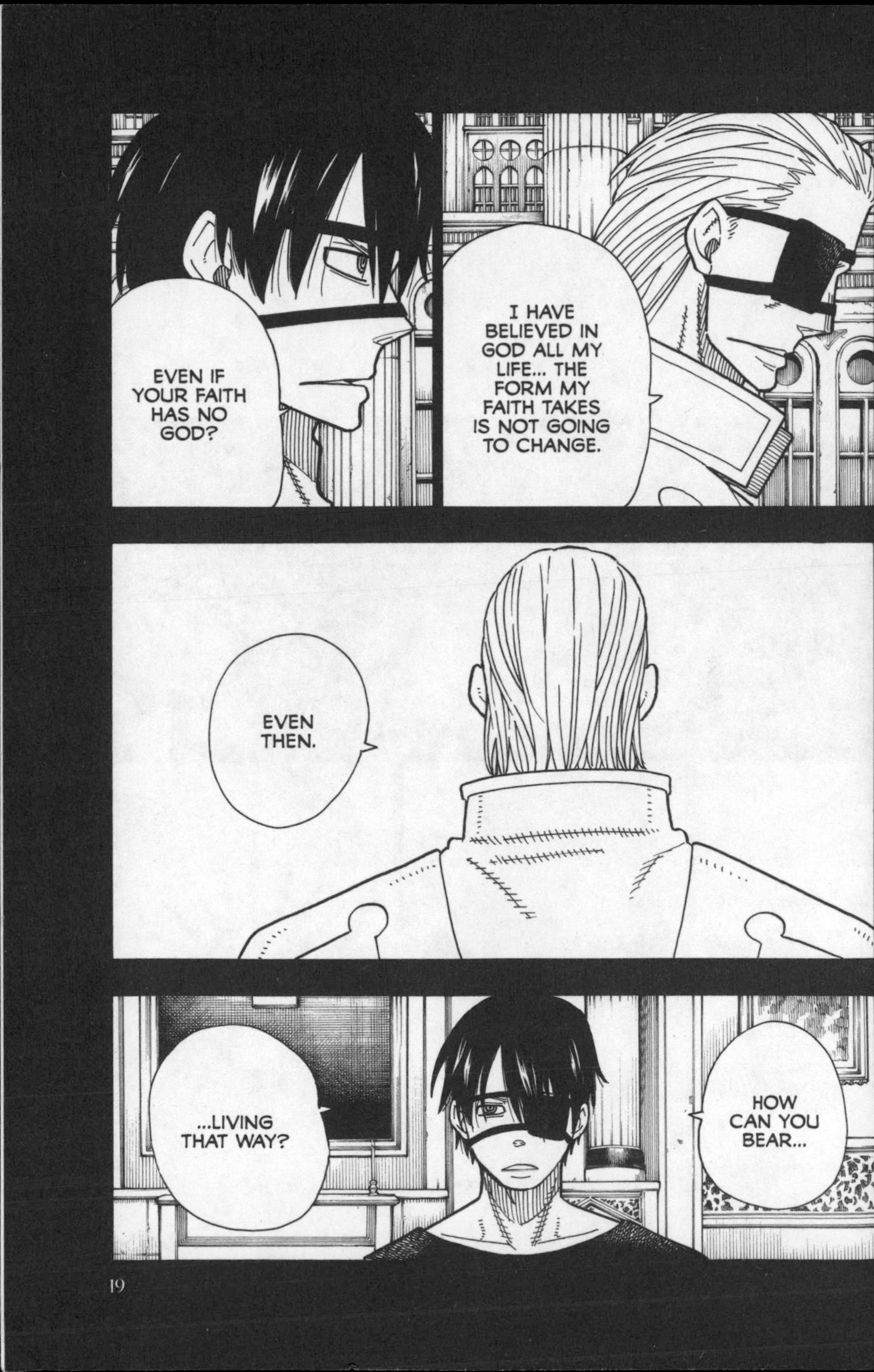
I HAVE BELIEVED IN GOD ALL MY LIFE... THE FORM MY FAITH TAKES IS NOT GOING TO CHANGE.
EVEN IF YOUR FAITH HAS NO GOD?
EVEN THEN.
HOW CAN YOU BEAR...
...LIVING THAT WAY?

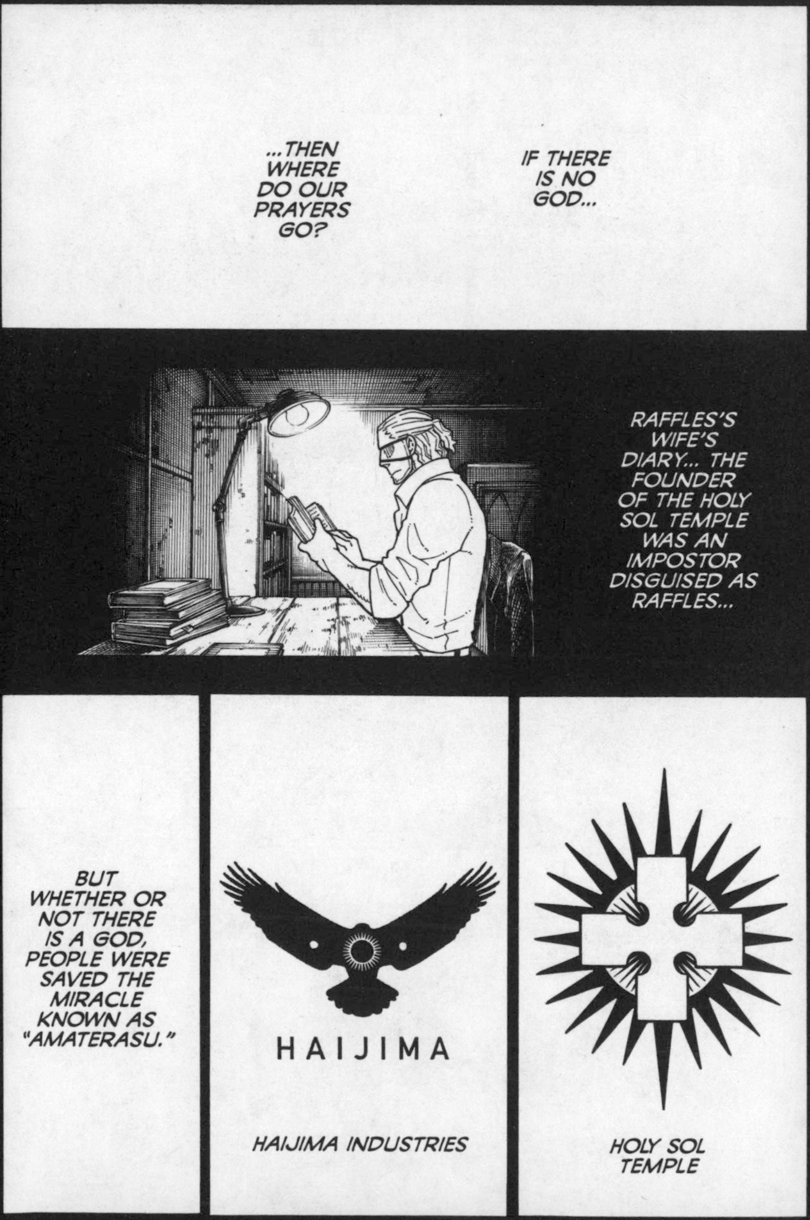
IF THERE IS NO GOD...
...THEN WHERE DO OUR PRAYERS GO?
RAFFLES'S WIFE'S DIARY... THE FOUNDER OF THE HOLY SOL TEMPLE WAS AN IMPOSTOR DISGUISED AS RAFFLES...
HOLY SOL TEMPLE
HAIJIMA
HAIJIMA INDUSTRIES
BUT WHETHER OR NOT THERE IS A GOD, PEOPLE WERE SAVED THE MIRACLE KNOWN AS "AMATERASU."

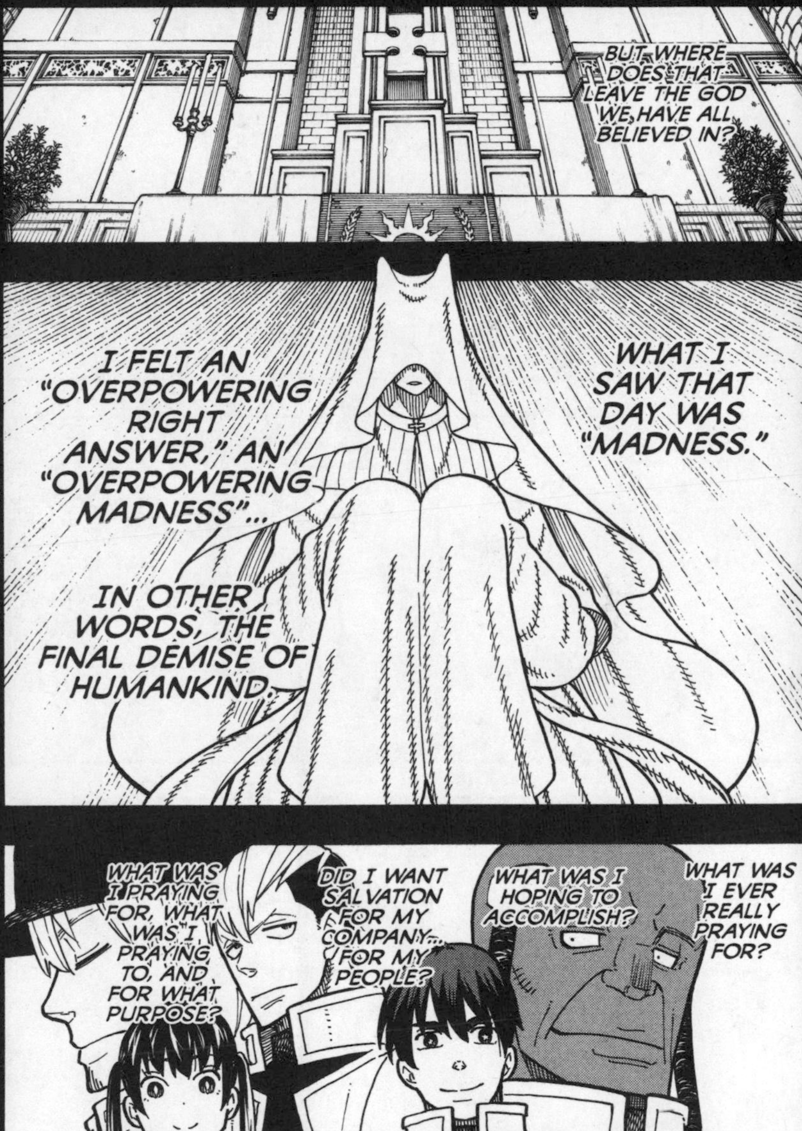
BUT WHERE DOES THAT LEAVE THE GOD WE HAVE ALL BELIEVED IN?
WHAT I SAW THAT DAY WAS "MADNESS."
I FELT AN "OVERPOWERING RIGHT ANSWER," AN "OVERPOWERING MADNESS"...
IN OTHER WORDS, THE FINAL DEMISE OF HUMANKIND.
WHAT WAS I EVER REALLY PRAYING FOR?
WHAT WAS I HOPING TO ACCOMPLISH?
DID I WANT SALVATION FOR MY COMPANY... FOR MY PEOPLE?
WHAT WAS I PRAYING FOR, WHAT WAS I PRAYING TO, AND FOR WHAT PURPOSE?

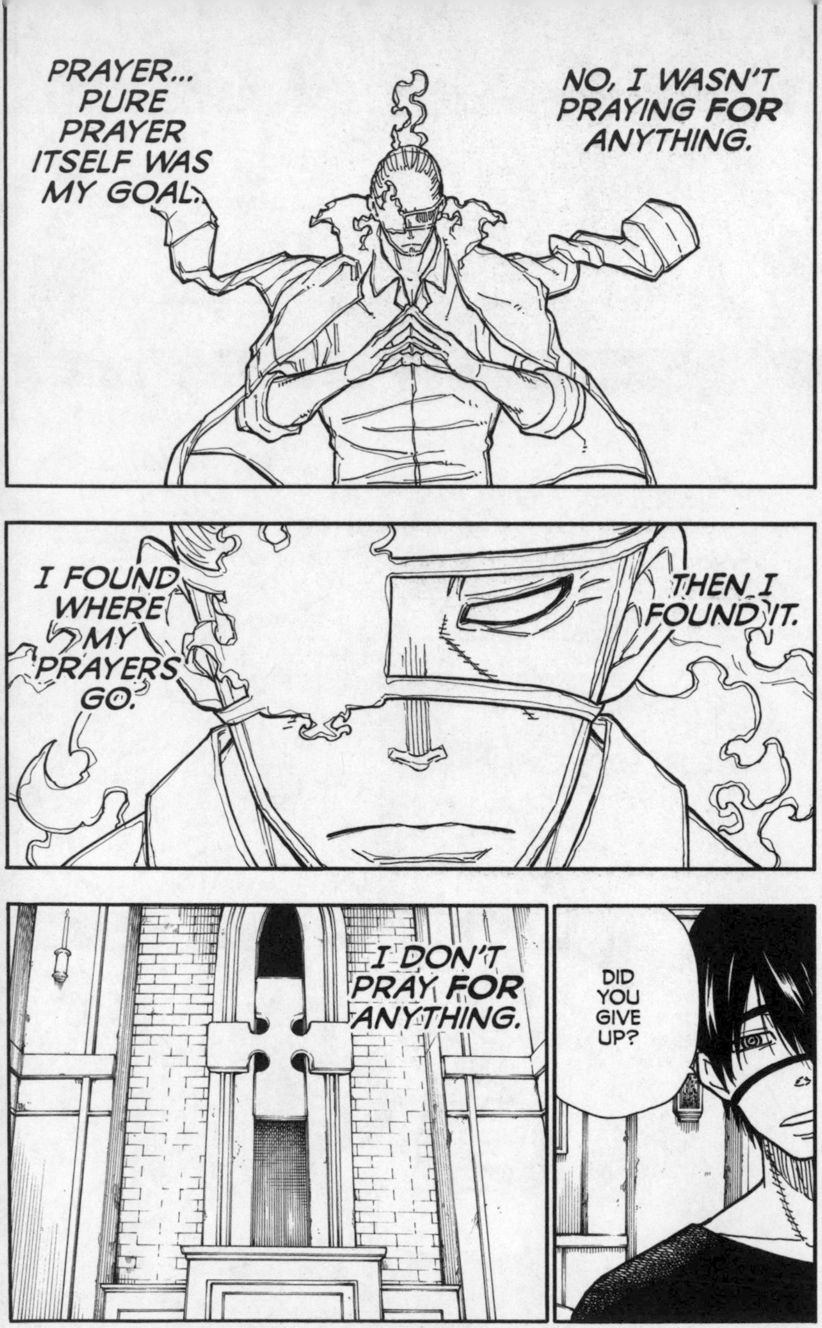
NO, I WASN'T PRAYING FOR ANYTHING.
PRAYER... PURE PRAYER ITSELF WAS MY GOAL.
THEN I FOUND IT.
I FOUND WHERE MY PRAYERS GO.
DID YOU GIVE UP?
I DON'T PRAY FOR ANYTHING.

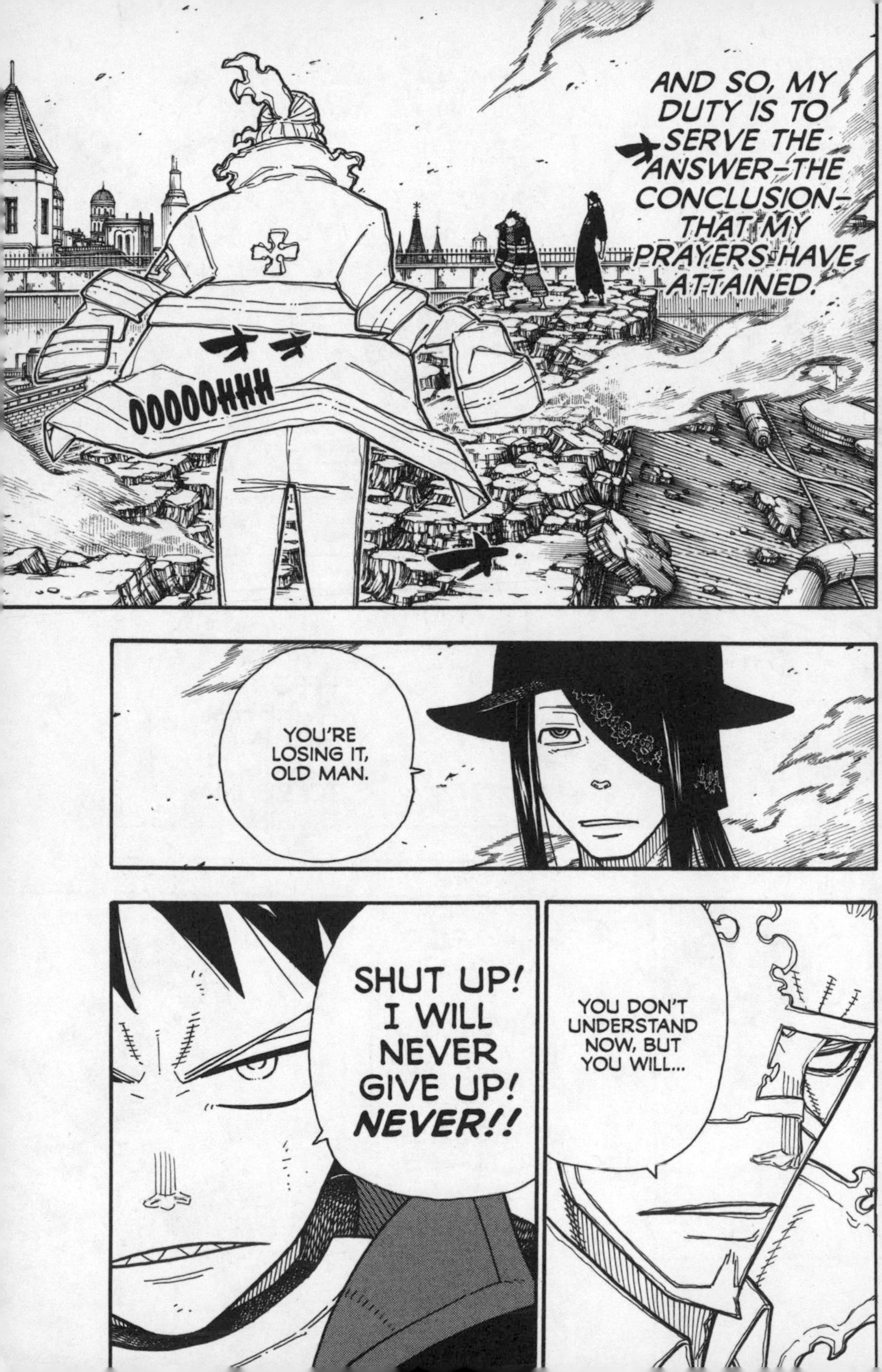
AND SO, MY DUTY IS TO SERVE THE ANSWER–THE CONCLUSION–THAT MY PRAYERS HAVE ATTAINED.
OOOOOHHH
YOU'RE LOSING IT, OLD MAN.
YOU DON'T UNDERSTAND NOW, BUT YOU WILL...
SHUT UP! I WILL NEVER GIVE UP! NEVER!!

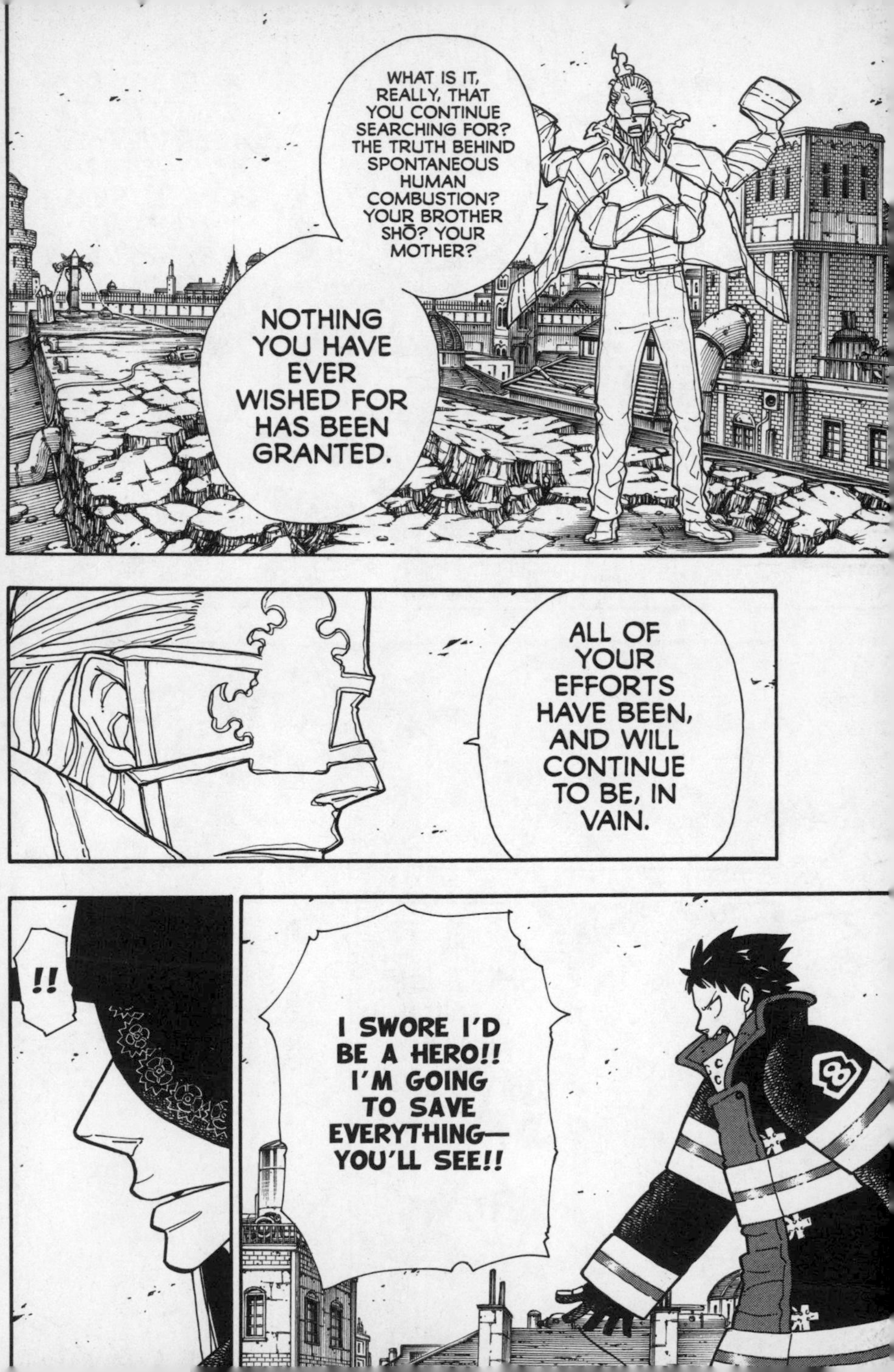
WHAT IS IT, REALLY, THAT YOU CONTINUE SEARCHING FOR? THE TRUTH BEHIND SPONTANEOUS HUMAN COMBUSTION? YOUR BROTHER SHŌ? YOUR MOTHER?
NOTHING YOU HAVE EVER WISHED FOR HAS BEEN GRANTED.
ALL OF YOUR EFFORTS HAVE BEEN, AND WILL CONTINUE TO BE, IN VAIN.
I SWORE I'D BE A HERO!! I'M GOING TO SAVE EVERYTHING— YOU'LL SEE!!
!!

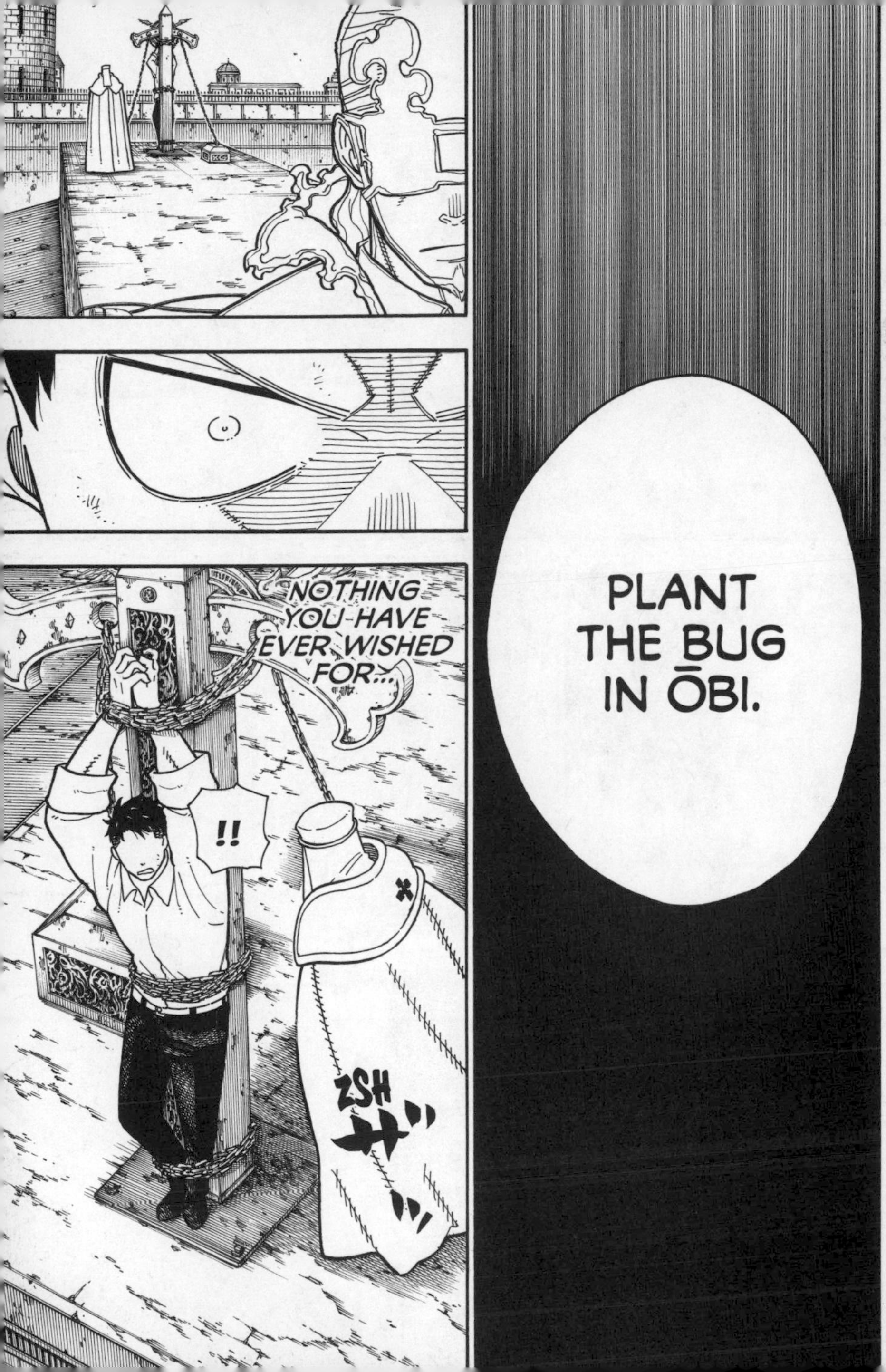
PLANT THE BUG IN ŌBI.
NOTHING YOU HAVE EVER WISHED FOR...
!!
ZSH

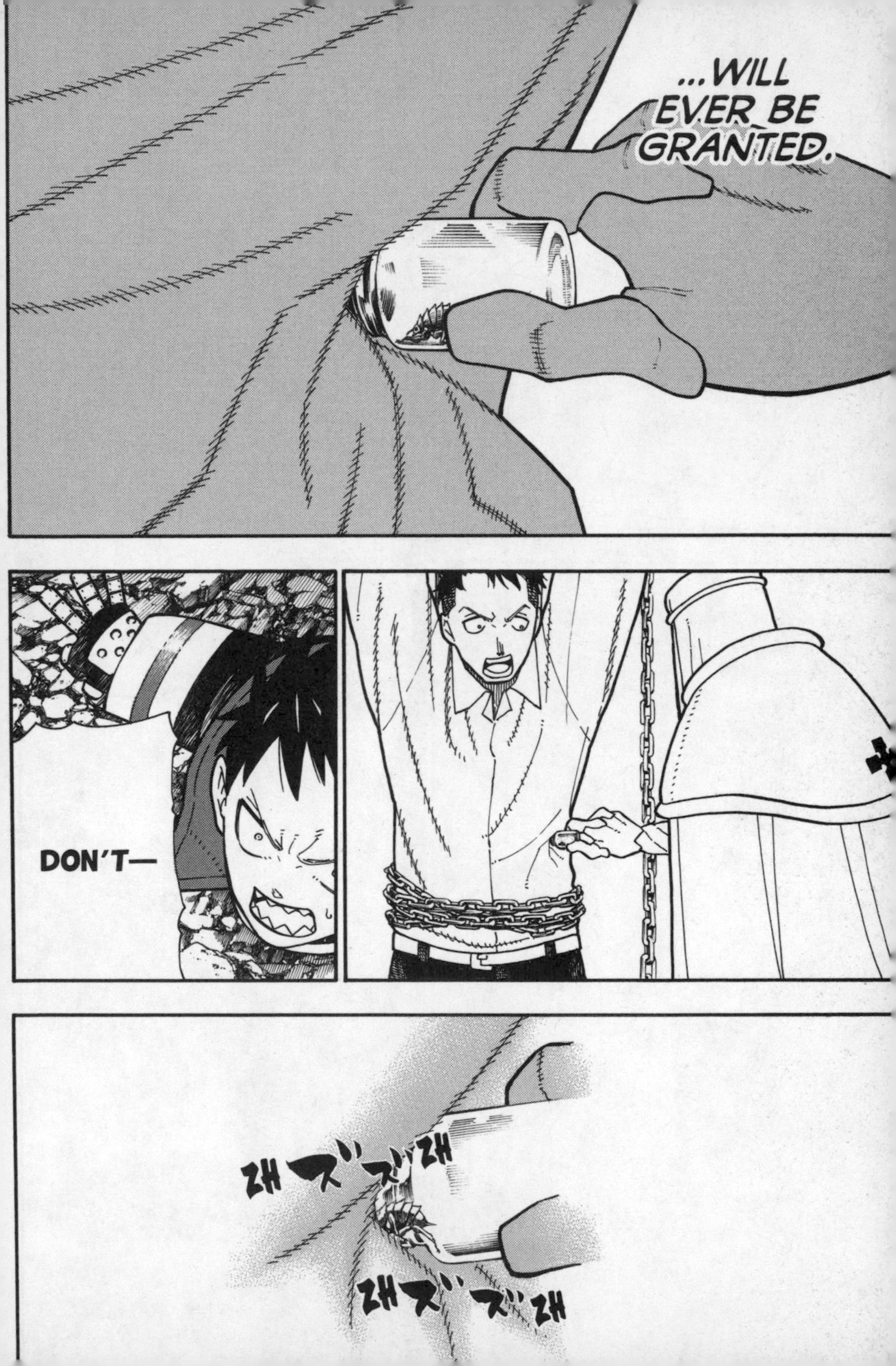
...WILL EVER BE GRANTED.
DON'T—
ZH ズ ズ ZH
ZH ズ ズ ZH

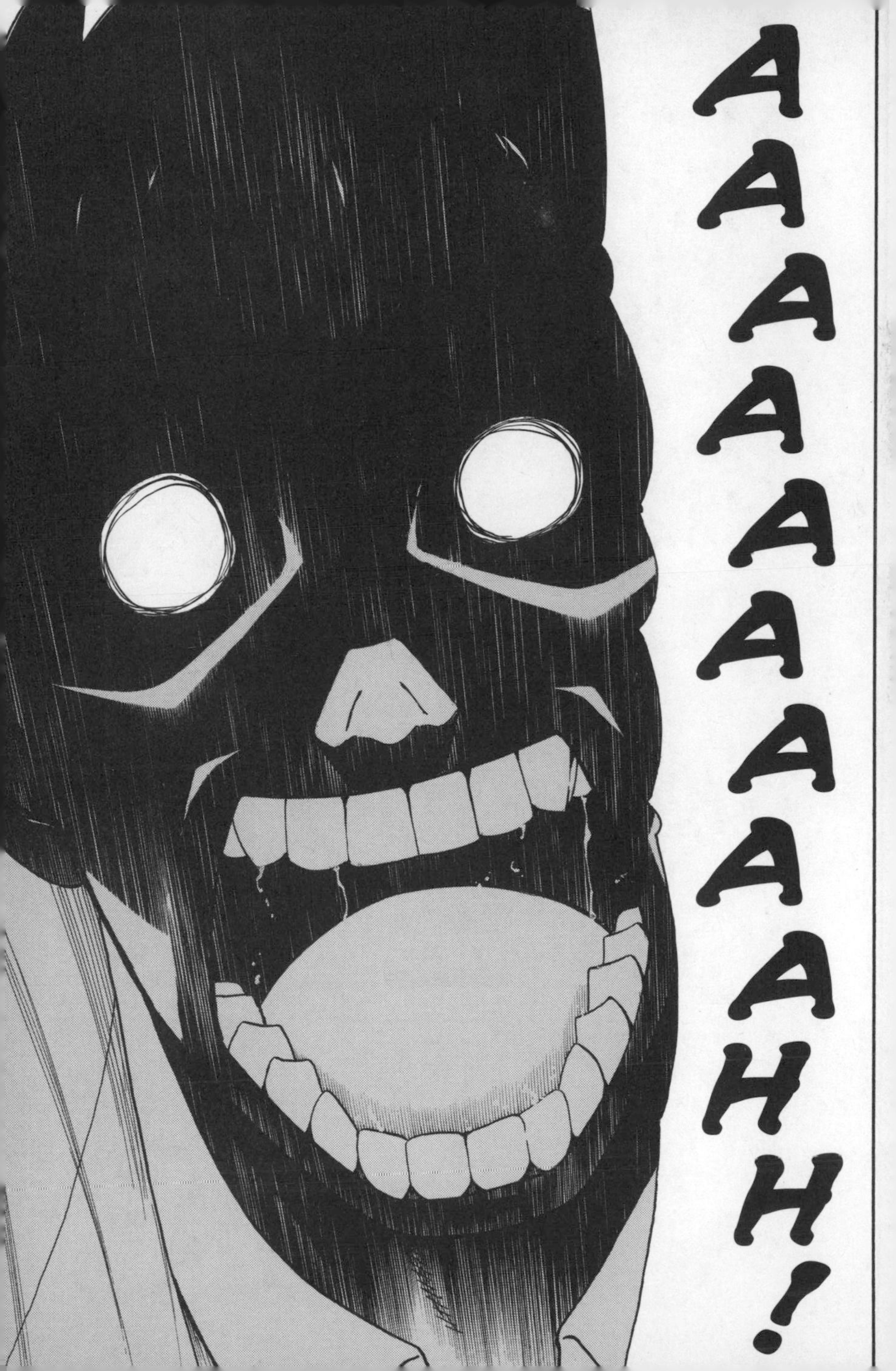
AAAAAAAAAH!

FIRE FORCE

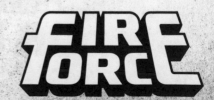

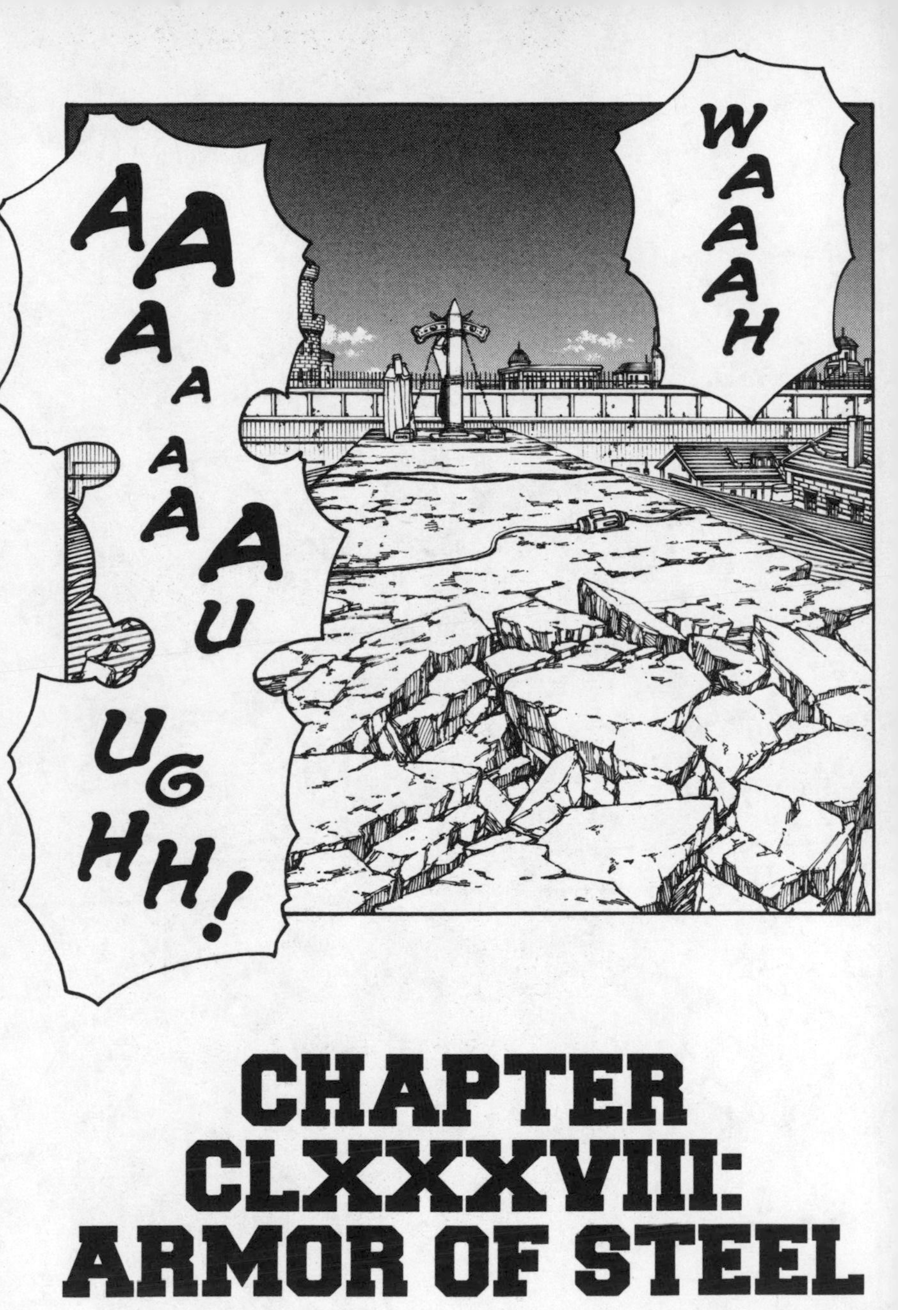
WAAAH
AAAAAAUUGHH!

CHAPTER CLXXVIII: ARMOR OF STEEL

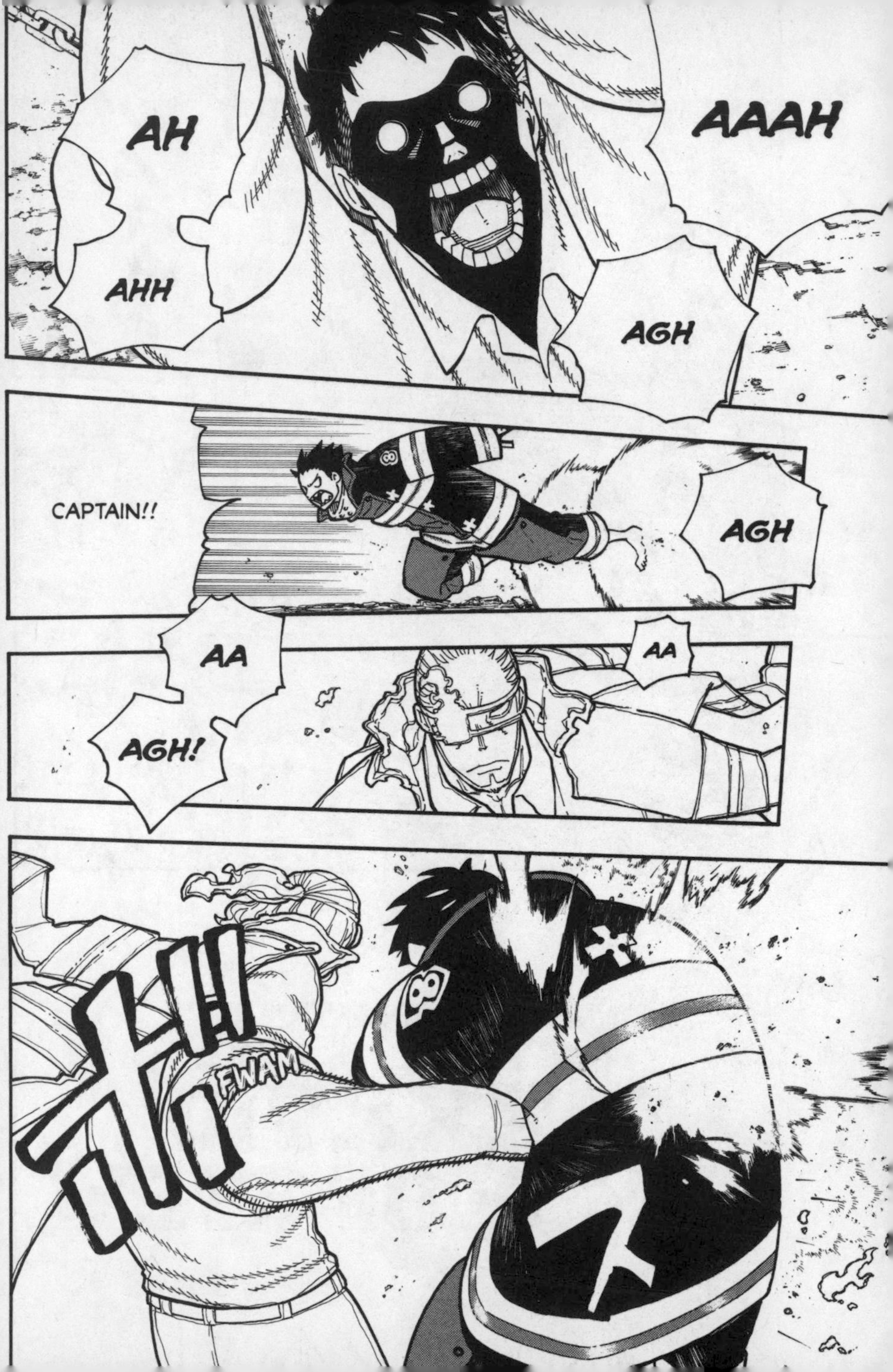
AAAH
AGH
AH
AHH
AGH
CAPTAIN!!
AA
AA
AGH!
FWAM

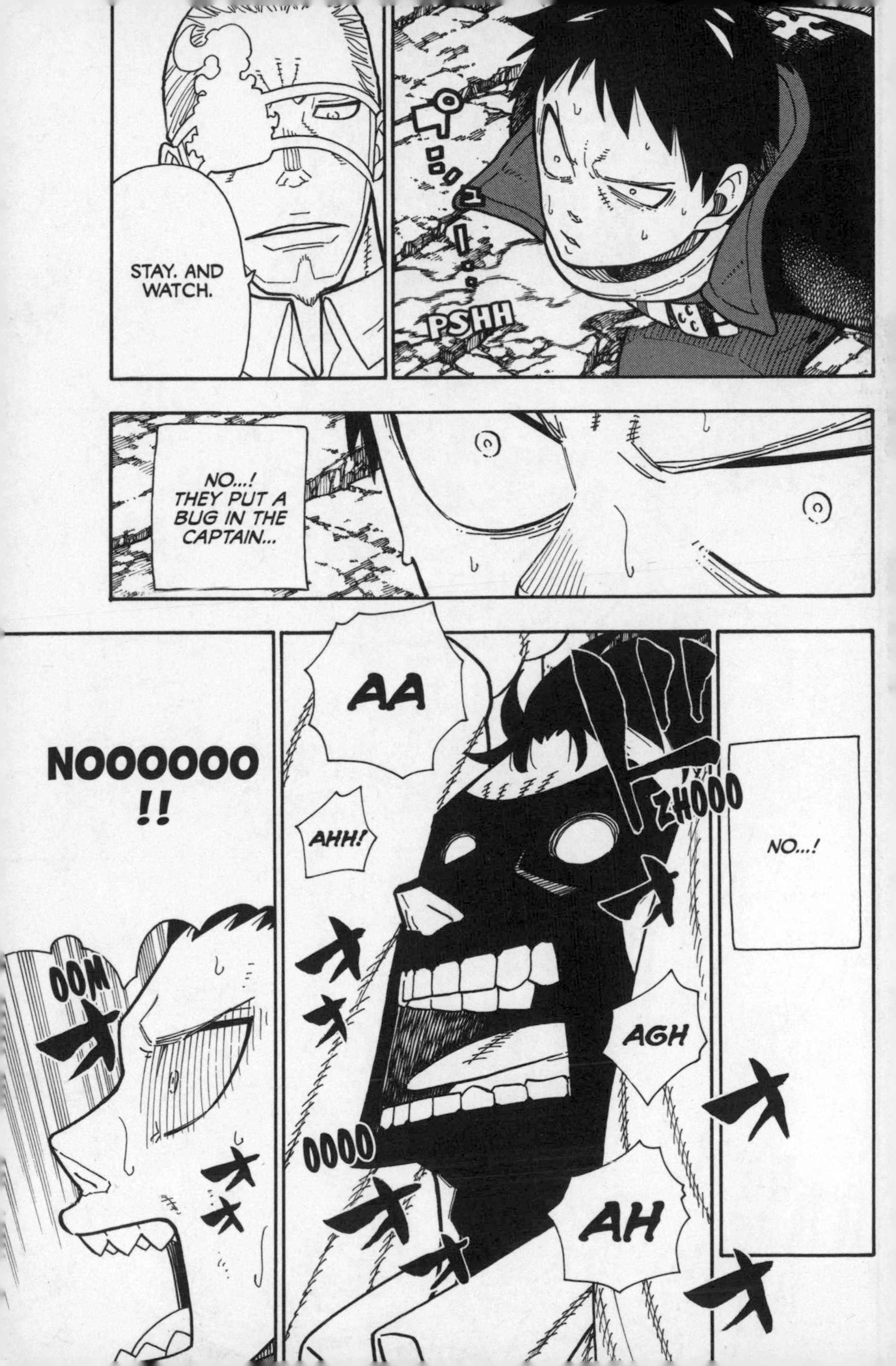
PSHH
STAY. AND WATCH.
NO...! THEY PUT A BUG IN THE CAPTAIN...
NO...!
AA
ZHOOO
AHH!
AGH
OOOO
AH
NOOOOOO!!
OOM

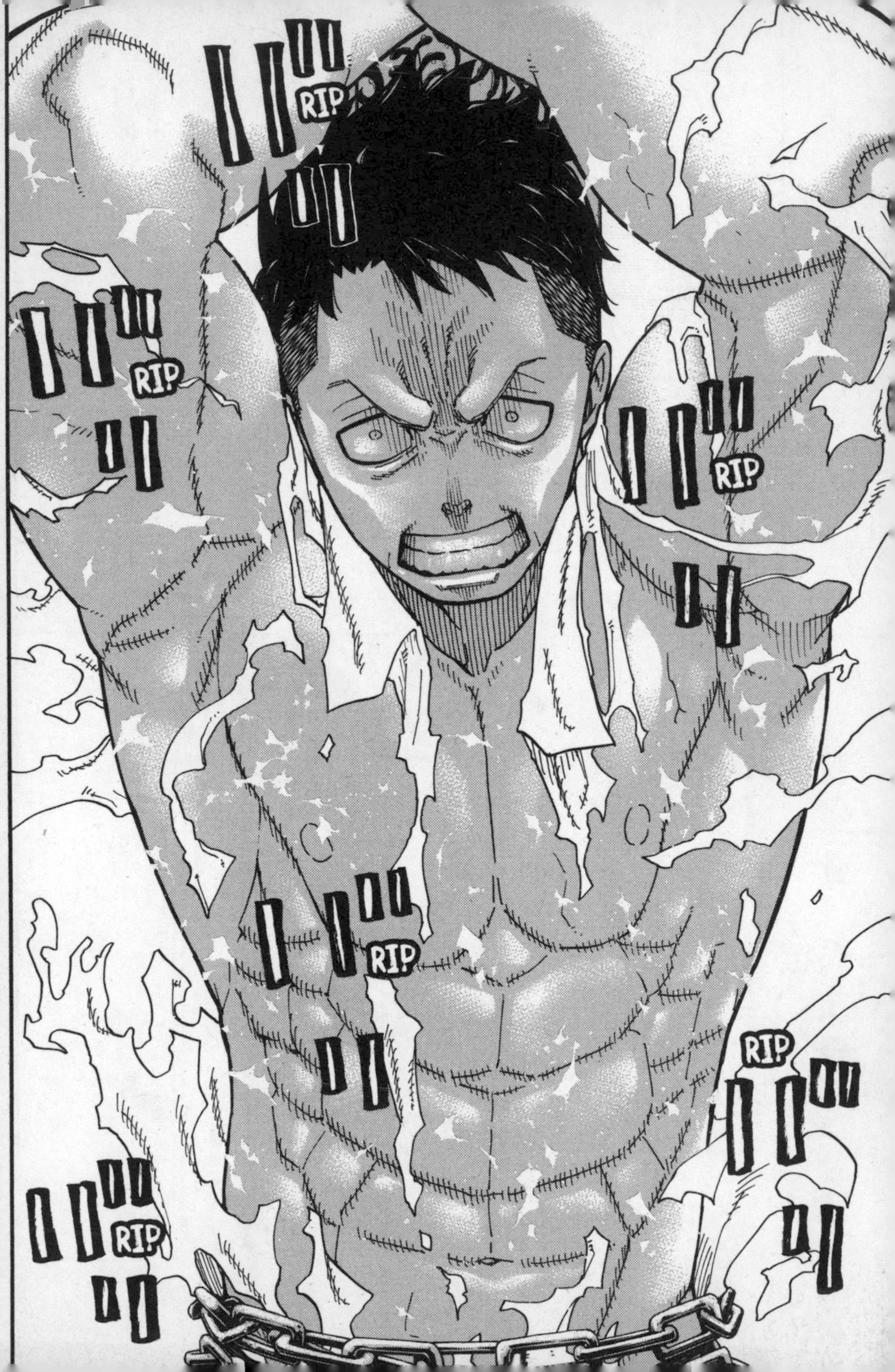
RIP
RIP
RIP
RIP
RIP
RIP

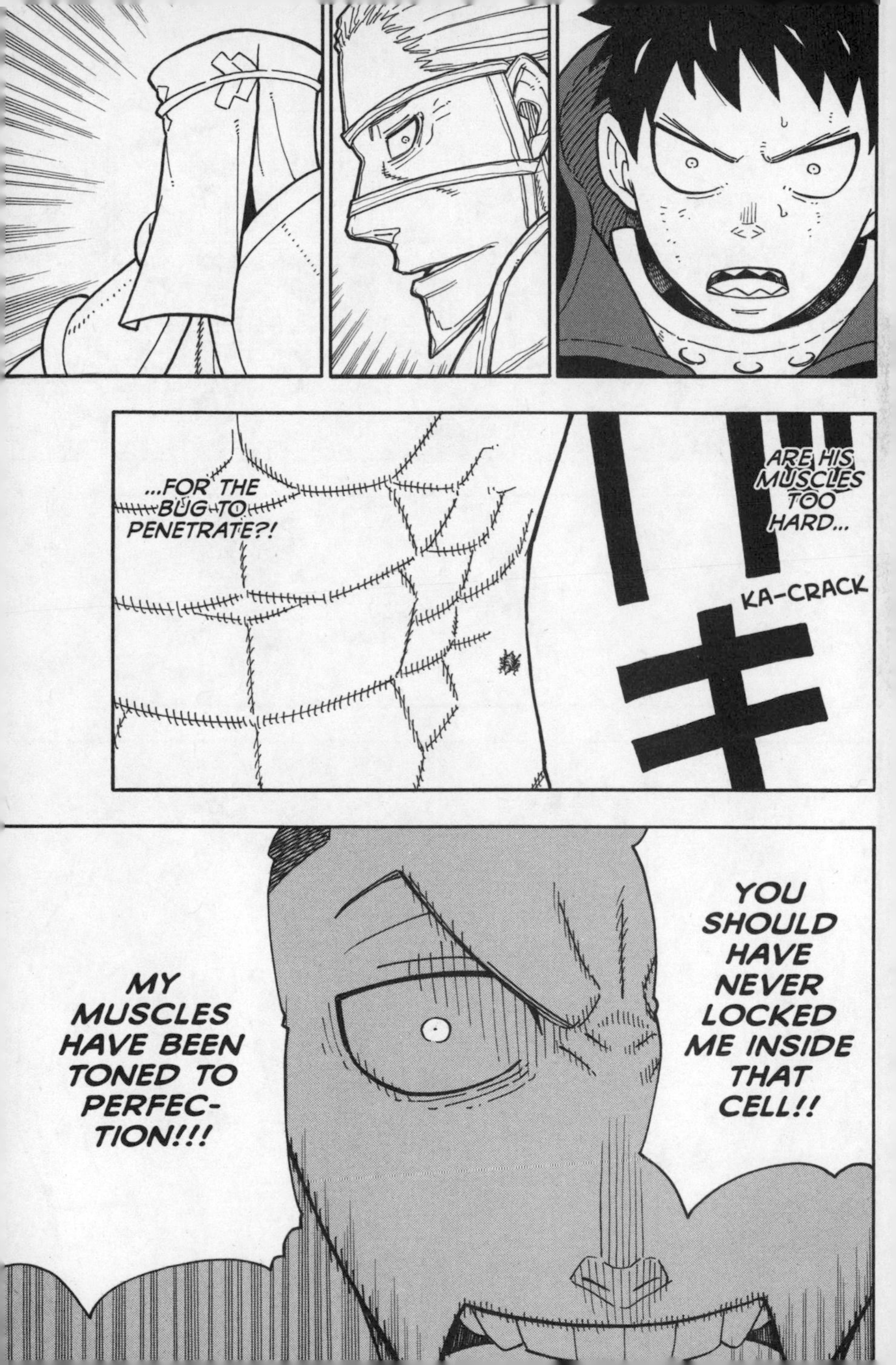
ARE HIS MUSCLES TOO HARD...
KA-CRACK
...FOR THE BUG TO PENETRATE?!
YOU SHOULD HAVE NEVER LOCKED ME INSIDE THAT CELL!!
MY MUSCLES HAVE BEEN TONED TO PERFEC-TION!!!

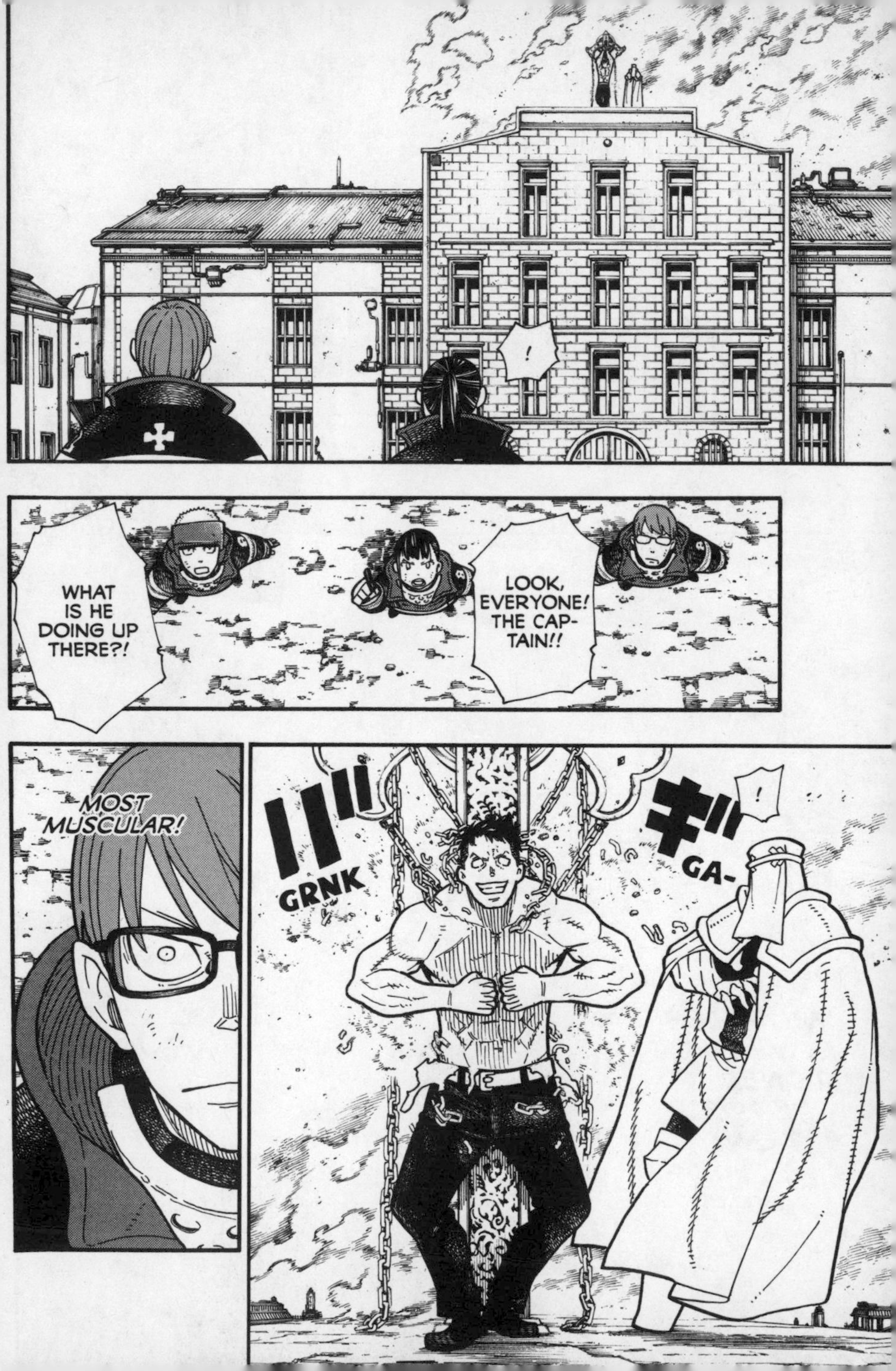
!
LOOK, EVERYONE! THE CAPTAIN!!
WHAT IS HE DOING UP THERE?!
!
GA-
GRNK
MOST MUSCULAR!

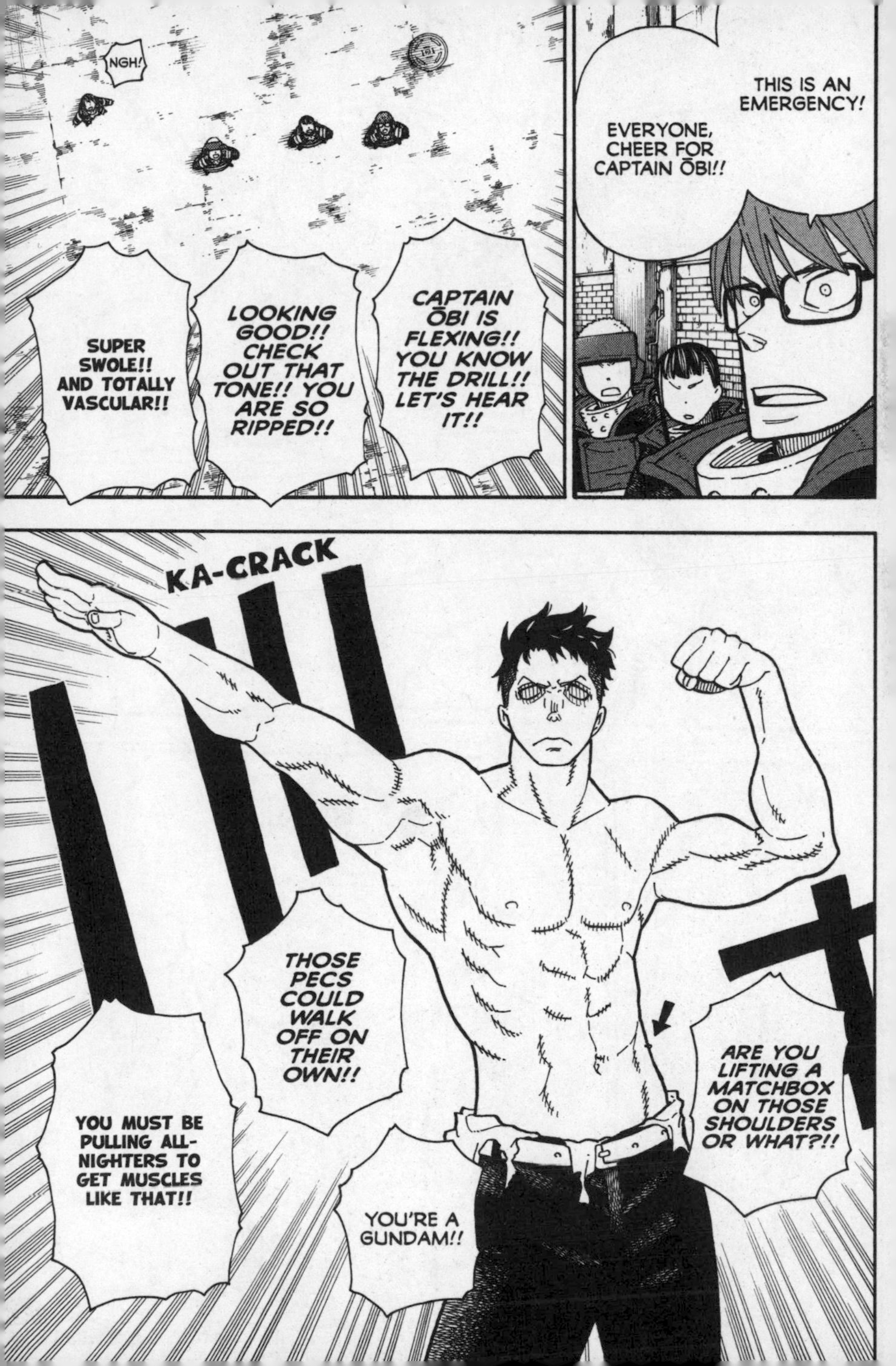
THIS IS AN EMERGENCY!
EVERYONE, CHEER FOR CAPTAIN ŌBI!!
NGH!
CAPTAIN ŌBI IS FLEXING!! YOU KNOW THE DRILL!! LET'S HEAR IT!!
LOOKING GOOD!! CHECK OUT THAT TONE!! YOU ARE SO RIPPED!!
SUPER SWOLE!! AND TOTALLY VASCULAR!!
KA-CRACK
ARE YOU LIFTING A MATCHBOX ON THOSE SHOULDERS OR WHAT?!!
THOSE PECS COULD WALK OFF ON THEIR OWN!!
YOU'RE A GUNDAM!!
YOU MUST BE PULLING ALL-NIGHTERS TO GET MUSCLES LIKE THAT!!

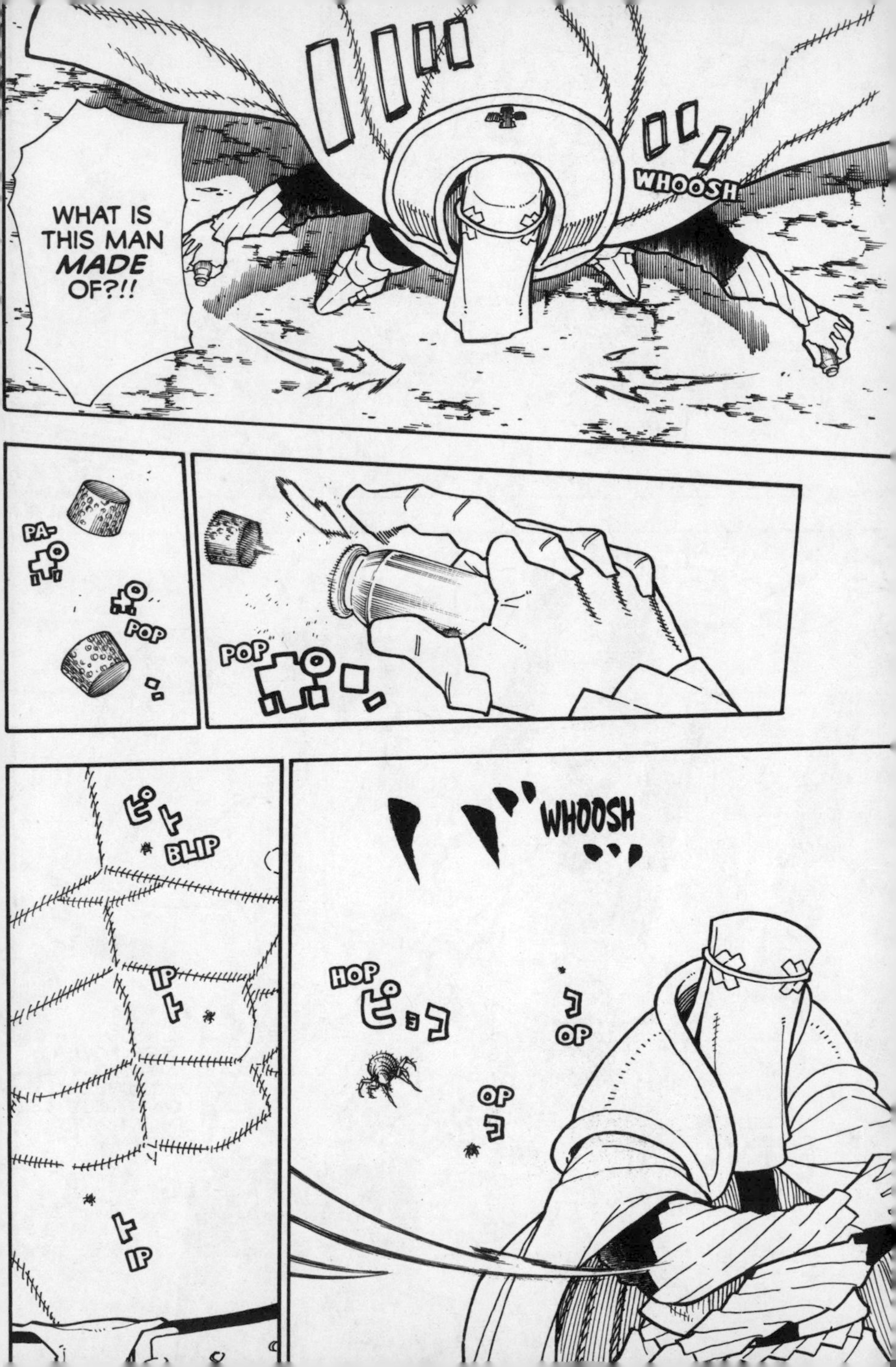
WHAT IS THIS MAN *MADE* OF?!!
WHOOSH
POP
PA-
POP
WHOOSH
HOP
OP
OP
BLIP
IP
IP

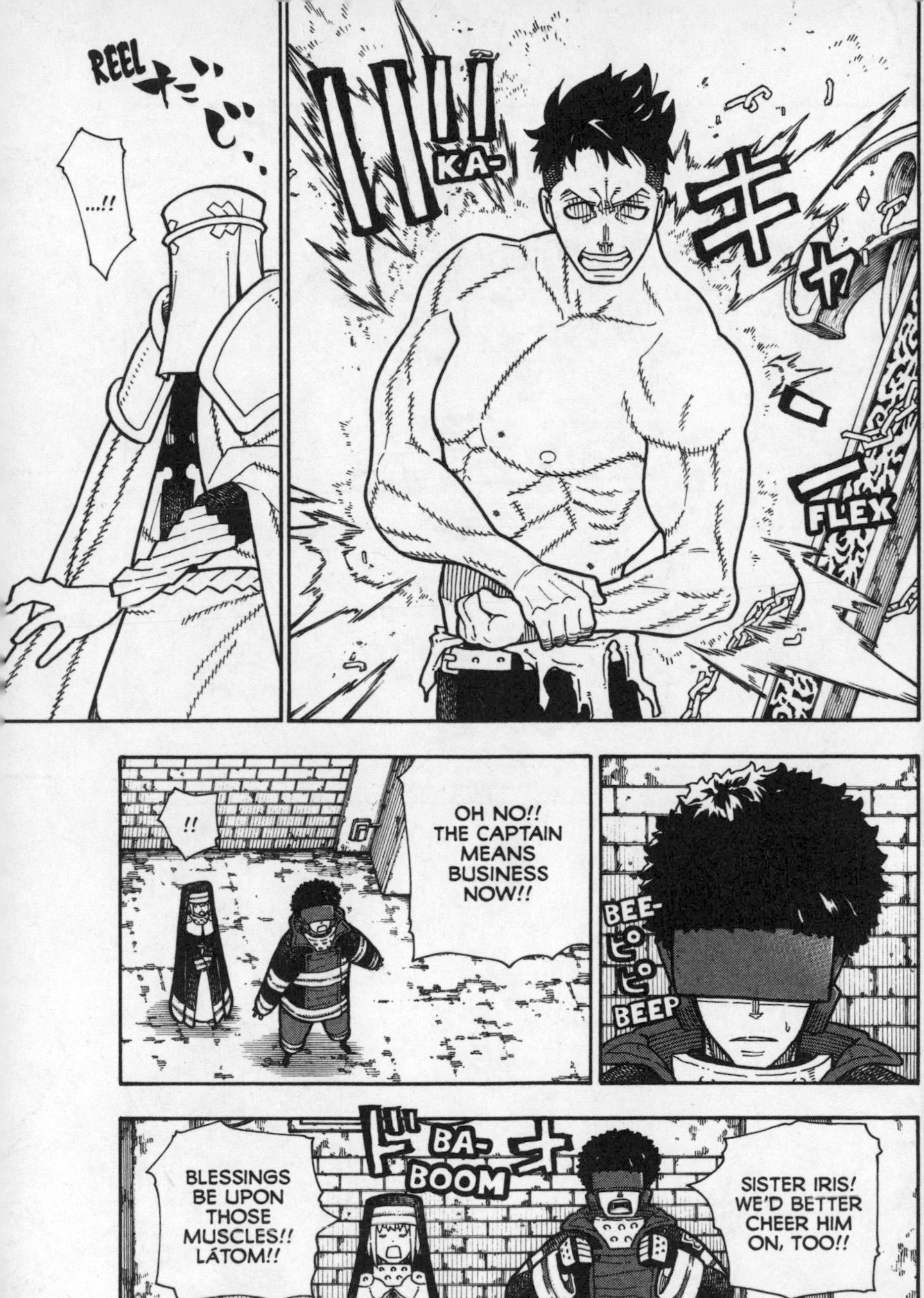
KA-
FLEX
REEL
...!!
BEE-
BEEP
OH NO!! THE CAPTAIN MEANS BUSINESS NOW!!
!!
SISTER IRIS! WE'D BETTER CHEER HIM ON, TOO!!
BA-BOOM
BLESSINGS BE UPON THOSE MUSCLES!! LÁTOM!!

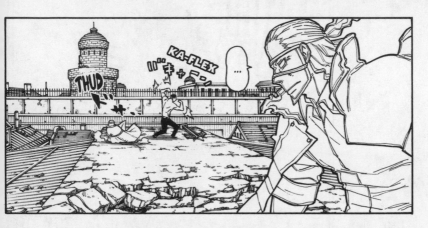

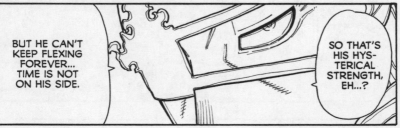

...
KA-FLEX
THUD
SO THAT'S HIS HYS-TERICAL STRENGTH, EH...?
BUT HE CAN'T KEEP FLEXING FOREVER... TIME IS NOT ON HIS SIDE.
CAPTAIN BURNS...
PREPARE TO HAVE YOUR ASS KICKED!!

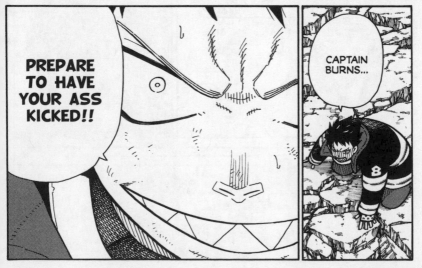

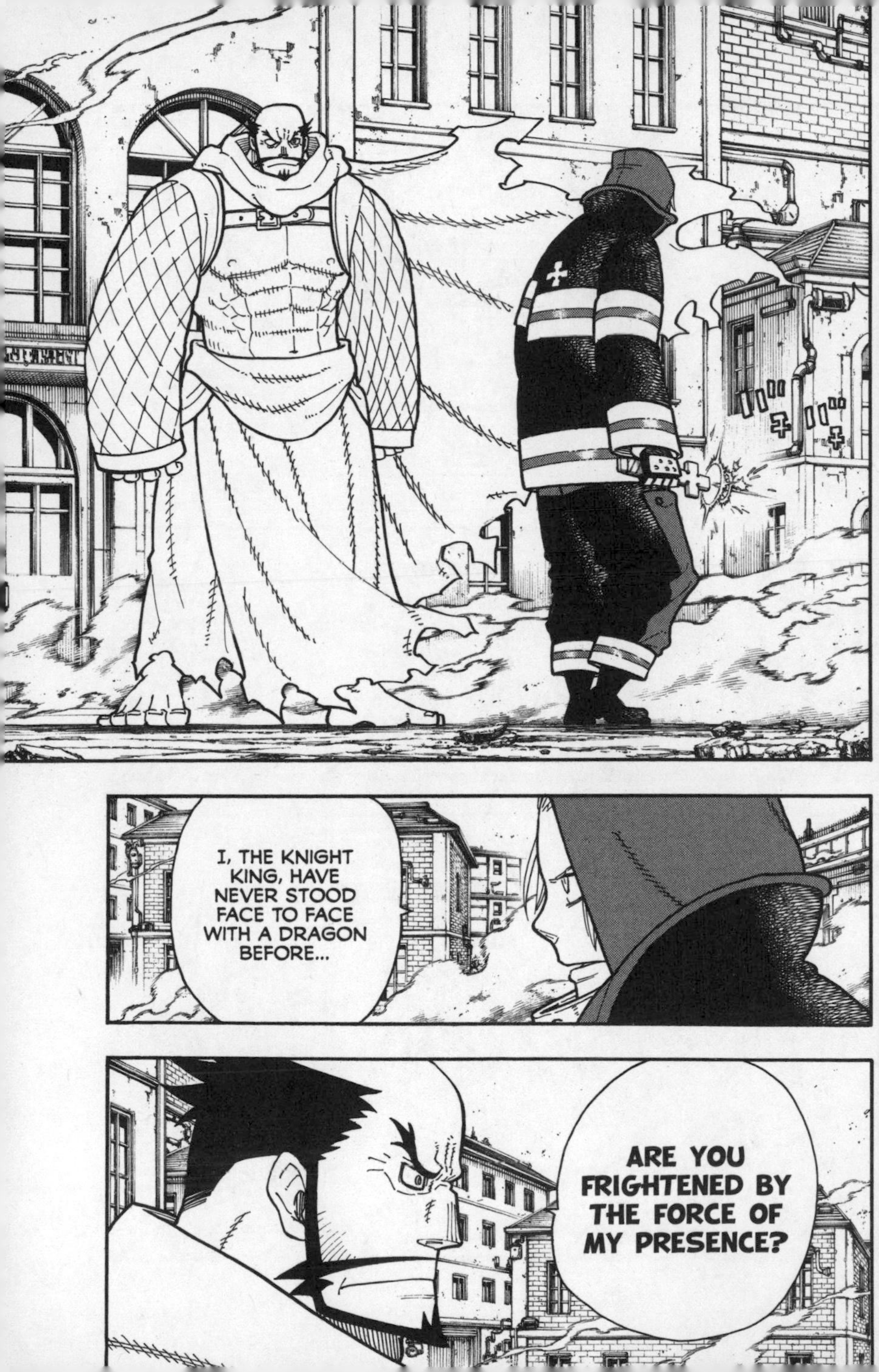
I, THE KNIGHT KING, HAVE NEVER STOOD FACE TO FACE WITH A DRAGON BEFORE...
ARE YOU FRIGHTENED BY THE FORCE OF MY PRESENCE?

Z-ZSH

ZSH

...

IF YOU
INSIST...

ONLY A
SELECT FEW
WARRIORS
MAY STAND
BEFORE A
DRAGON...
VULCAN,
STEP BACK.

GH

GH

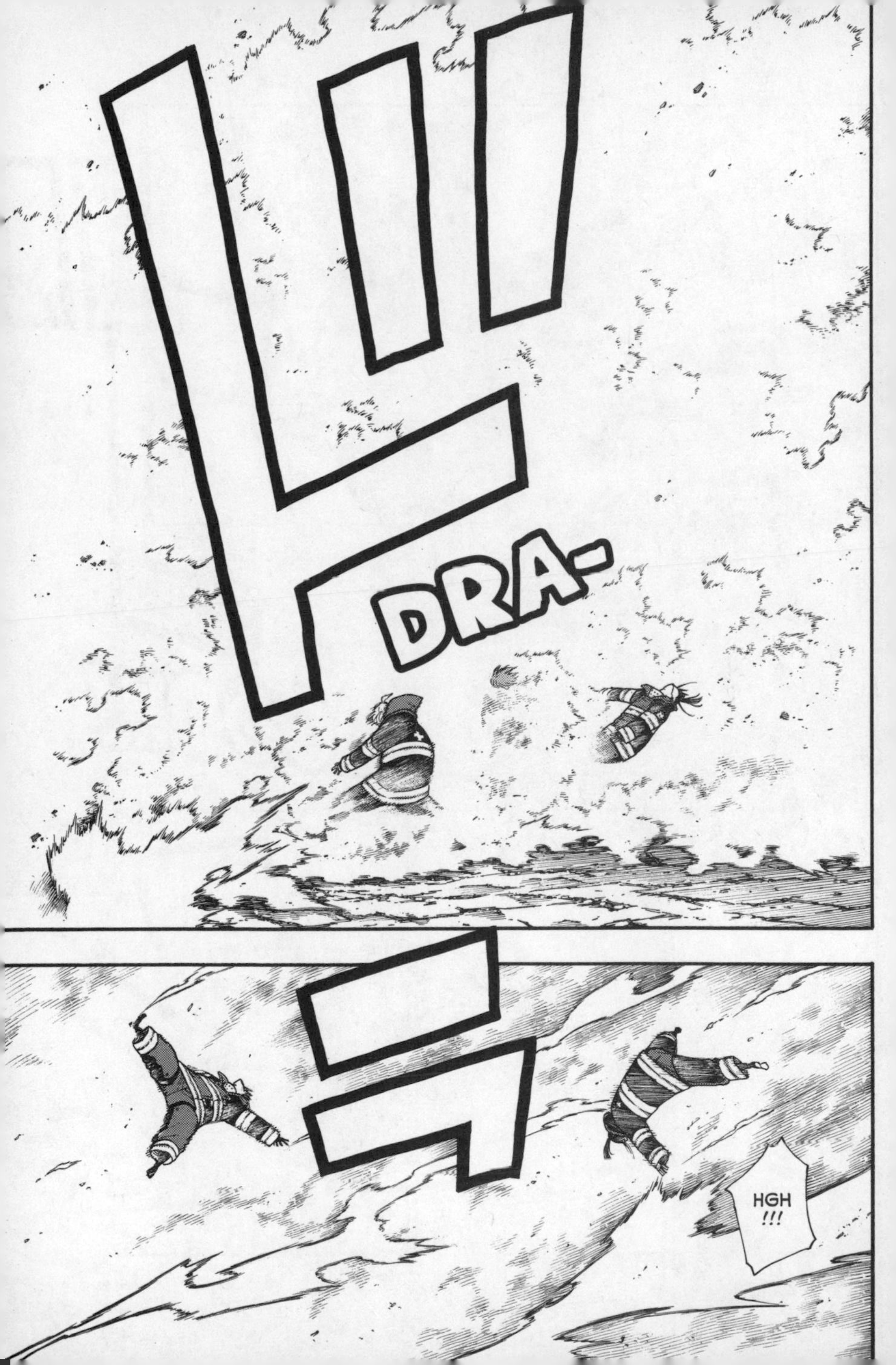
DRA-
HGH !!!

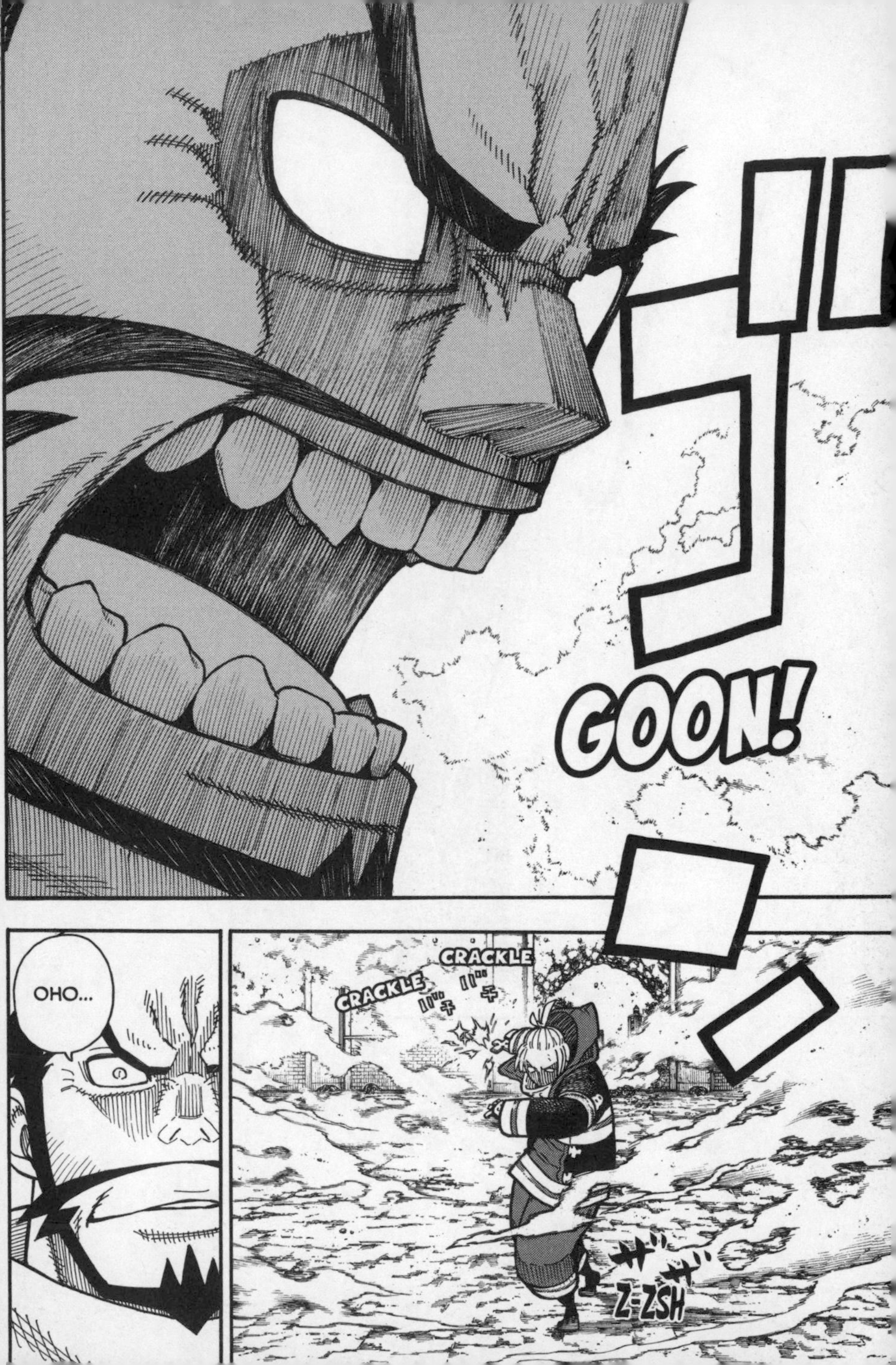
GOON!
CRACKLE
CRACKLE
Z-ZSH
OHO...

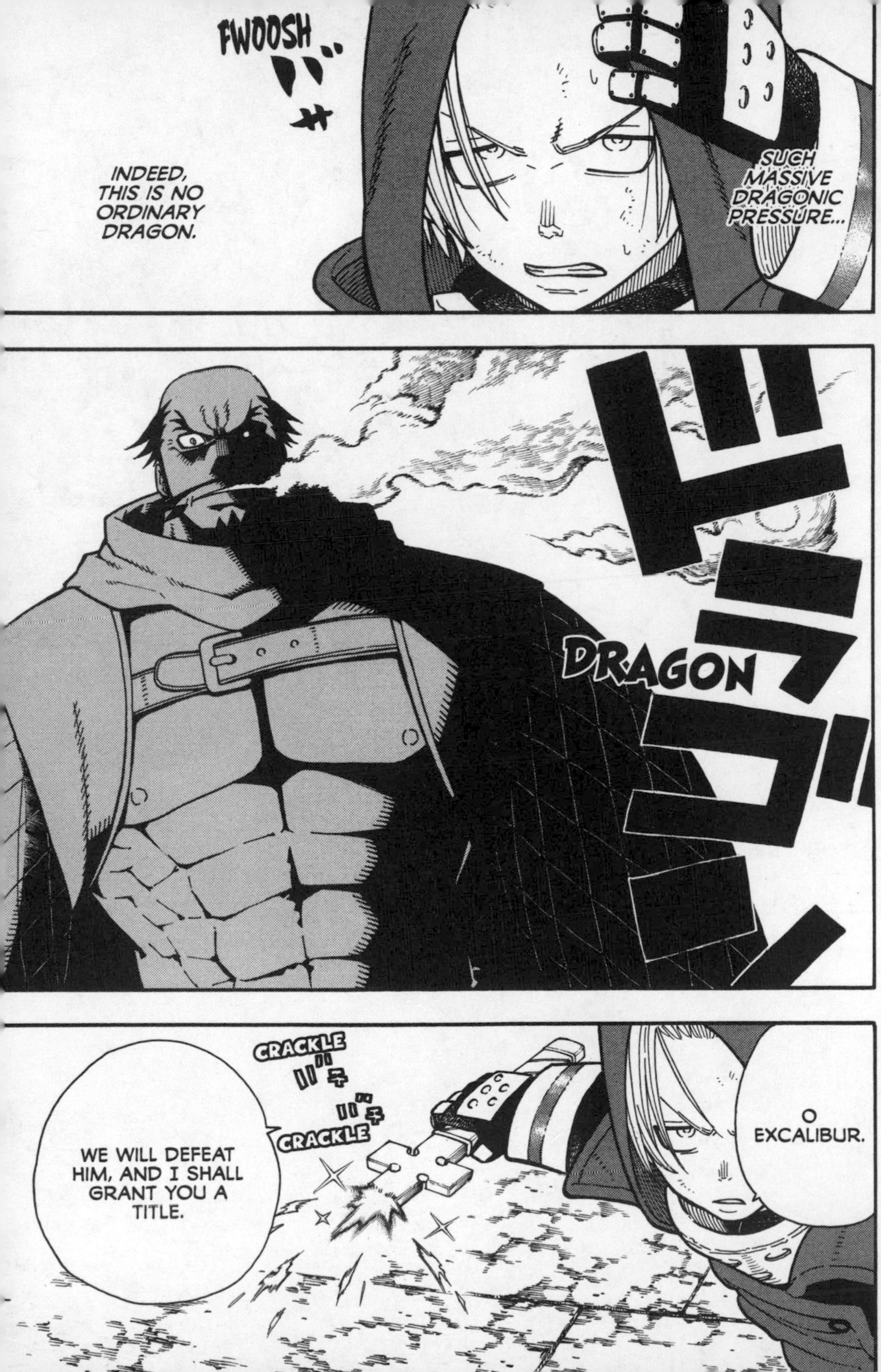
FWOOSH
バッ
SUCH MASSIVE DRAGONIC PRESSURE...
INDEED, THIS IS NO ORDINARY DRAGON.
ドラゴン
DRAGON
O EXCALIBUR.
CRACKLE
CRACKLE
WE WILL DEFEAT HIM, AND I SHALL GRANT YOU A TITLE.

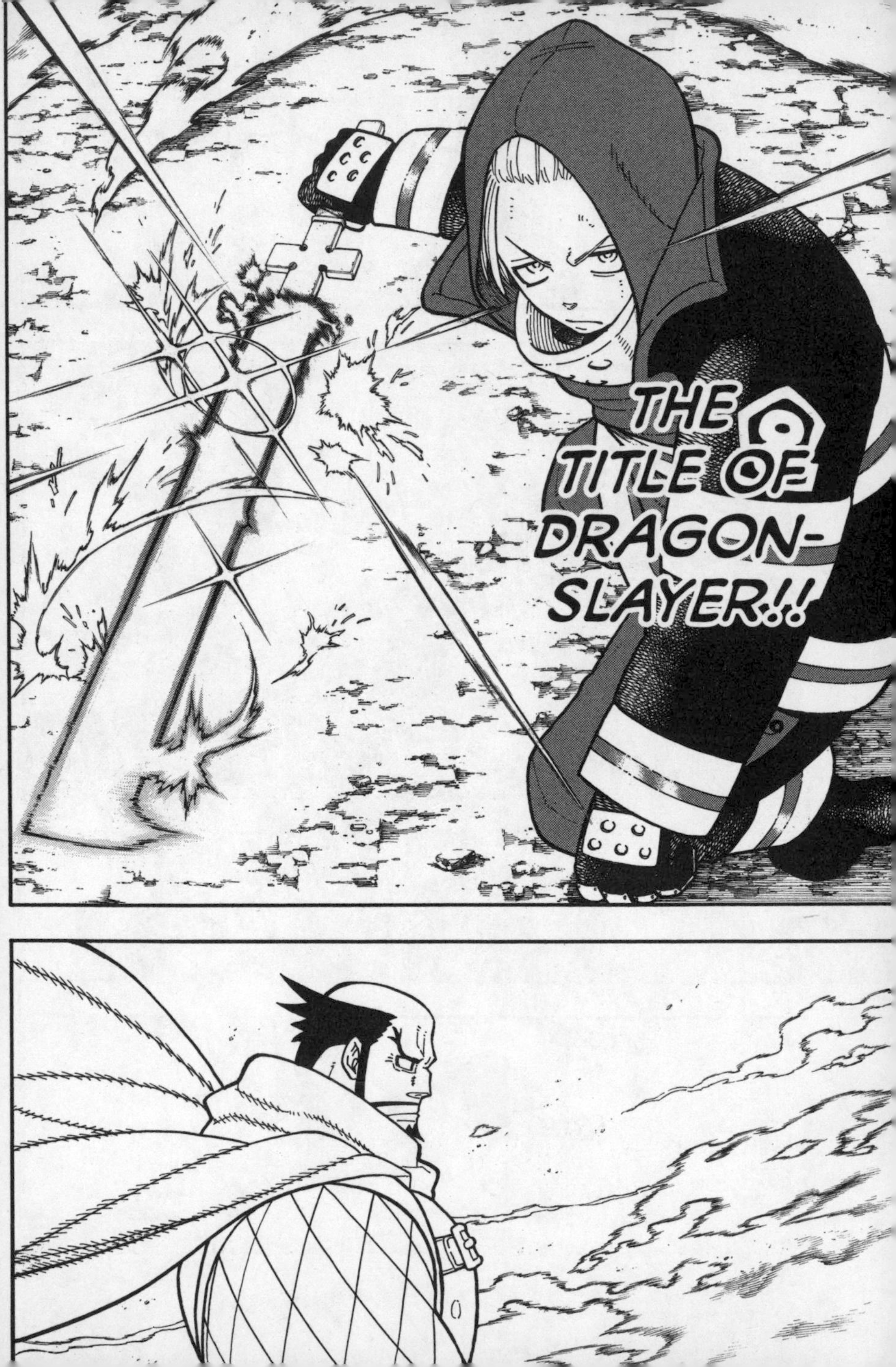
THE TITLE OF DRAGON-SLAYER!!

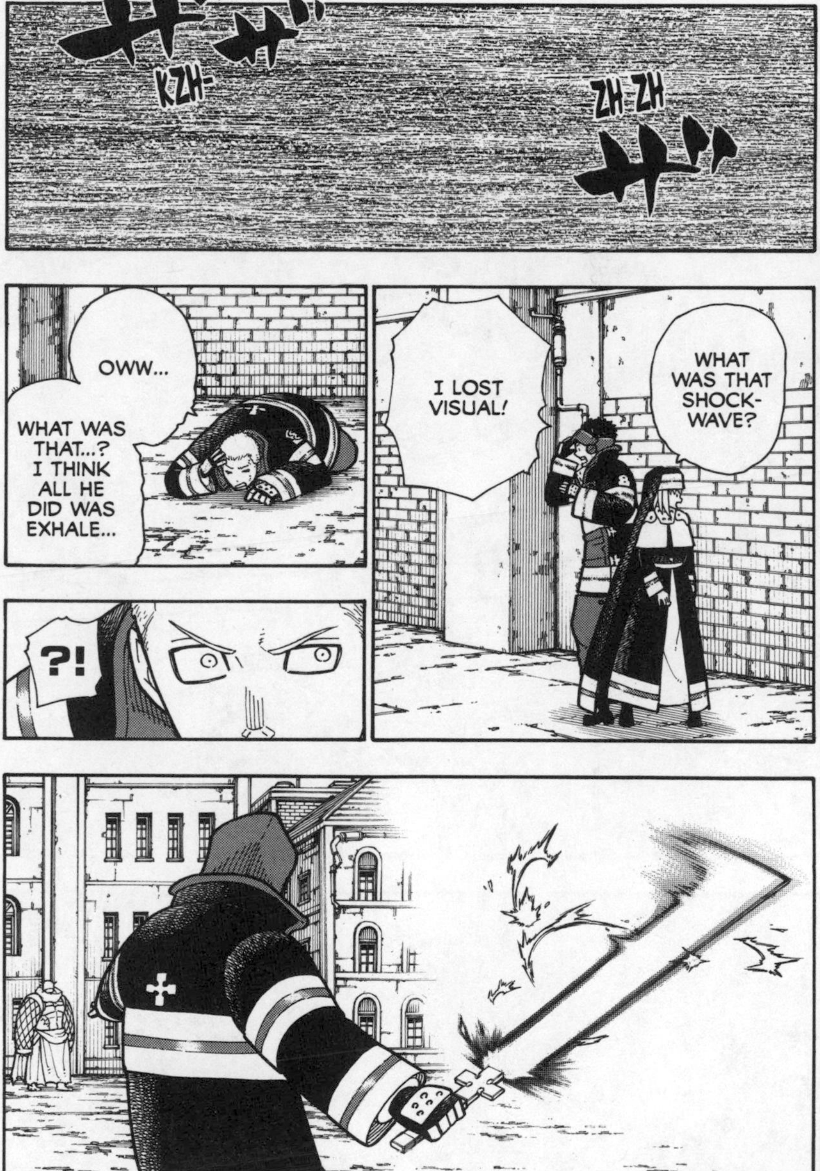
KZH-
ZH ZH
WHAT WAS THAT SHOCK-WAVE?
I LOST VISUAL!
OWW...
WHAT WAS THAT...? I THINK ALL HE DID WAS EXHALE...
?!

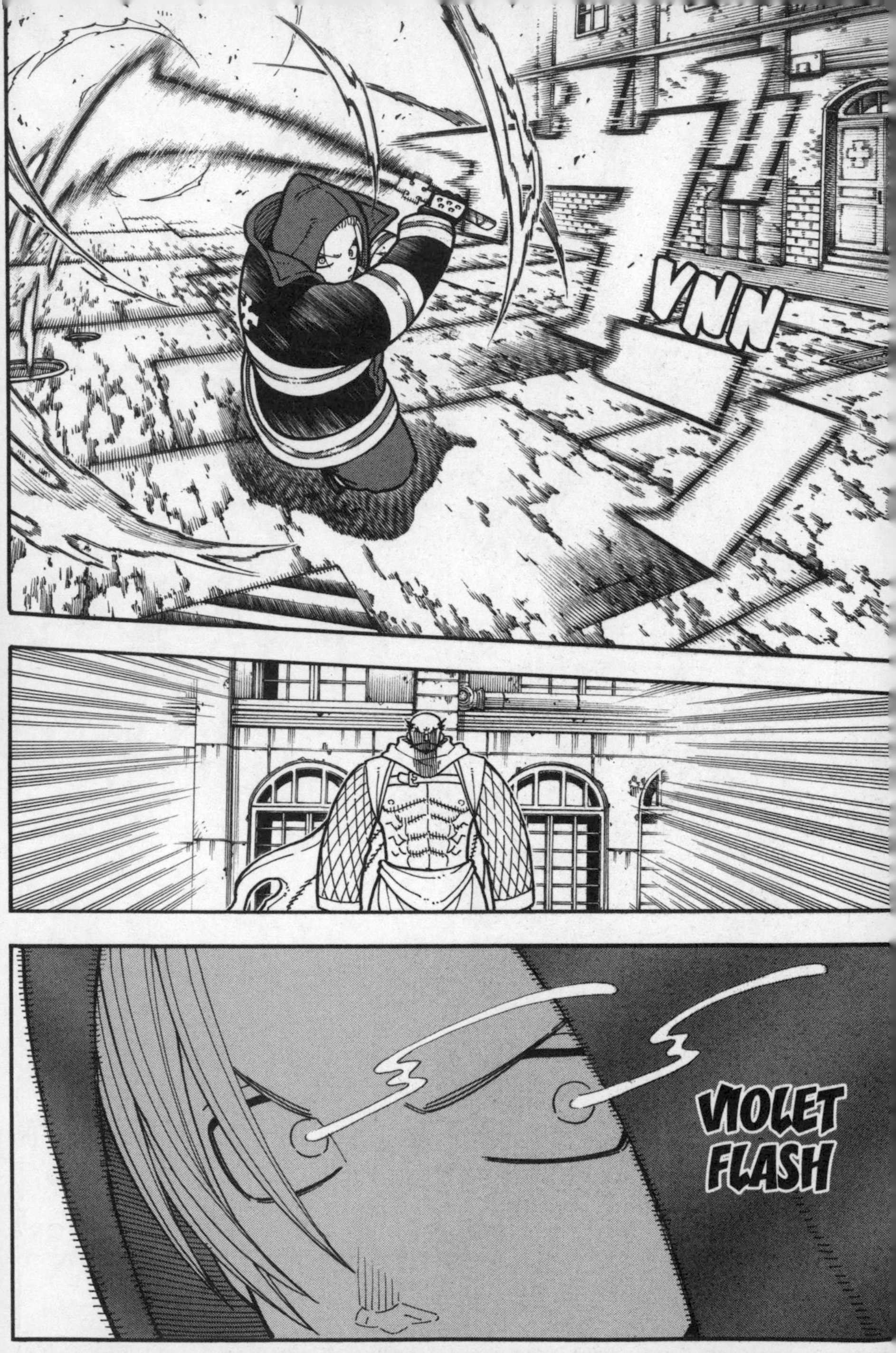
VNN
VIOLET FLASH

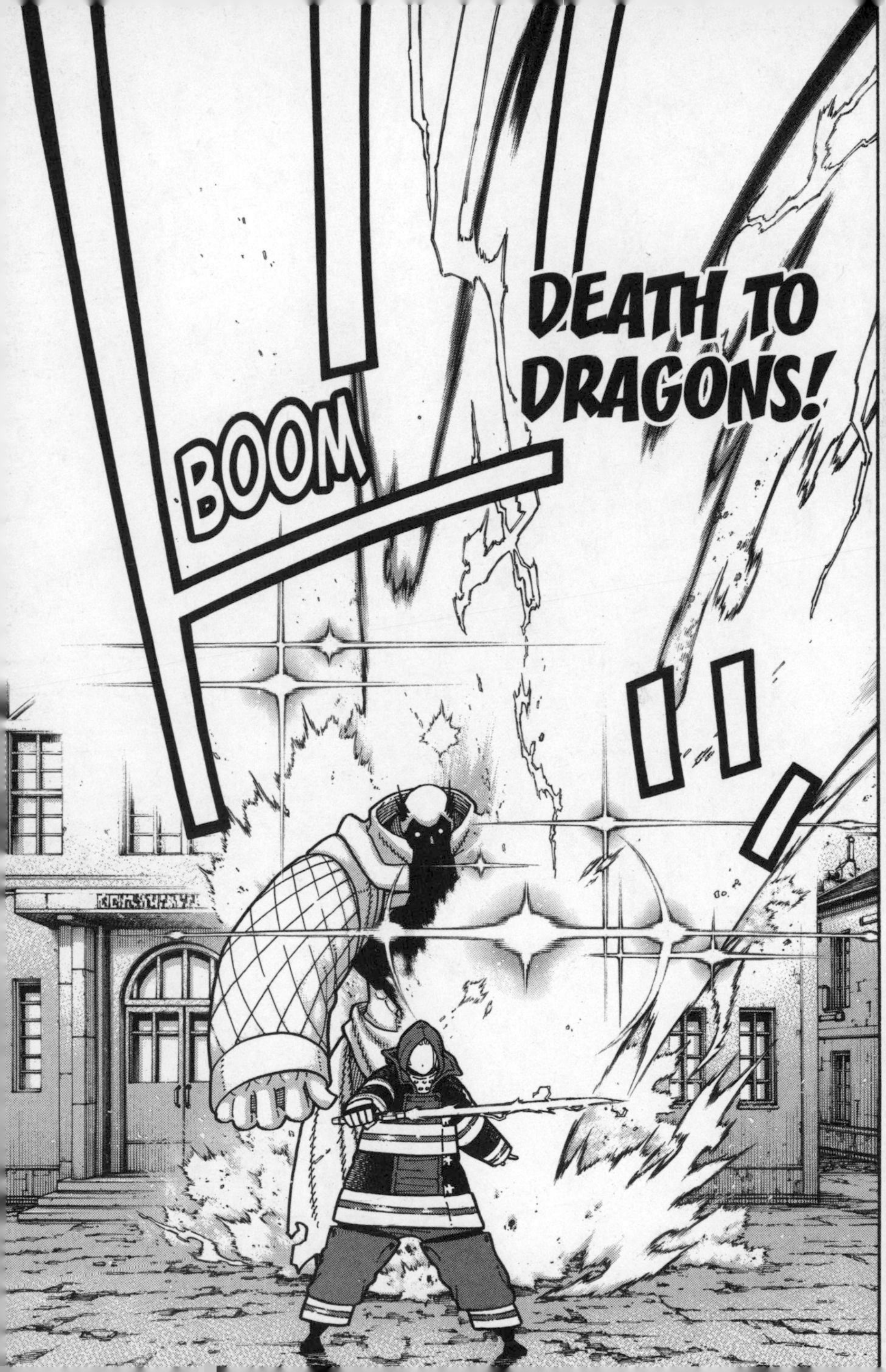
DEATH TO DRAGONS!
BOOM

FIRE FORCE

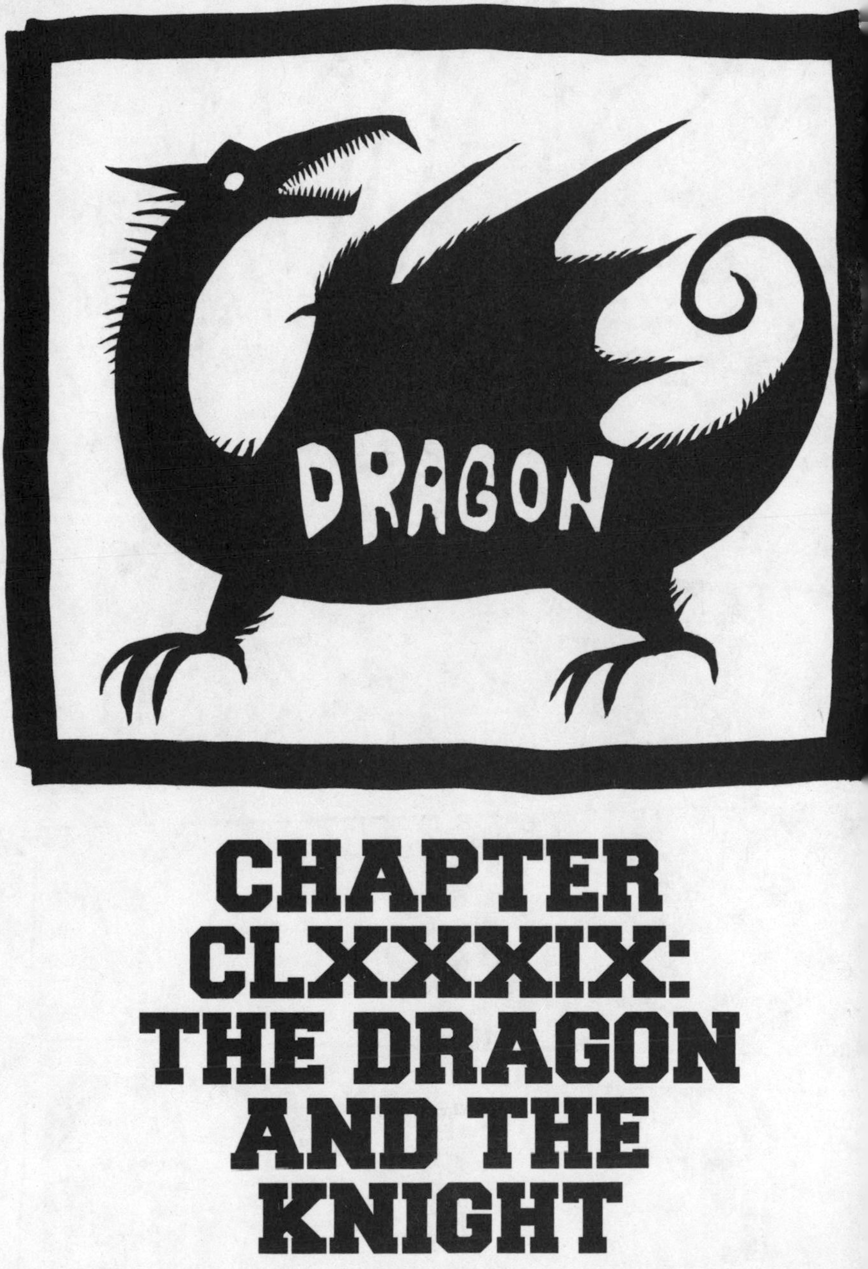
DRAGON

CHAPTER CLXXXIX: THE DRAGON AND THE KNIGHT

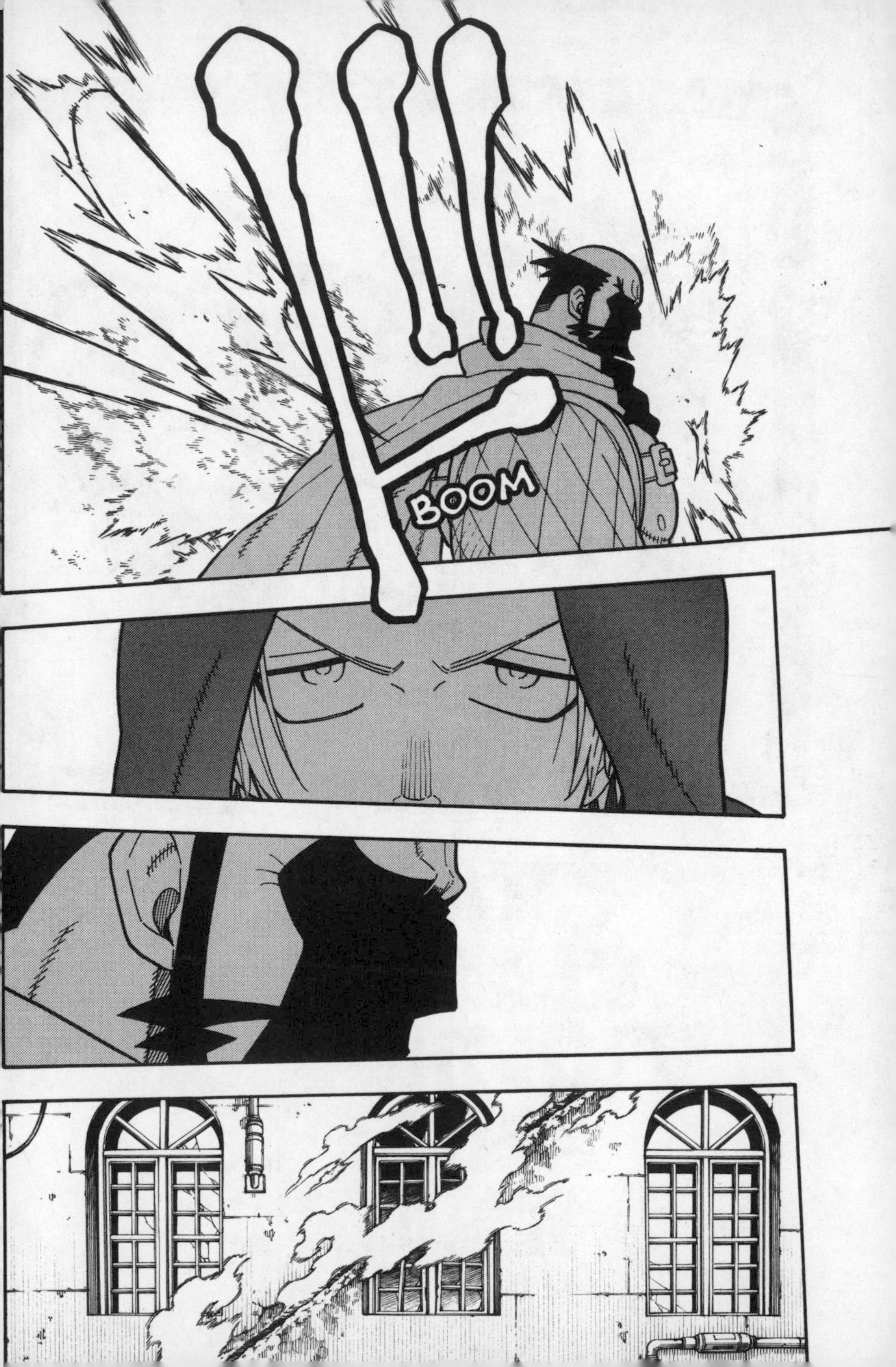
BOOM

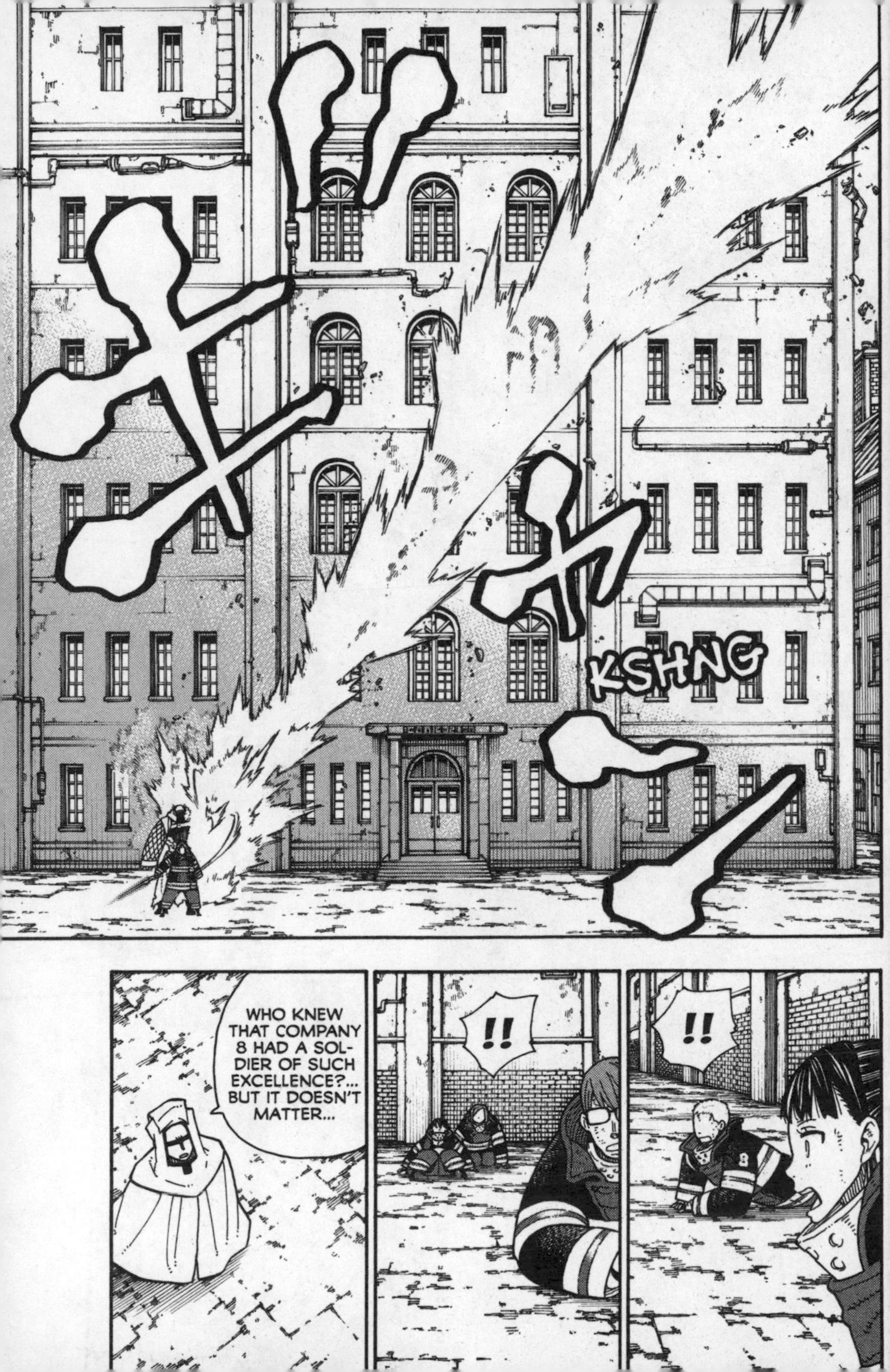
KSHNG
!!
!!
WHO KNEW THAT COMPANY 8 HAD A SOLDIER OF SUCH EXCELLENCE?... BUT IT DOESN'T MATTER...

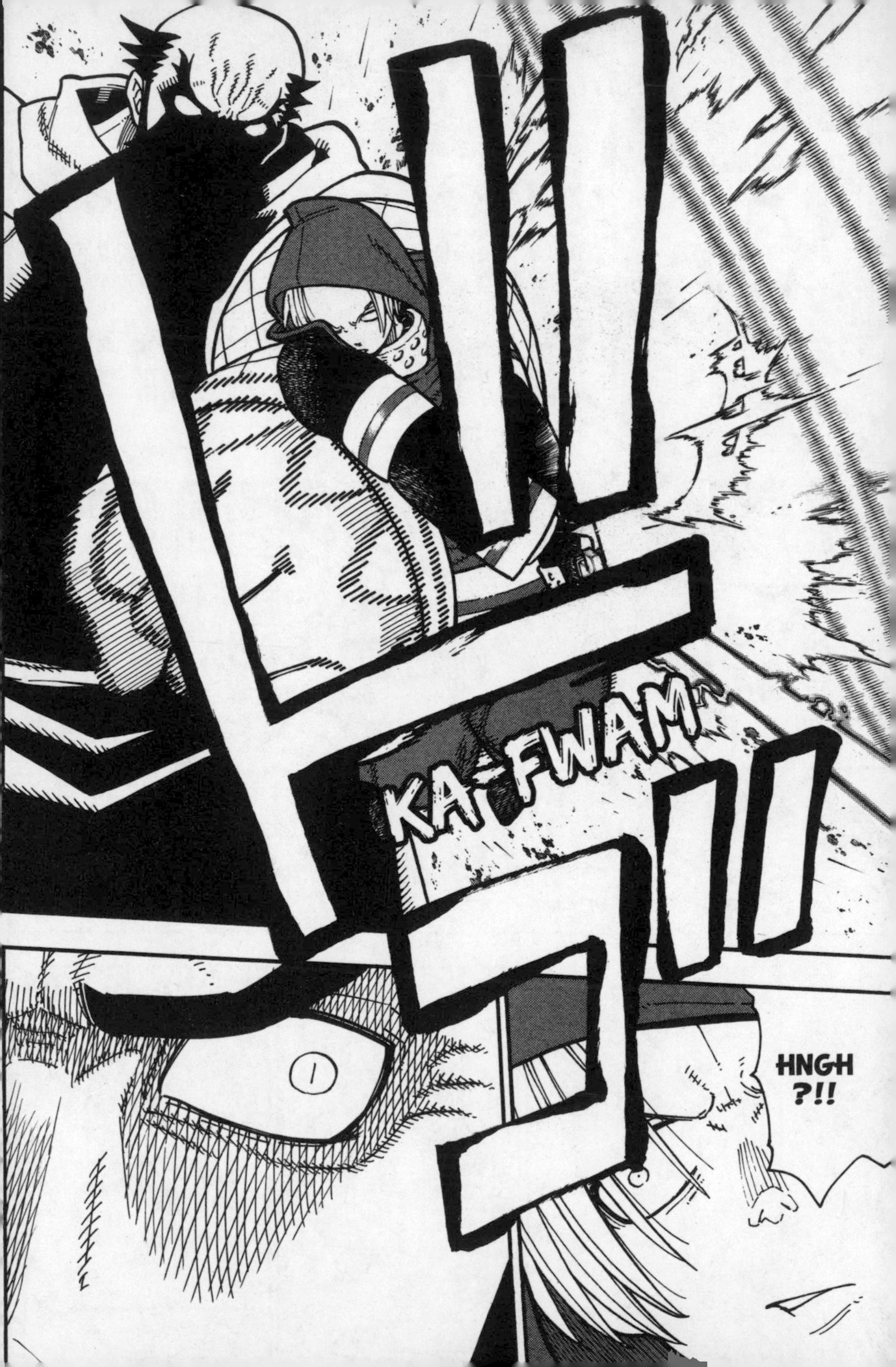
KA-FWAM
HNGH ?!!

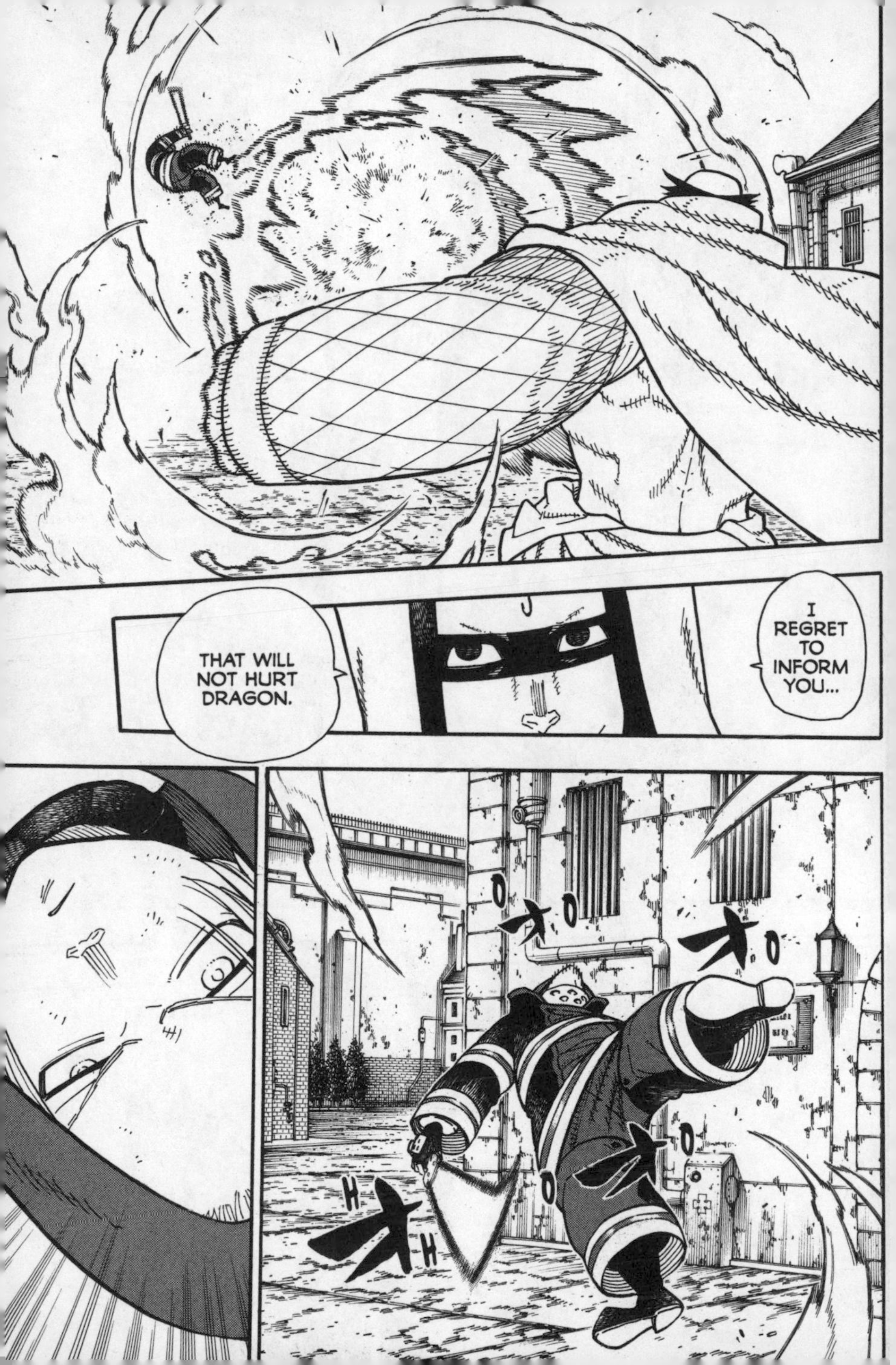
I REGRET TO INFORM YOU...
THAT WILL NOT HURT DRAGON.

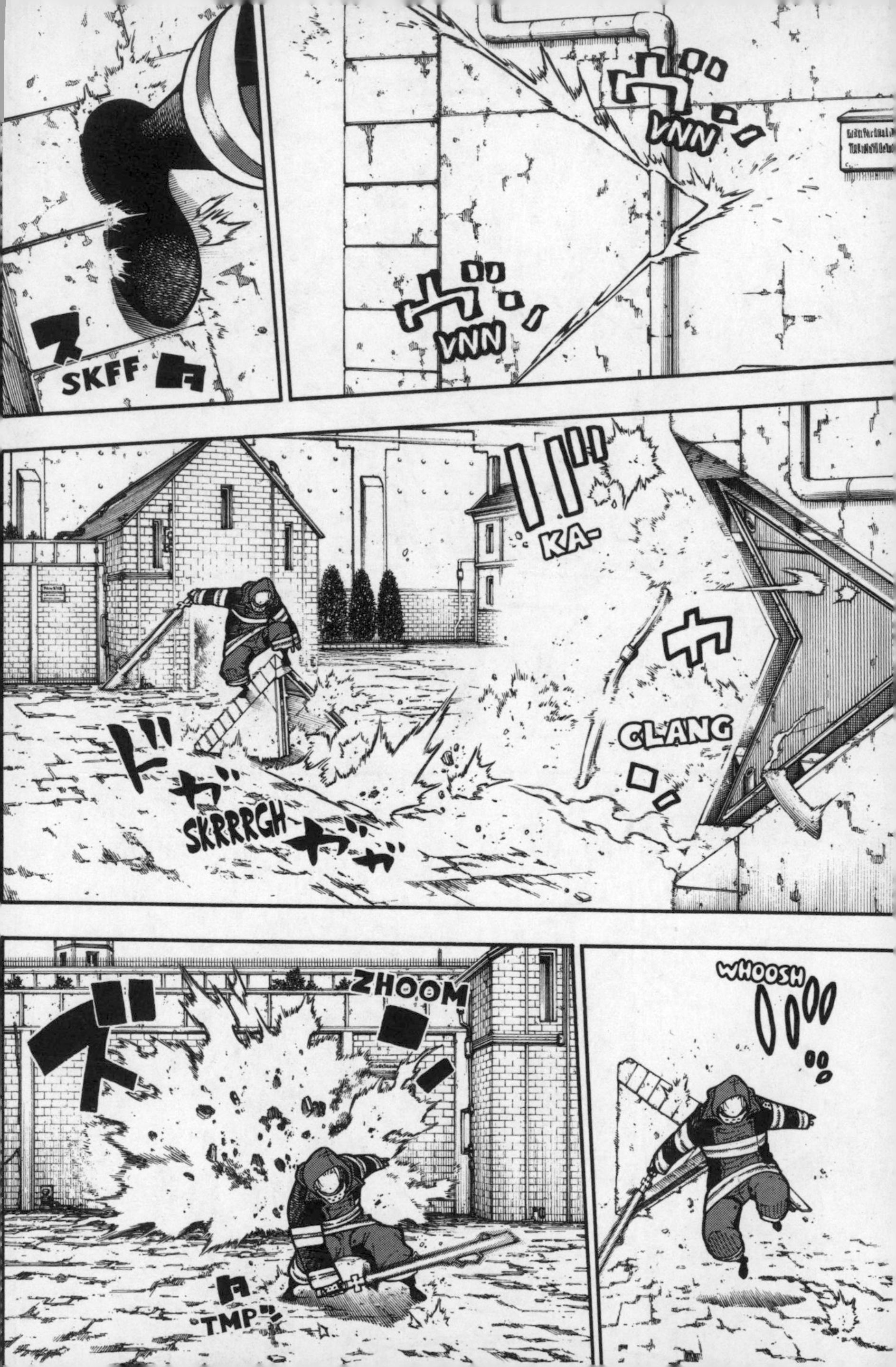
VNN
VNN
SKFF
KA-
CLANG
SKRRRGH
WHOOSH
ZHOOM
TMP

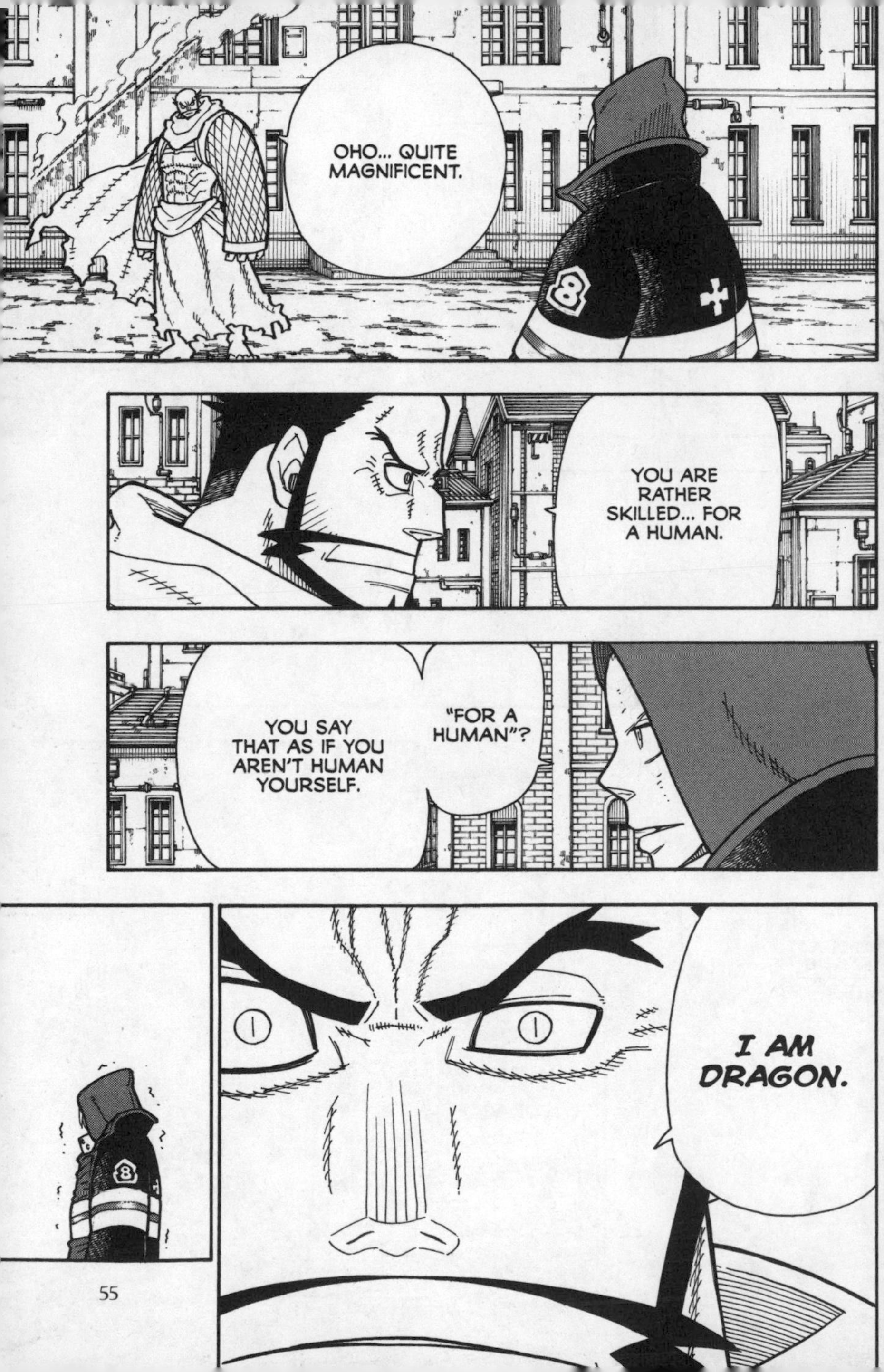
OHO... QUITE MAGNIFICENT.
YOU ARE RATHER SKILLED... FOR A HUMAN.
"FOR A HUMAN"?
YOU SAY THAT AS IF YOU AREN'T HUMAN YOURSELF.
I AM DRAGON.

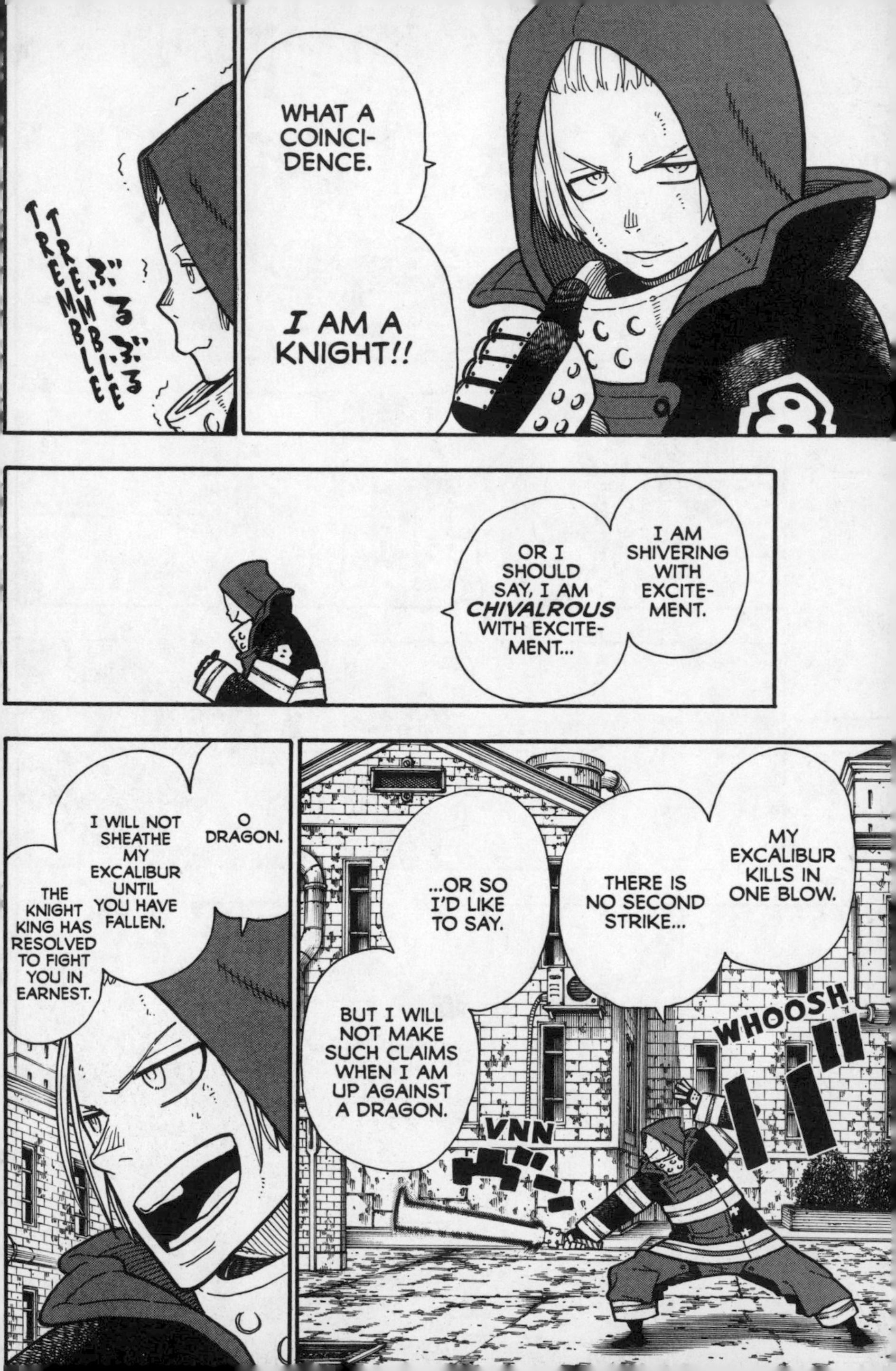
WHAT A COINCIDENCE.
I AM A KNIGHT!!
TREMBLE TREMBLE
ぶるぶる
I AM SHIVERING WITH EXCITEMENT.
OR I SHOULD SAY, I AM CHIVALROUS WITH EXCITEMENT...
MY EXCALIBUR KILLS IN ONE BLOW.
THERE IS NO SECOND STRIKE...
...OR SO I'D LIKE TO SAY.
BUT I WILL NOT MAKE SUCH CLAIMS WHEN I AM UP AGAINST A DRAGON.
WHOOSH
VNN
O DRAGON.
I WILL NOT SHEATHE MY EXCALIBUR UNTIL YOU HAVE FALLEN.
THE KNIGHT KING HAS RESOLVED TO FIGHT YOU IN EARNEST.

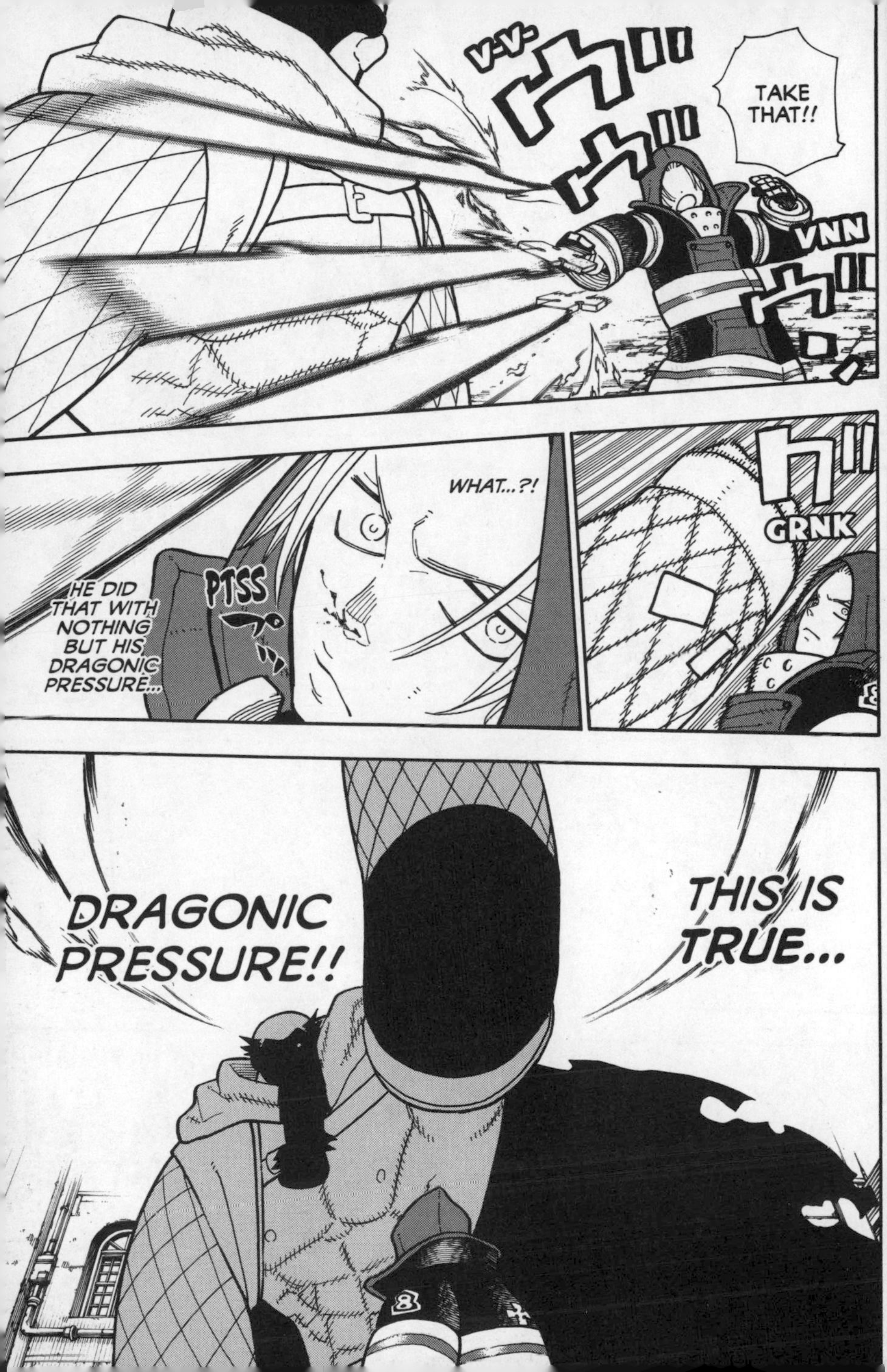
TAKE THAT!!
V-V-
VNN
GRNK
WHAT...?!
PTSS
HE DID THAT WITH NOTHING BUT HIS DRAGONIC PRESSURE...
THIS IS TRUE...
DRAGONIC PRESSURE!!

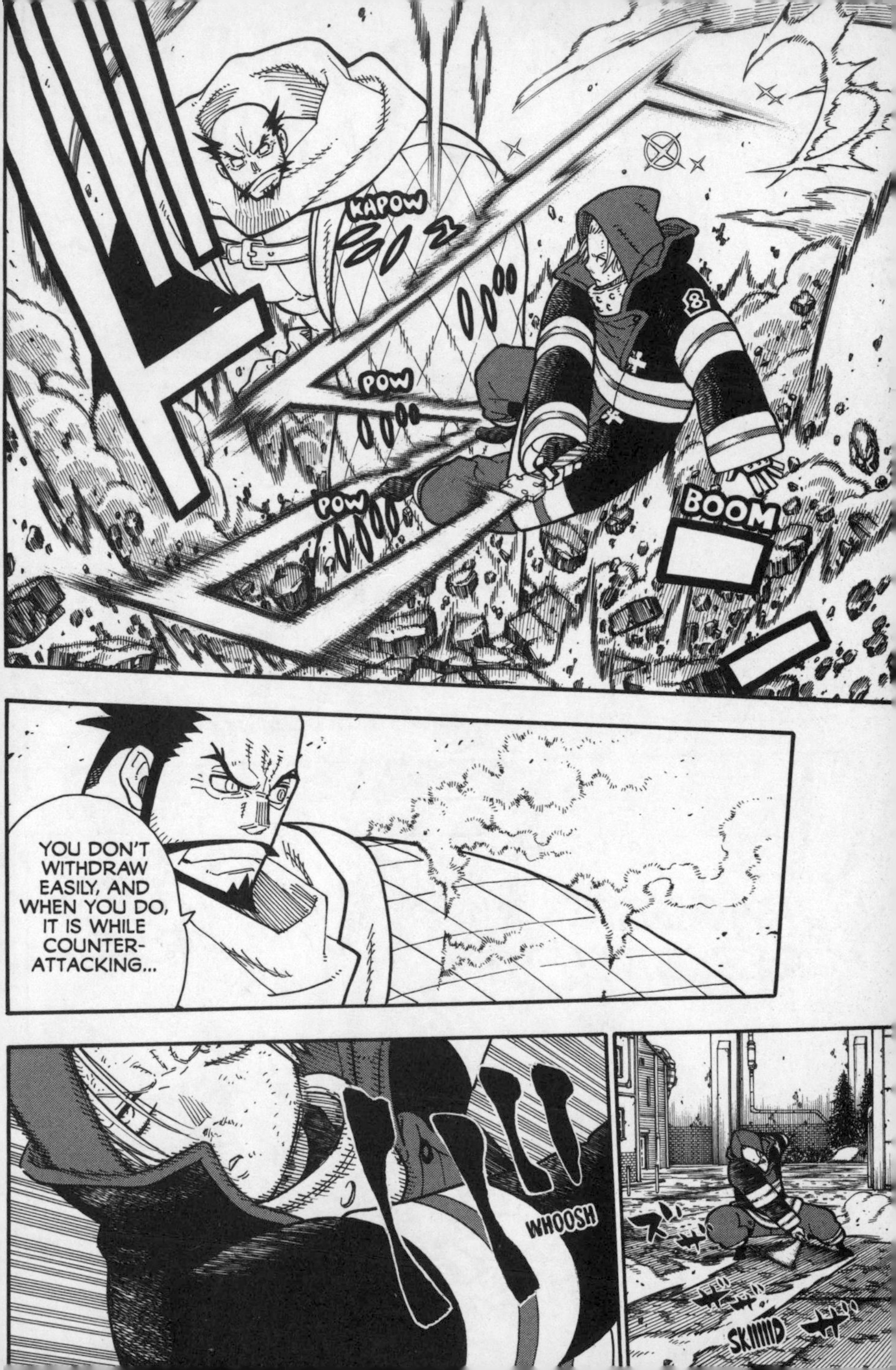
KAPOW
POW
BOOM
POW
YOU DON'T WITHDRAW EASILY, AND WHEN YOU DO, IT IS WHILE COUNTER-ATTACKING...
SKIIIIID
WHOOSH

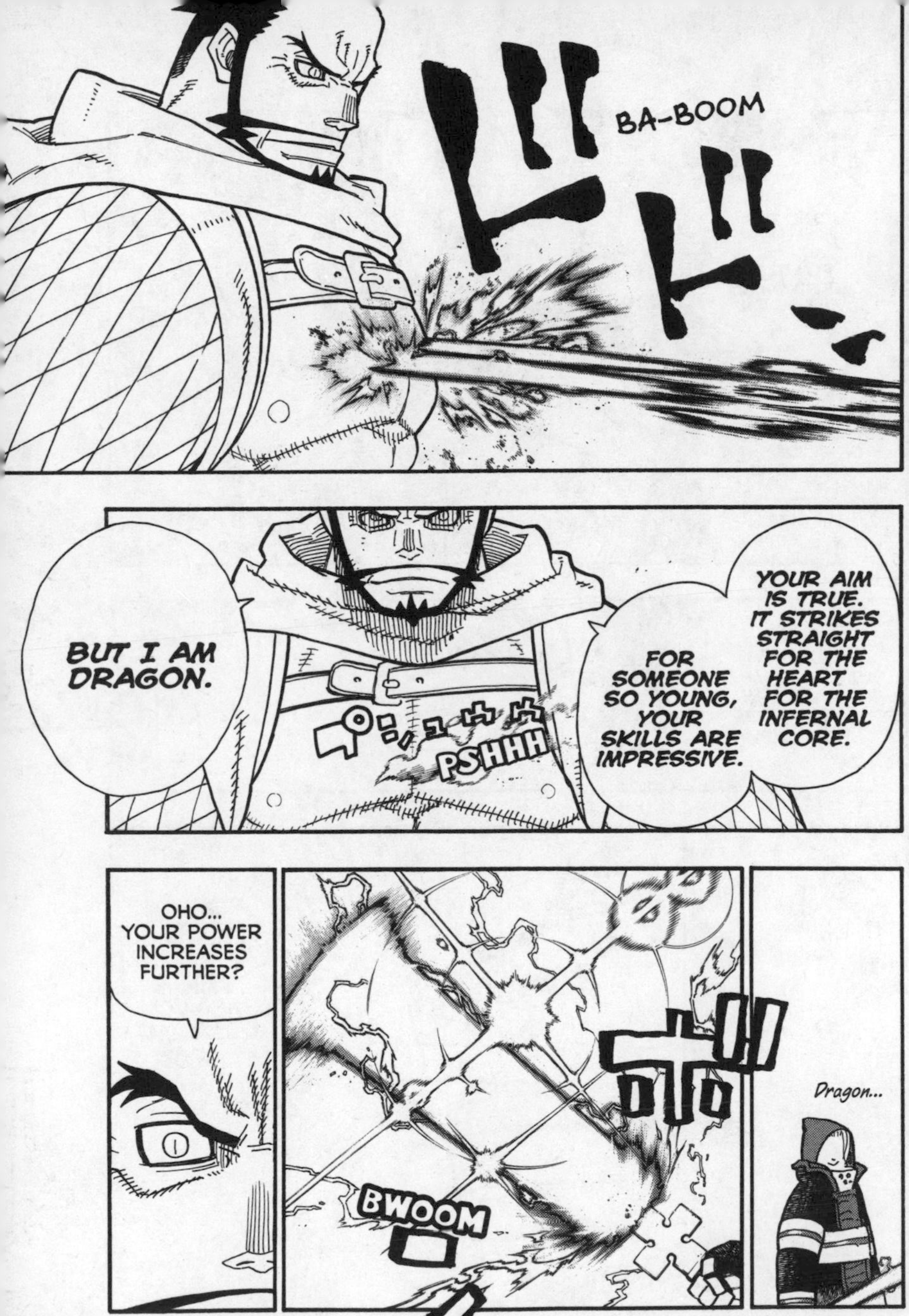
BA-BOOM
YOUR AIM IS TRUE. IT STRIKES STRAIGHT FOR THE HEART FOR THE INFERNAL CORE.
FOR SOMEONE SO YOUNG, YOUR SKILLS ARE IMPRESSIVE.
PSHHH
BUT I AM DRAGON.
Dragon...
BWOOM
OHO... YOUR POWER INCREASES FURTHER?

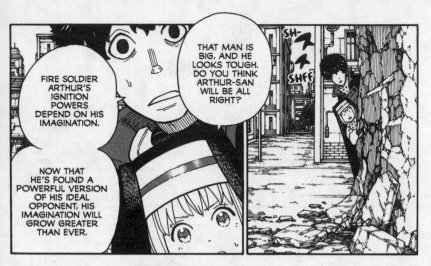

SH-
スス
SHFF
THAT MAN IS BIG, AND HE LOOKS TOUGH. DO YOU THINK ARTHUR-SAN WILL BE ALL RIGHT?
FIRE SOLDIER ARTHUR'S IGNITION POWERS DEPEND ON HIS IMAGINATION.
NOW THAT HE'S FOUND A POWERFUL VERSION OF HIS IDEAL OPPONENT, HIS IMAGINATION WILL GROW GREATER THAN EVER.
I'M NOT SURE THAT ANYONE CAN STOP HIM NOW.
THE POWER OF YOUR FLAMES, AND YOUR COMMAND OVER THEM, ARE THAT OF A TRUE MASTER.
HEH.
MY SWORD'S... MY BLADE WILL...

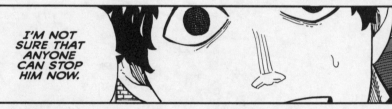

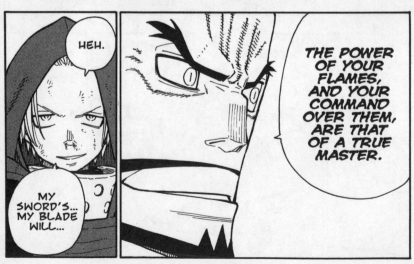

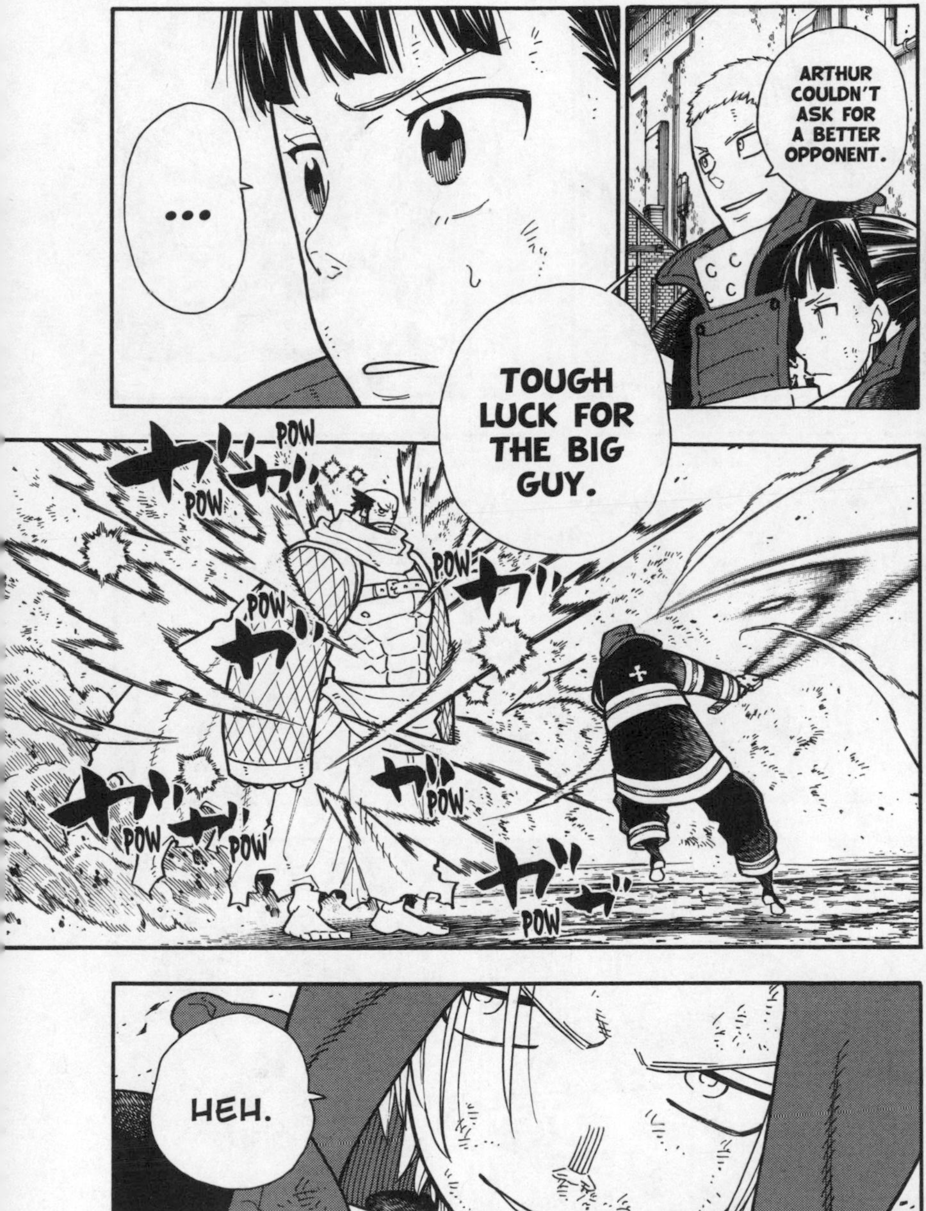

ARTHUR COULDN'T ASK FOR A BETTER OPPONENT.
...
TOUGH LUCK FOR THE BIG GUY.
POW
POW
POW
POW
POW
POW
POW
POW
HEH.

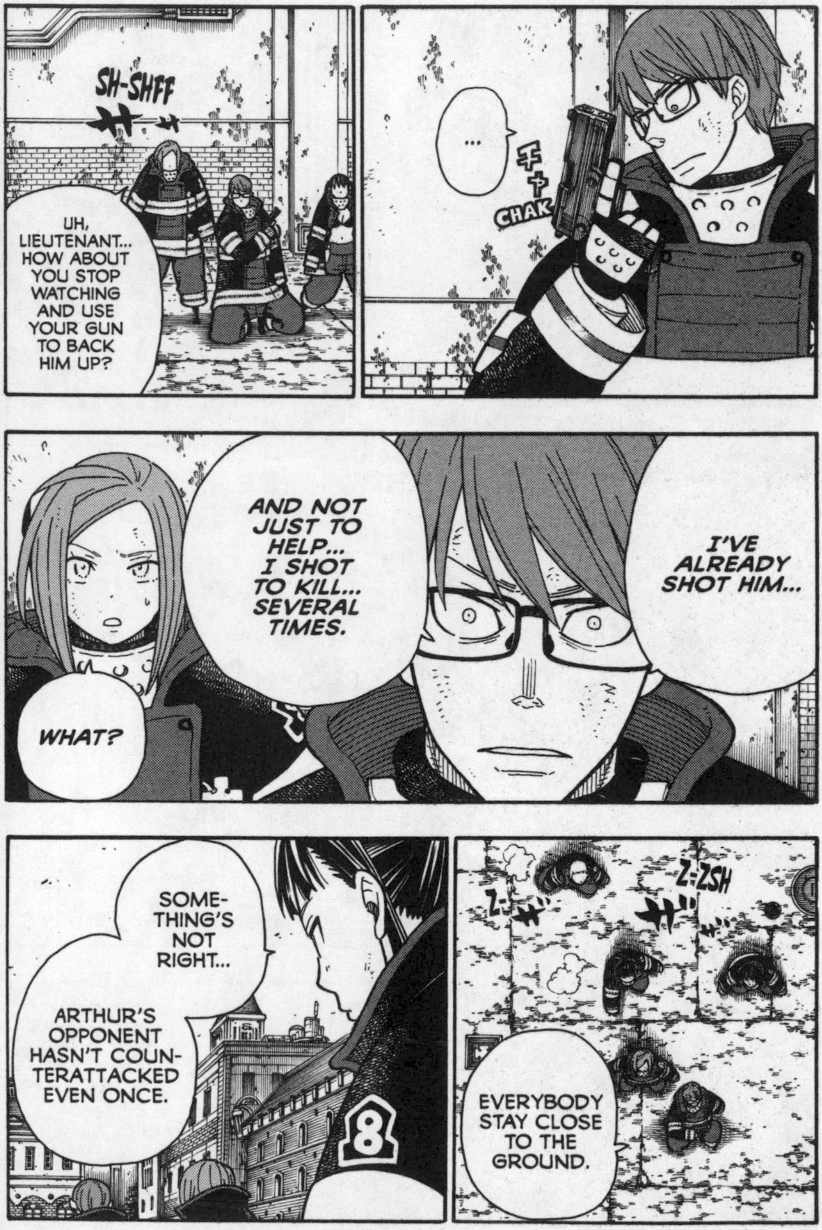
...
CHAK
SH-SHFF
UH, LIEUTENANT... HOW ABOUT YOU STOP WATCHING AND USE YOUR GUN TO BACK HIM UP?
I'VE ALREADY SHOT HIM...
AND NOT JUST TO HELP... I SHOT TO KILL... SEVERAL TIMES.
WHAT?
Z-ZSH
Z-
EVERYBODY STAY CLOSE TO THE GROUND.
SOME-THING'S NOT RIGHT...
ARTHUR'S OPPONENT HASN'T COUN-TERATTACKED EVEN ONCE.

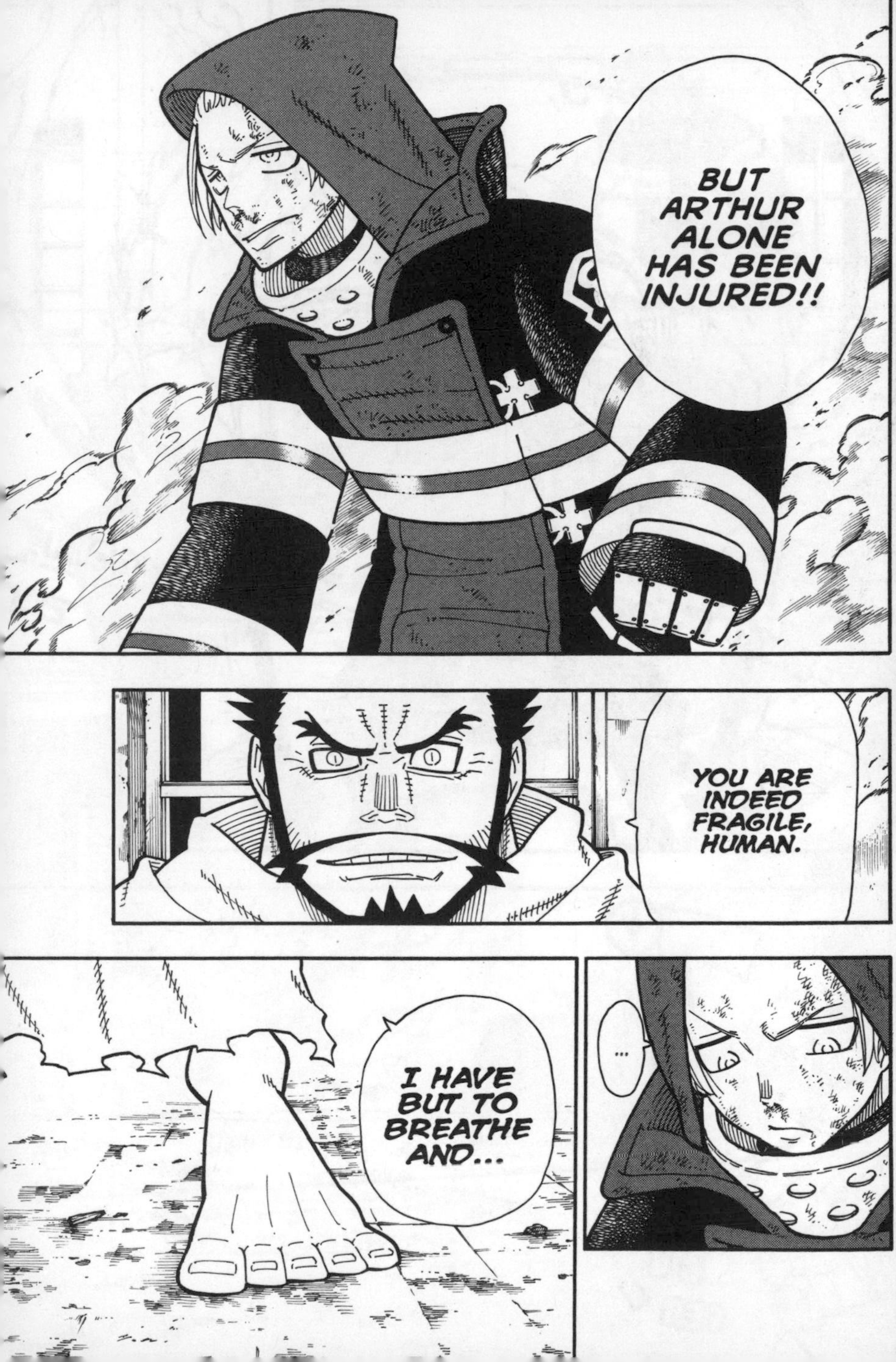
BUT ARTHUR ALONE HAS BEEN INJURED!!
YOU ARE INDEED FRAGILE, HUMAN.
...
I HAVE BUT TO BREATHE AND...

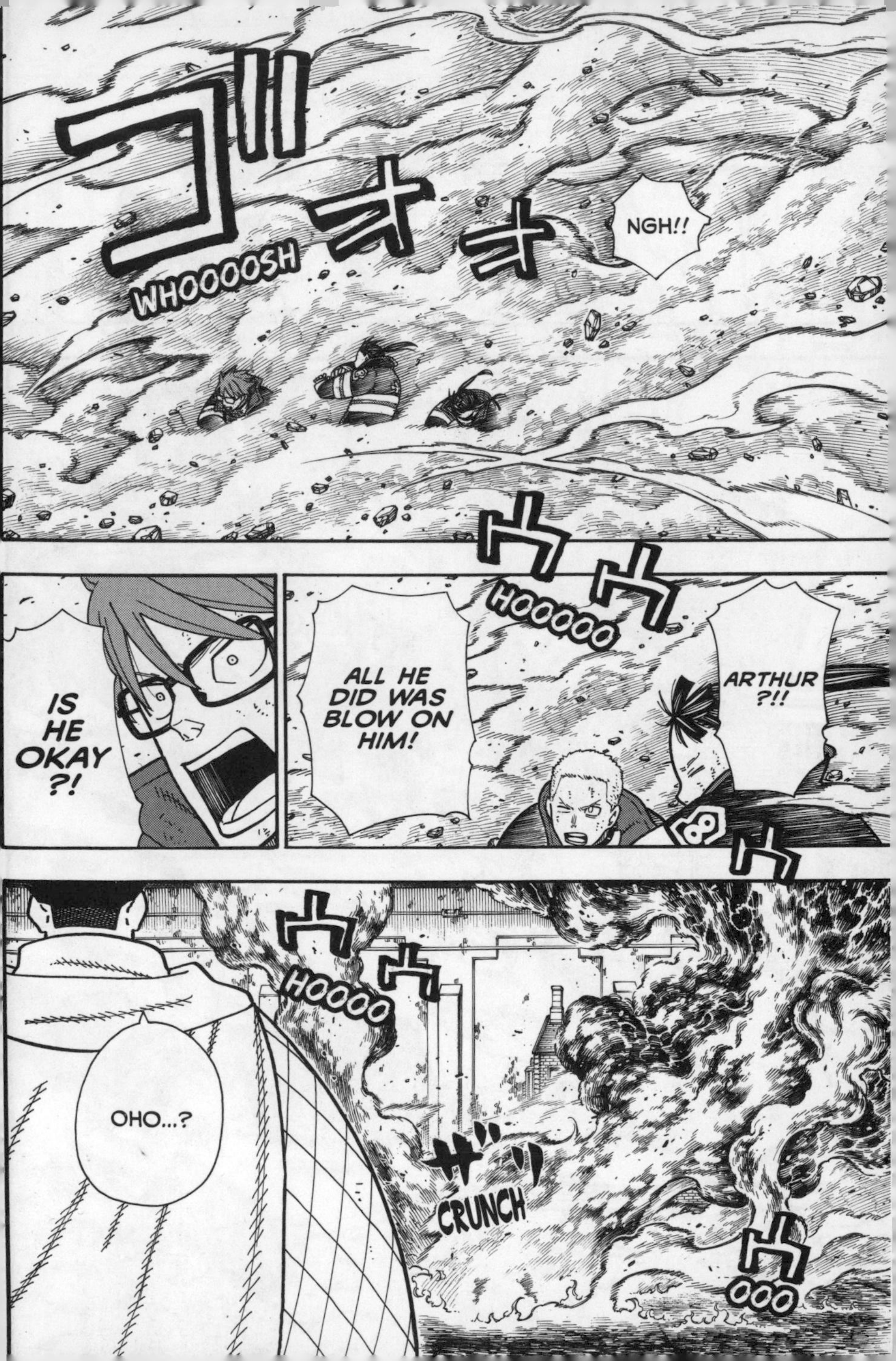
WHOOOOSH
NGH!!
HOOOOOO
ARTHUR?!!
ALL HE DID WAS BLOW ON HIM!
IS HE OKAY?!
HOOOO
OOO
CRUNCH
OHO...?

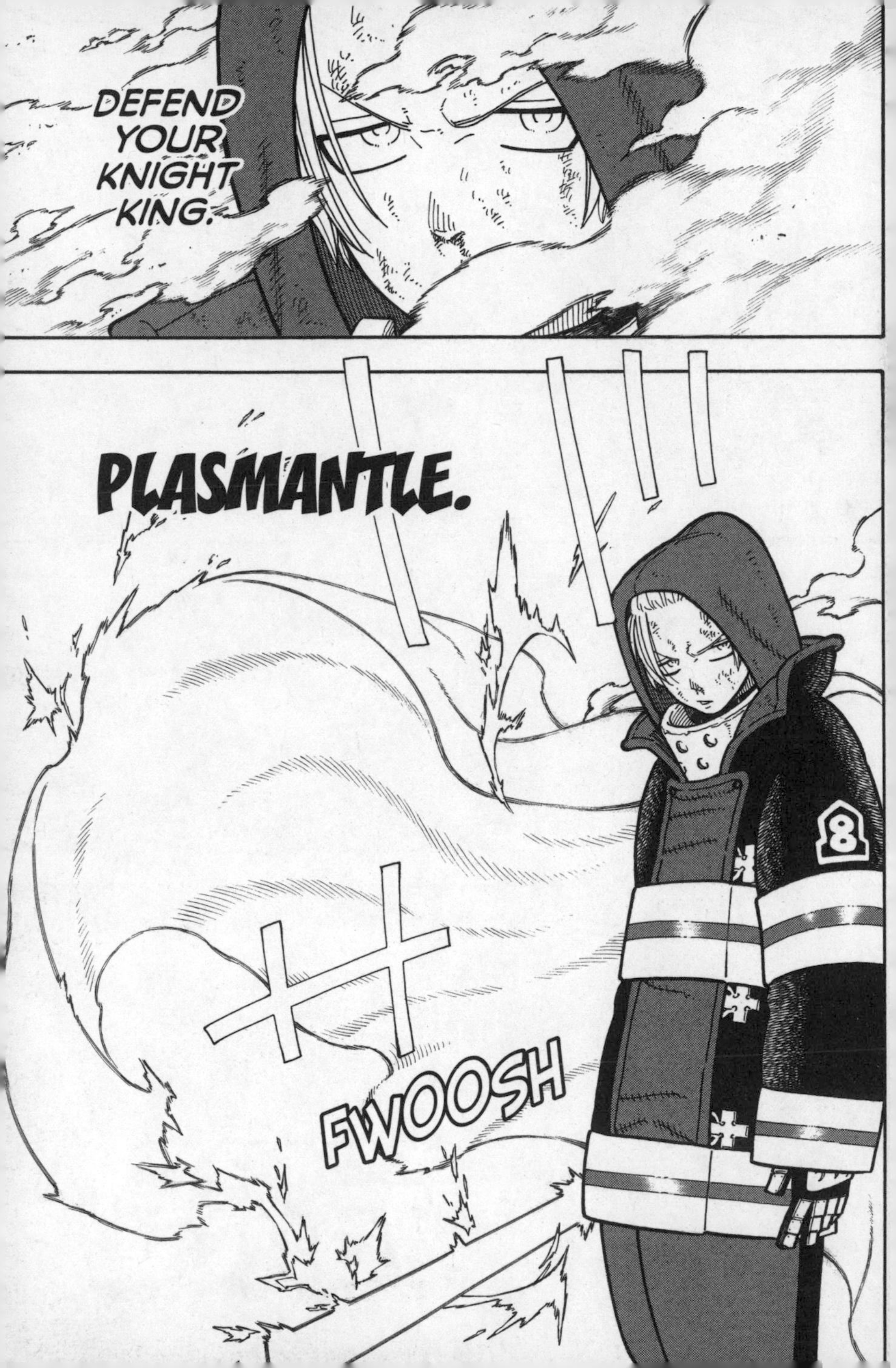
DEFEND YOUR KNIGHT KING.
PLASMANTLE.
FWOOSH

FIRE FORCE

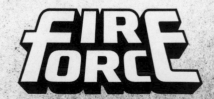

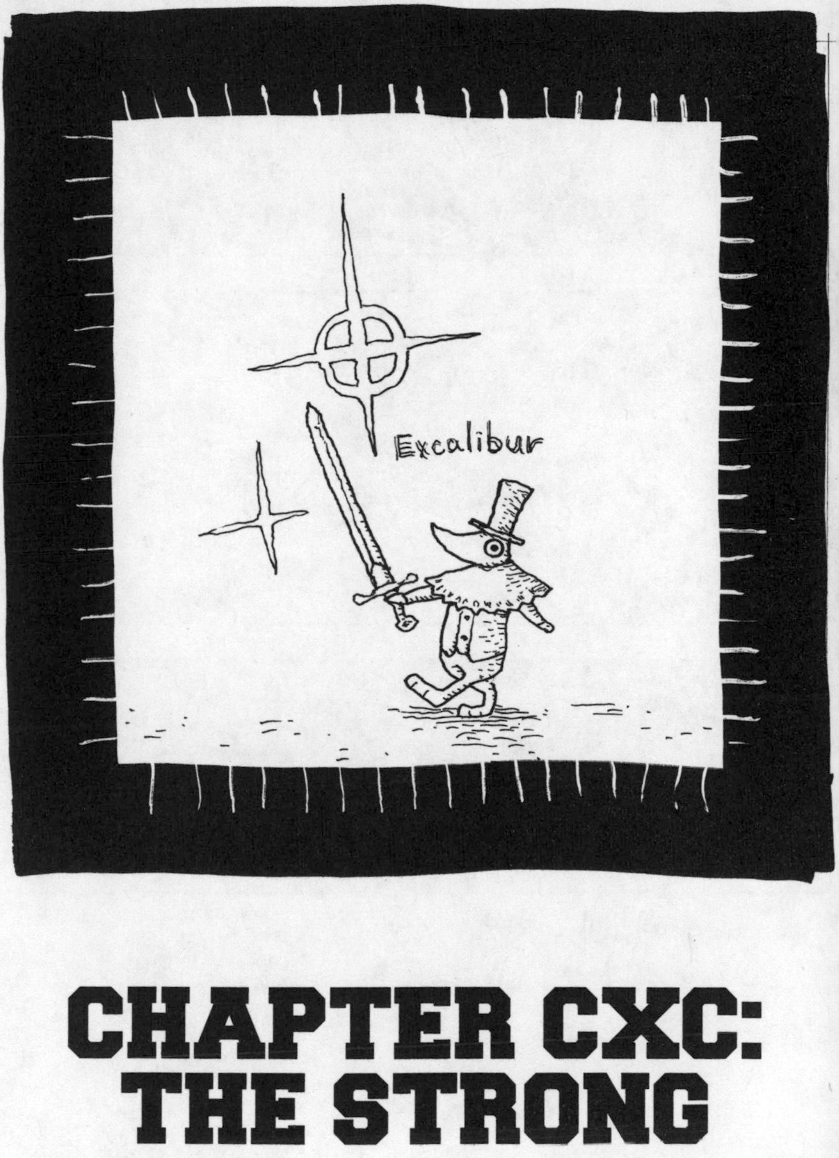
Excalibur

CHAPTER CXC: THE STRONG

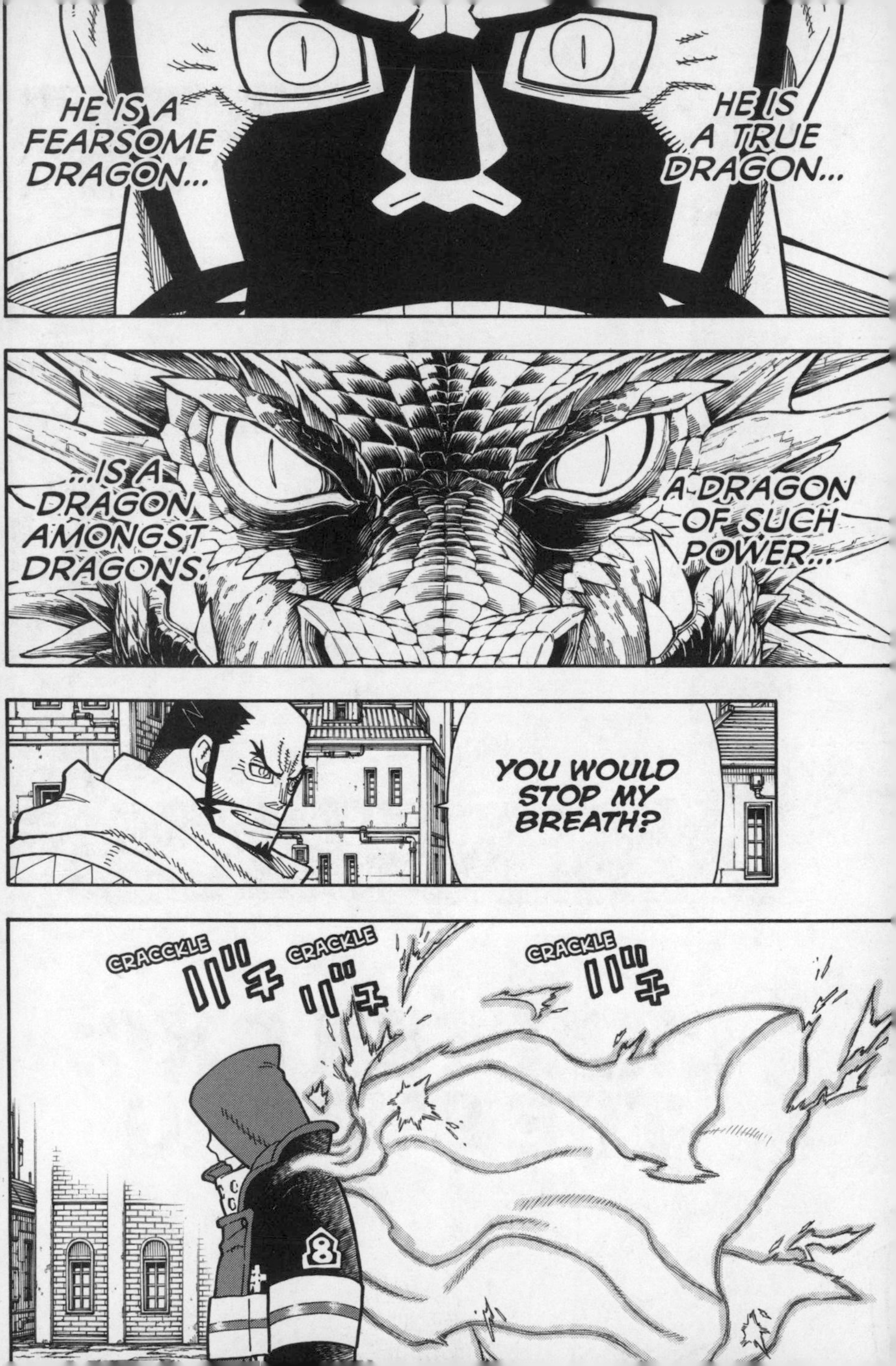
HE IS A TRUE DRAGON...
HE IS A FEARSOME DRAGON...
A DRAGON OF SUCH POWER...
...IS A DRAGON AMONGST DRAGONS.
YOU WOULD STOP MY BREATH?
CRACKLE
バチ
CRACKLE
バチ
CRACKLE
バチ

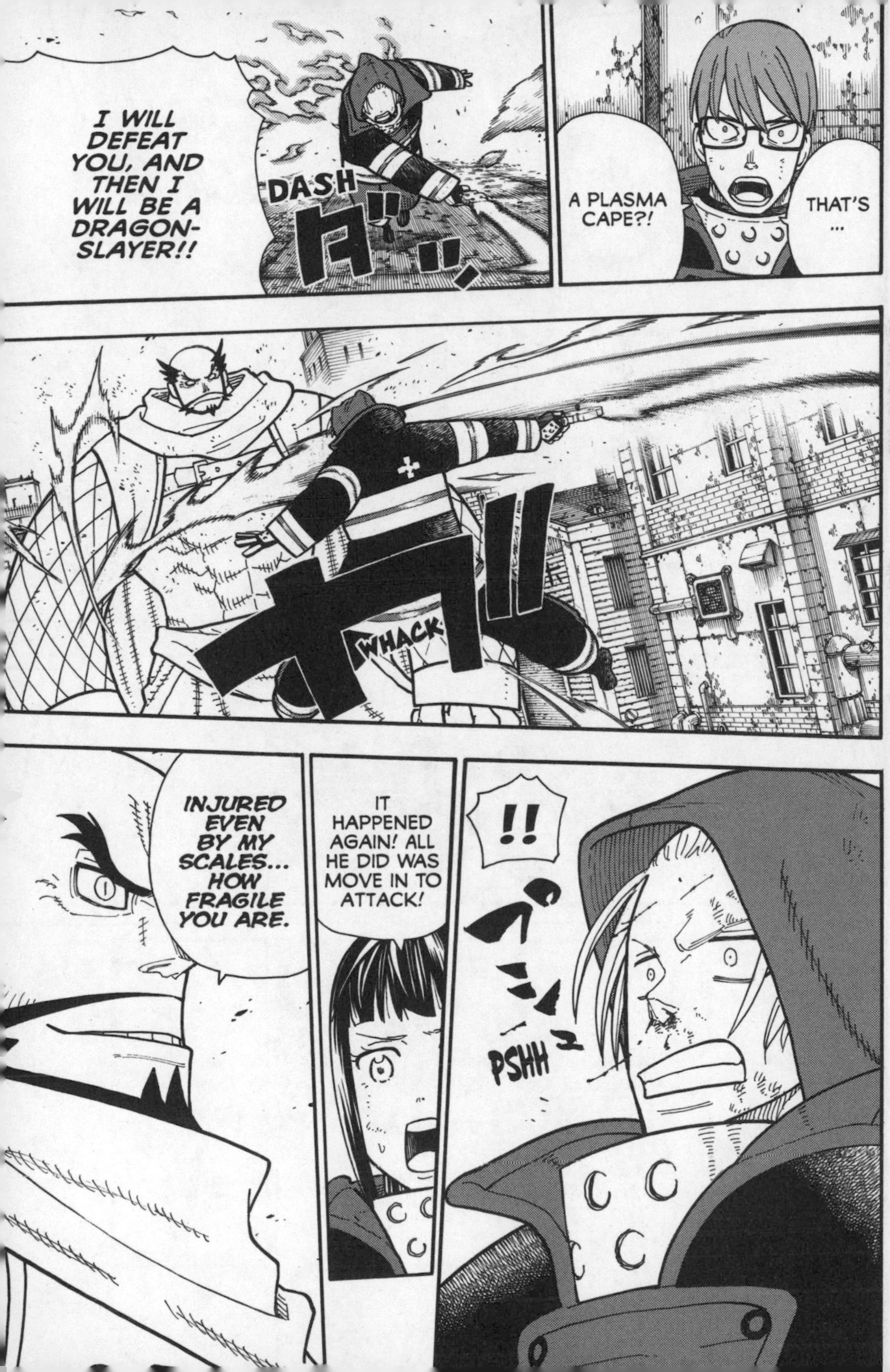
THAT'S ...
A PLASMA CAPE?!
I WILL DEFEAT YOU, AND THEN I WILL BE A DRAGON-SLAYER!!
DASH
WHACK
!!
PSHH
IT HAPPENED AGAIN! ALL HE DID WAS MOVE IN TO ATTACK!
INJURED EVEN BY MY SCALES... HOW FRAGILE YOU ARE.

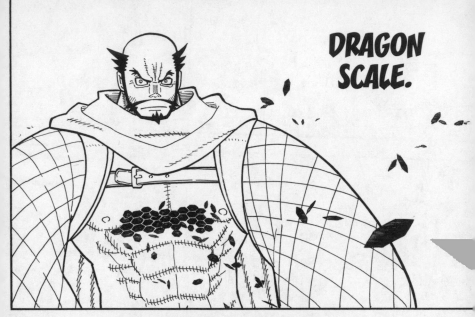

DRAGON SCALE.
PATTER
PATTER
WHERE ARTHUR SLASHED HIM, HE...
I'M TOO FAR AWAY TO GET A GOOD LOOK, BUT I THINK THOSE SCALES LOOK LIKE THE FLESH OF AN INFERNAL.
THE DREADED DRAGON SCALES.

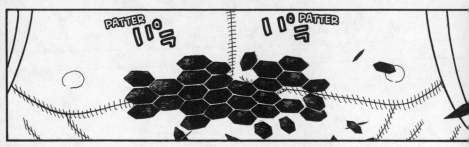

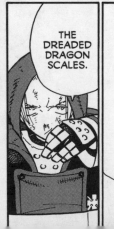

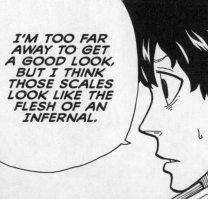

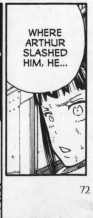

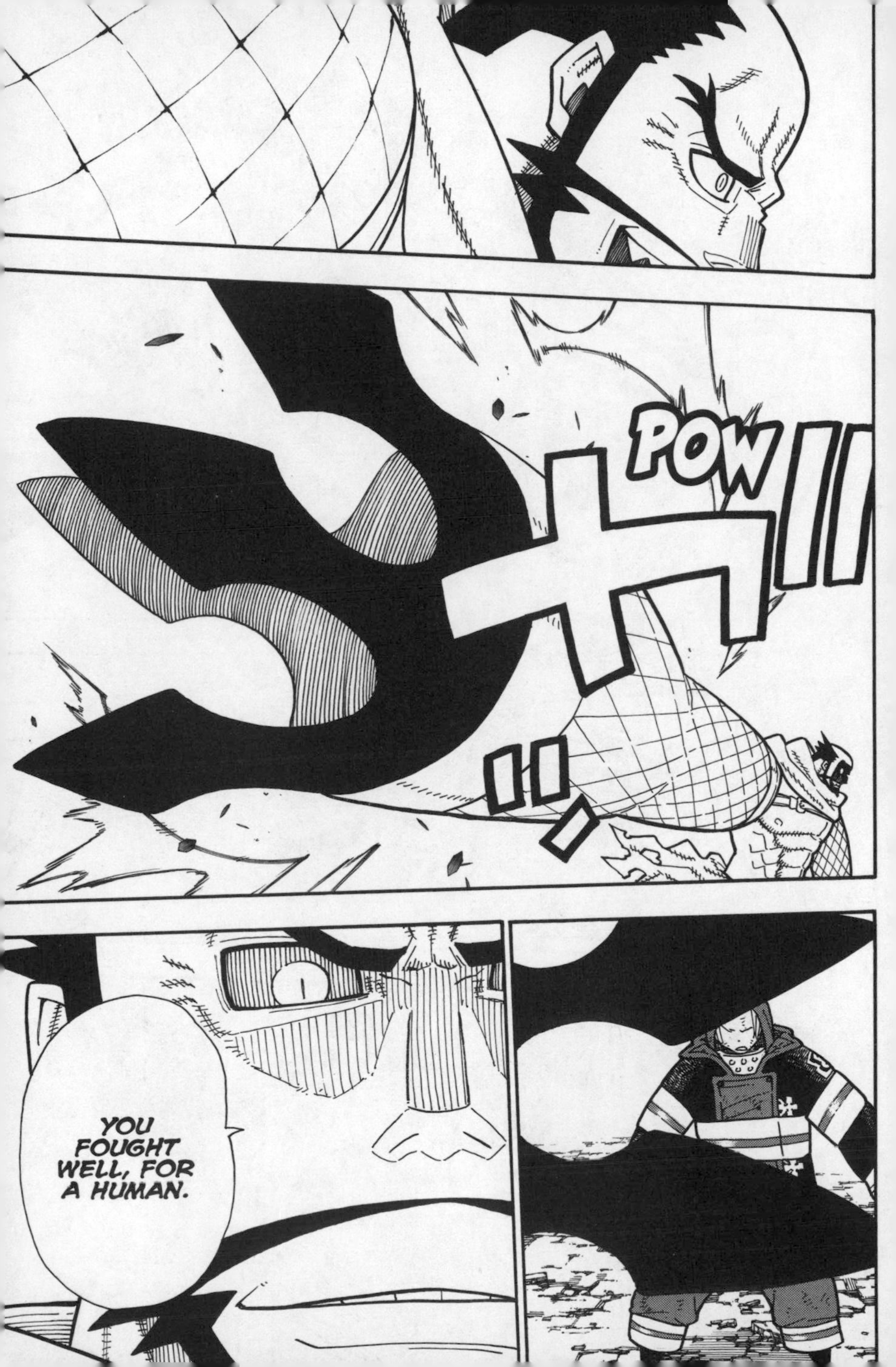
POW!!
YOU FOUGHT WELL, FOR A HUMAN.

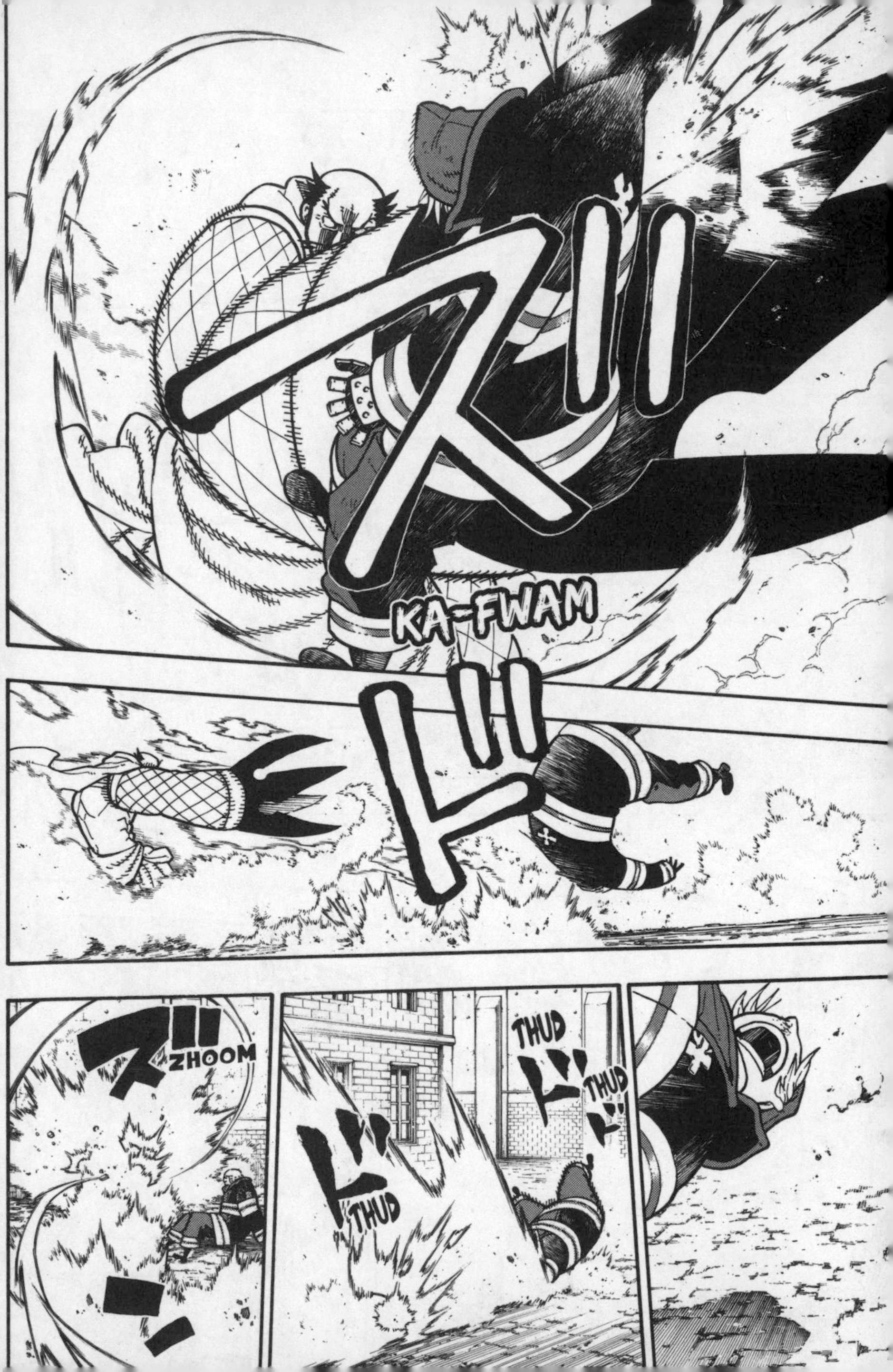
KA-FWAM
THUD
THUD
THUD
ZHOOM

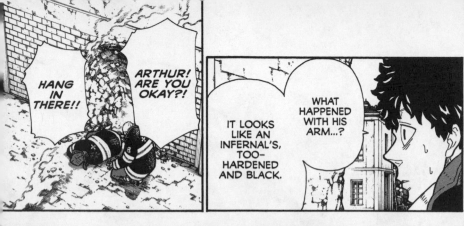

WHAT HAPPENED WITH HIS ARM...?
IT LOOKS LIKE AN INFERNAL'S, TOO— HARDENED AND BLACK.
ARTHUR! ARE YOU OKAY?!
HANG IN THERE!!
'TWAS NOT A BAD STRATEGY, ENHANCING YOUR IGNITION POWERS WITH THE MIGHT OF YOUR IMAGINATION.
BUT YOU HAVE YET TO GRASP ADOLLA.
WH...
WHAT ...?
YOU CANNOT GO ANY FARTHER WITH ONLY HALF OF YOUR POWER.

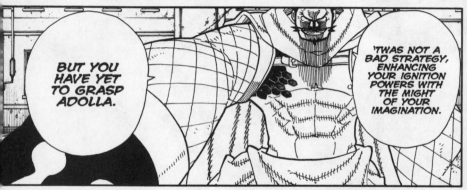

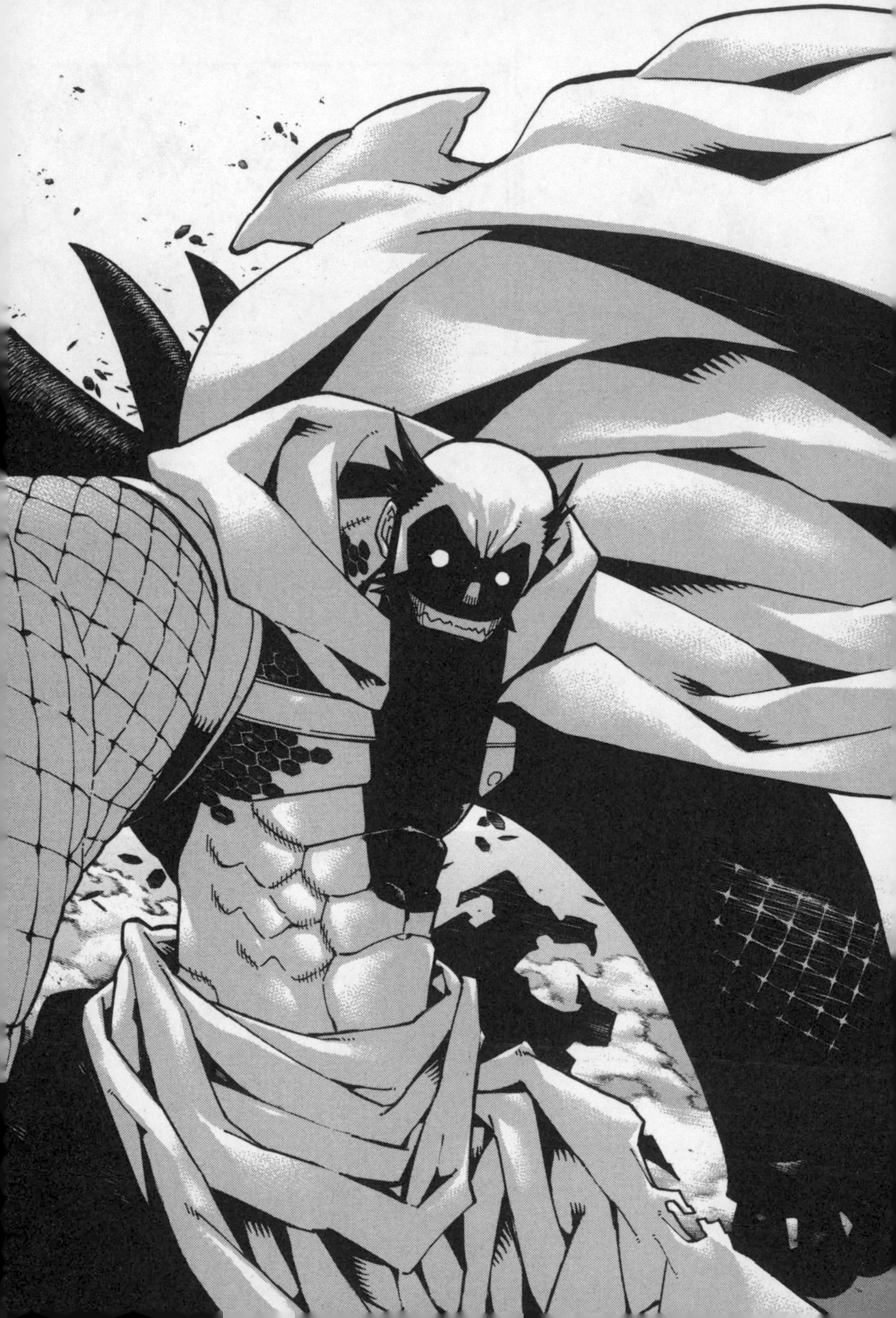

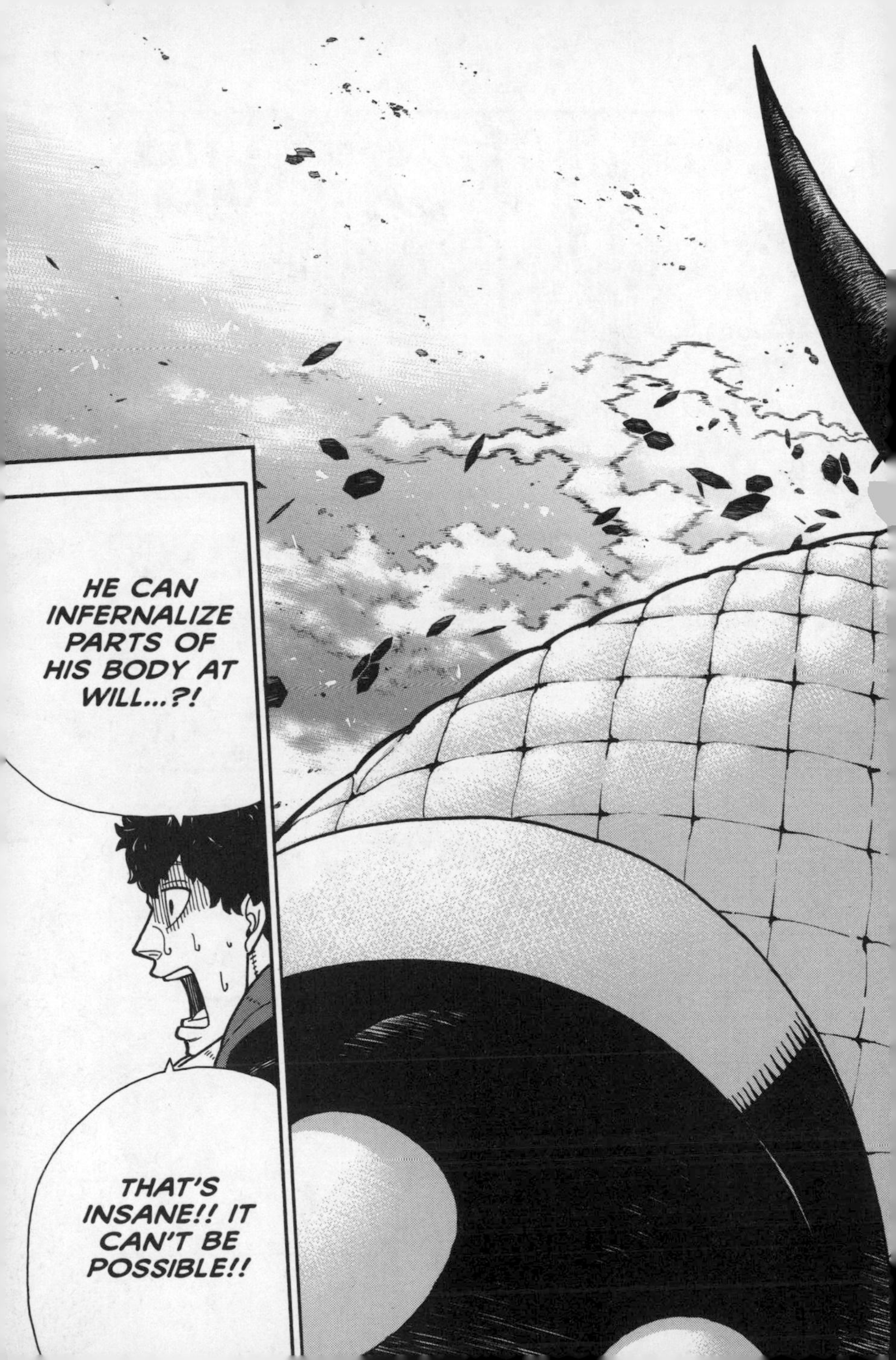
HE CAN INFERNALIZE PARTS OF HIS BODY AT WILL...?!
THAT'S INSANE!! IT CAN'T BE POSSIBLE!!

SPECIAL FIRE COMBINE 5
MIYA-MOTO... THE TALKING INFERNAL... DEMONS...
DOPPEL-GANGERS...
CLACK
WHY IS MY RESEARCH LEADING ME HERE...?

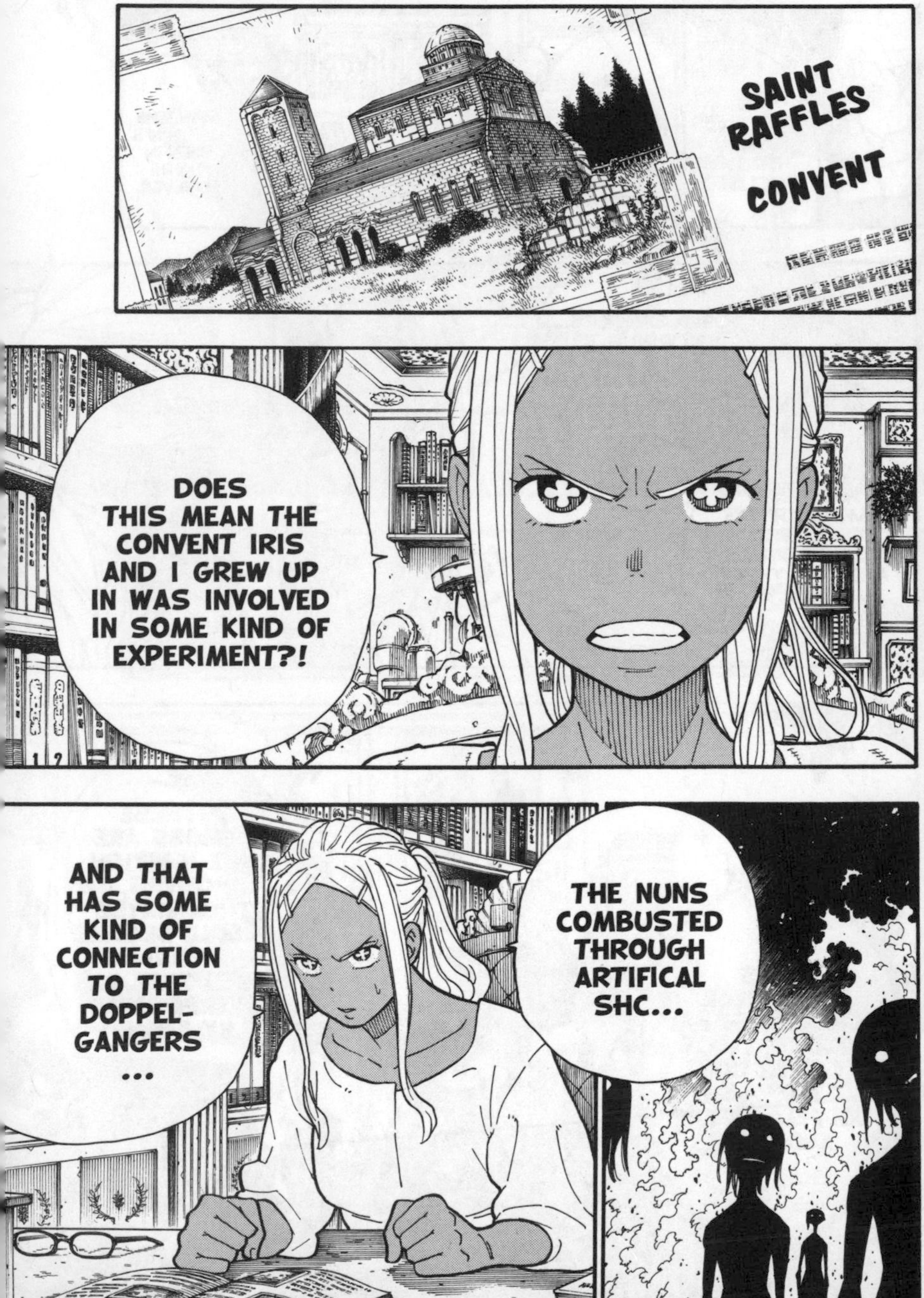
SAINT RAFFLES CONVENT
DOES THIS MEAN THE CONVENT IRIS AND I GREW UP IN WAS INVOLVED IN SOME KIND OF EXPERIMENT?!
THE NUNS COMBUSTED THROUGH ARTIFICAL SHC...
AND THAT HAS SOME KIND OF CONNECTION TO THE DOPPEL-GANGERS ...

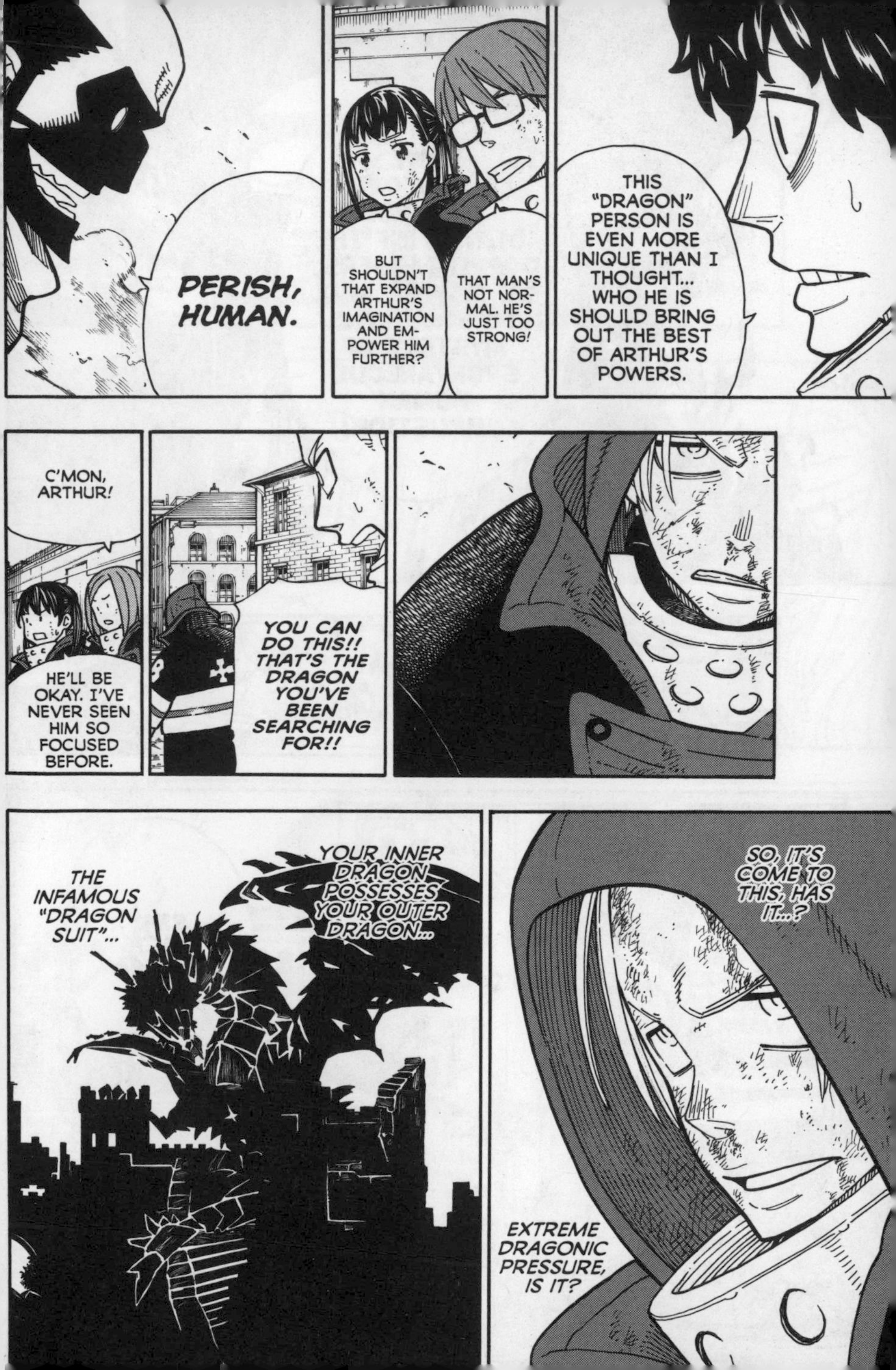
THIS "DRAGON" PERSON IS EVEN MORE UNIQUE THAN I THOUGHT... WHO HE IS SHOULD BRING OUT THE BEST OF ARTHUR'S POWERS.
THAT MAN'S NOT NORMAL. HE'S JUST TOO STRONG!
BUT SHOULDN'T THAT EXPAND ARTHUR'S IMAGINATION AND EMPOWER HIM FURTHER?
PERISH, HUMAN.
YOU CAN DO THIS!! THAT'S THE DRAGON YOU'VE BEEN SEARCHING FOR!!
C'MON, ARTHUR!
HE'LL BE OKAY. I'VE NEVER SEEN HIM SO FOCUSED BEFORE.
SO, IT'S COME TO THIS, HAS IT...?
EXTREME DRAGONIC PRESSURE, IS IT?
YOUR INNER DRAGON POSSESSES YOUR OUTER DRAGON...
THE INFAMOUS "DRAGON SUIT"...

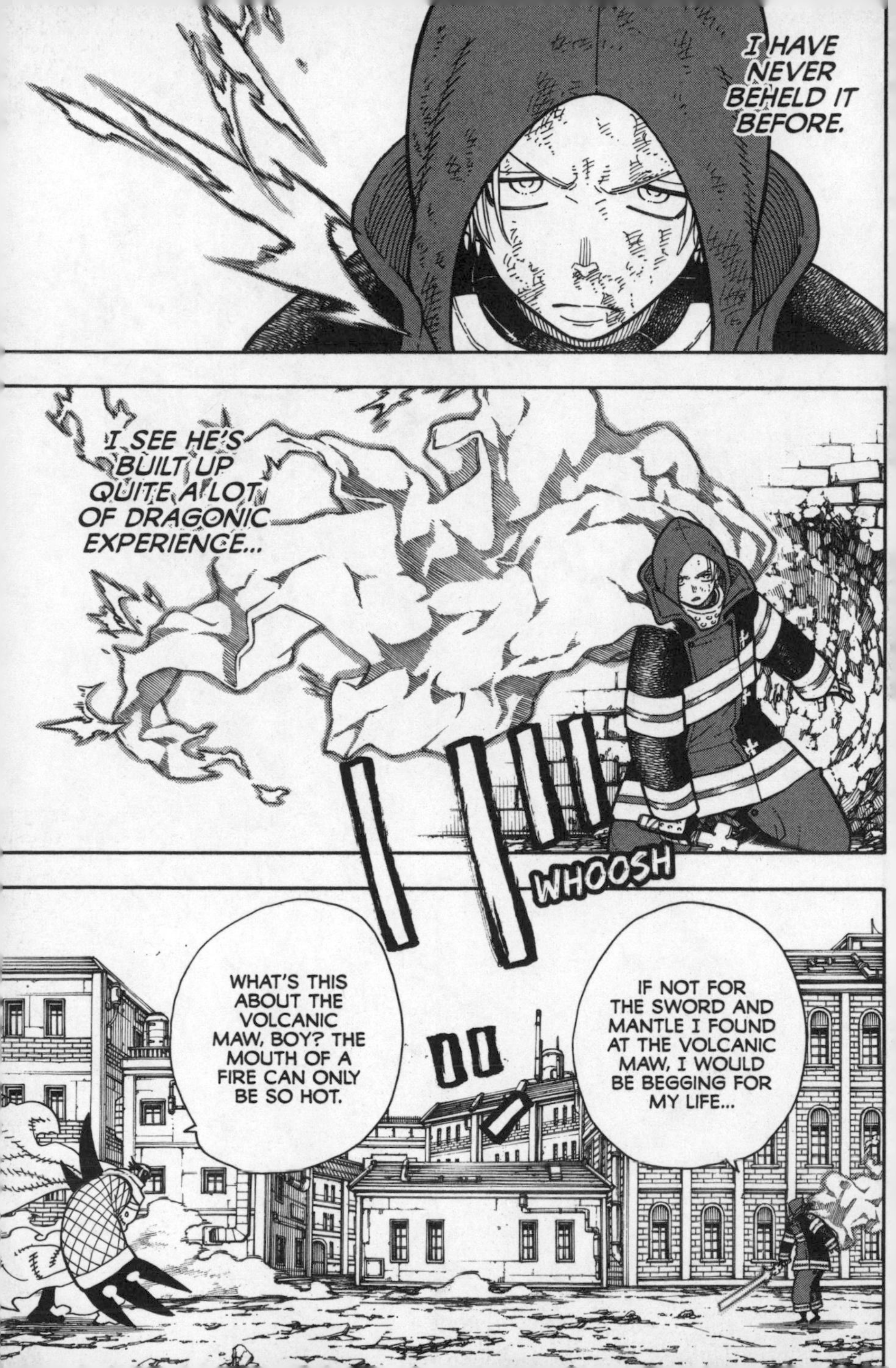
I HAVE NEVER BEHELD IT BEFORE.
I SEE HE'S BUILT UP QUITE A LOT OF DRAGONIC EXPERIENCE...
WHOOSH
IF NOT FOR THE SWORD AND MANTLE I FOUND AT THE VOLCANIC MAW, I WOULD BE BEGGING FOR MY LIFE...
WHAT'S THIS ABOUT THE VOLCANIC MAW, BOY? THE MOUTH OF A FIRE CAN ONLY BE SO HOT.

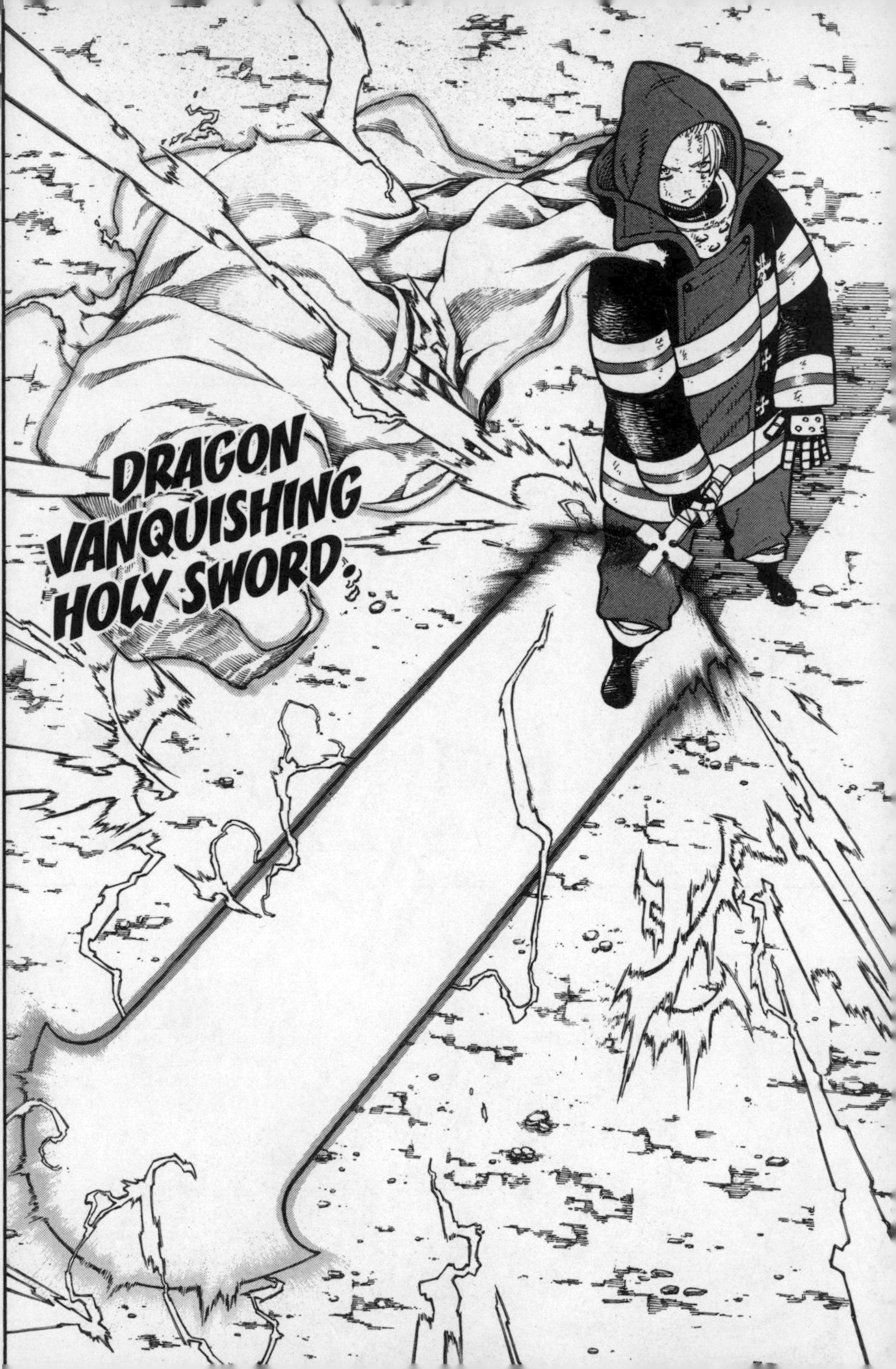
DRAGON VANQUISHING HOLY SWORD

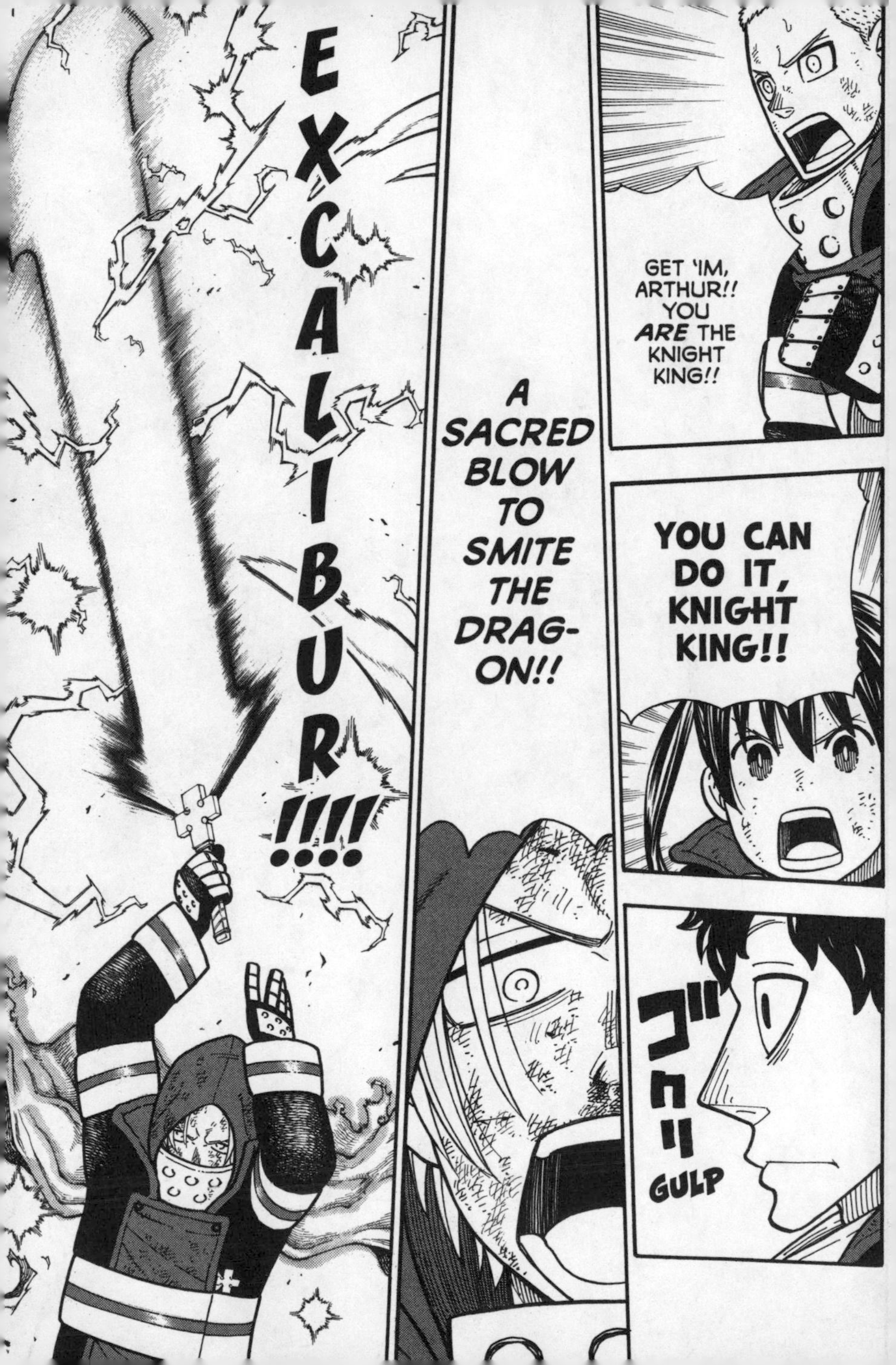
GET 'IM, ARTHUR!! YOU *ARE* THE KNIGHT KING!!
YOU CAN DO IT, KNIGHT KING!!
ゴクッ
GULP
A SACRED BLOW TO SMITE THE DRAG-ON!!
EXCALIBUR!!!!

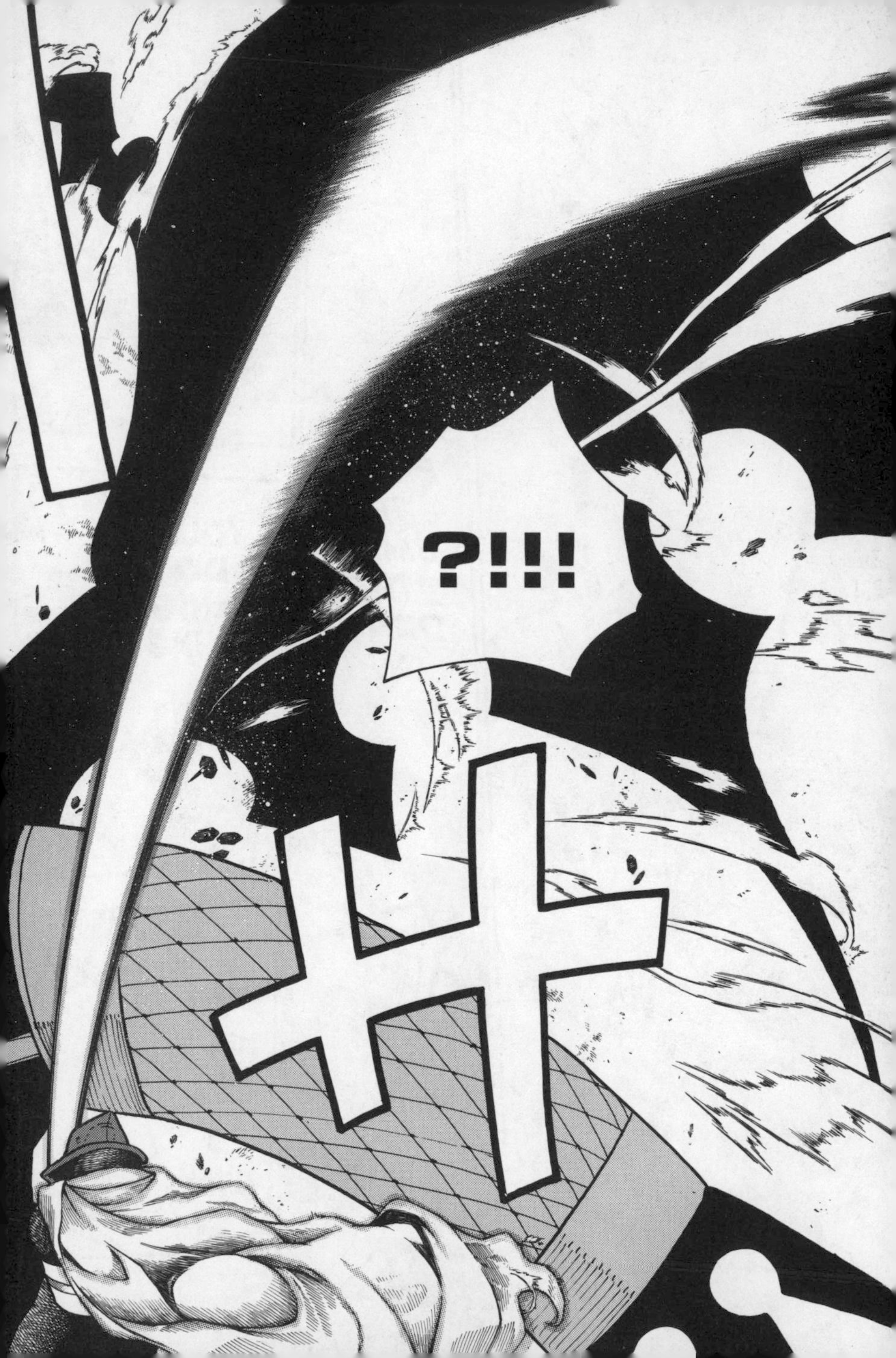
?!!!

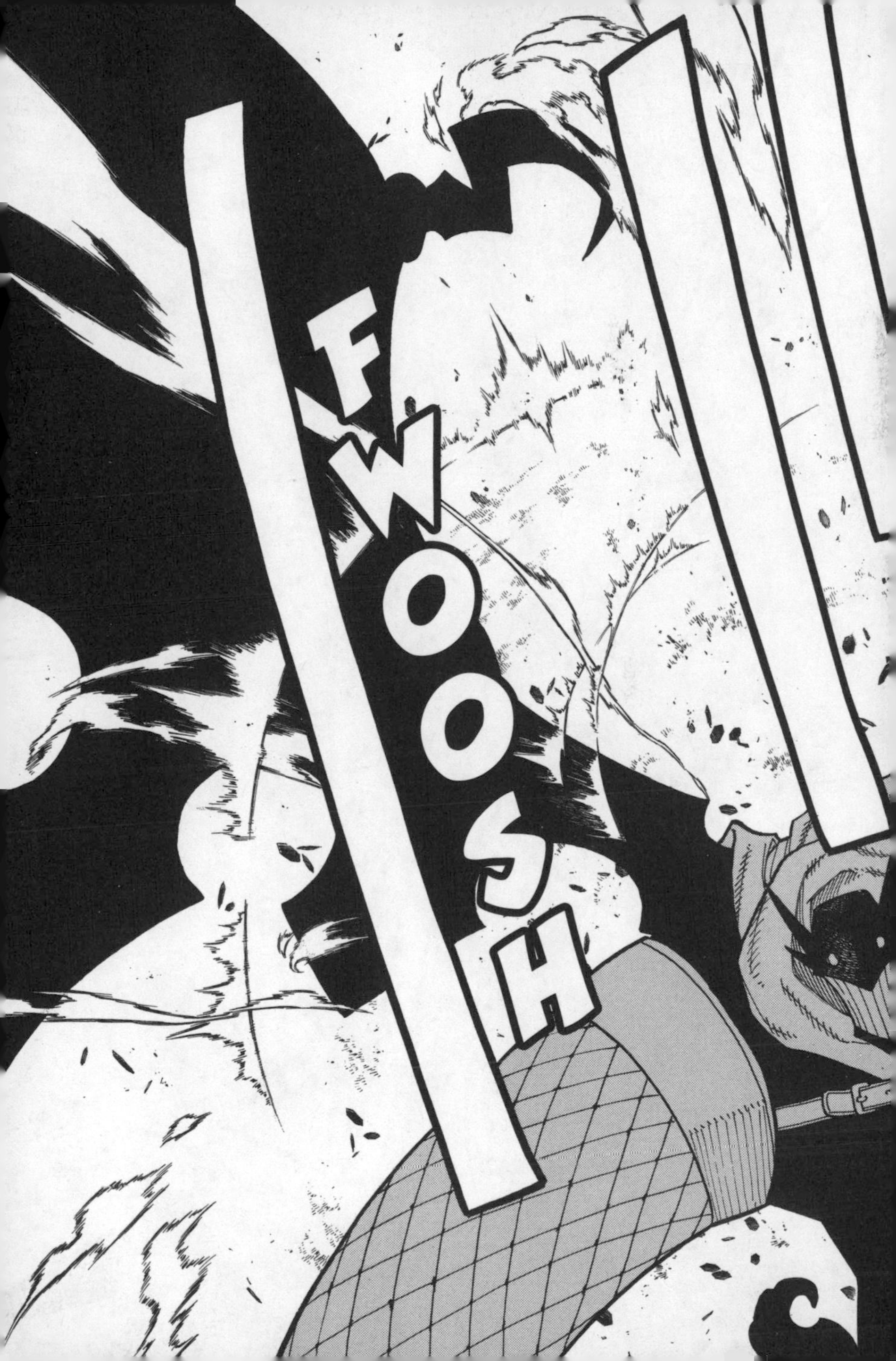
FWOOSH

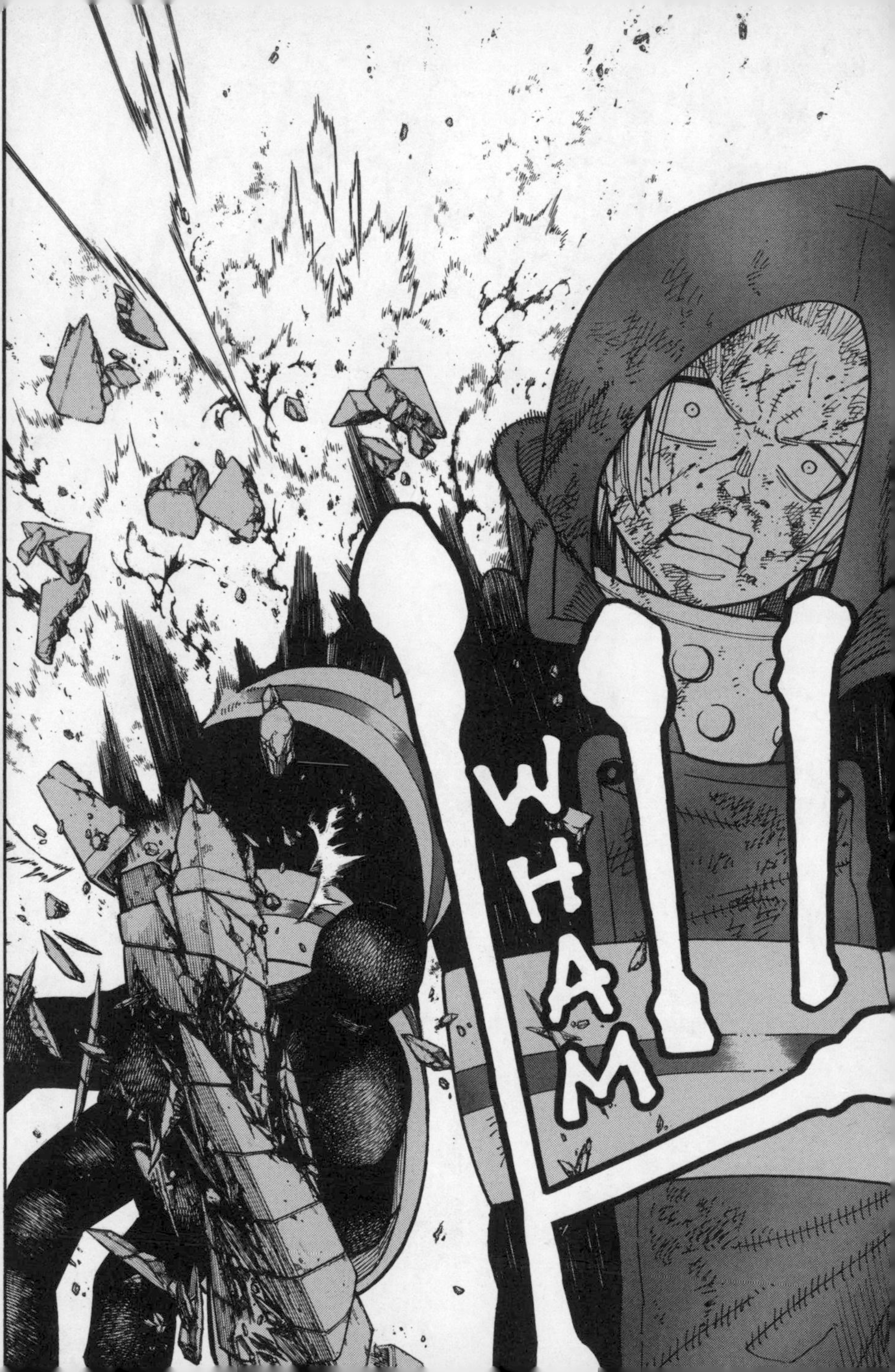
WHAM

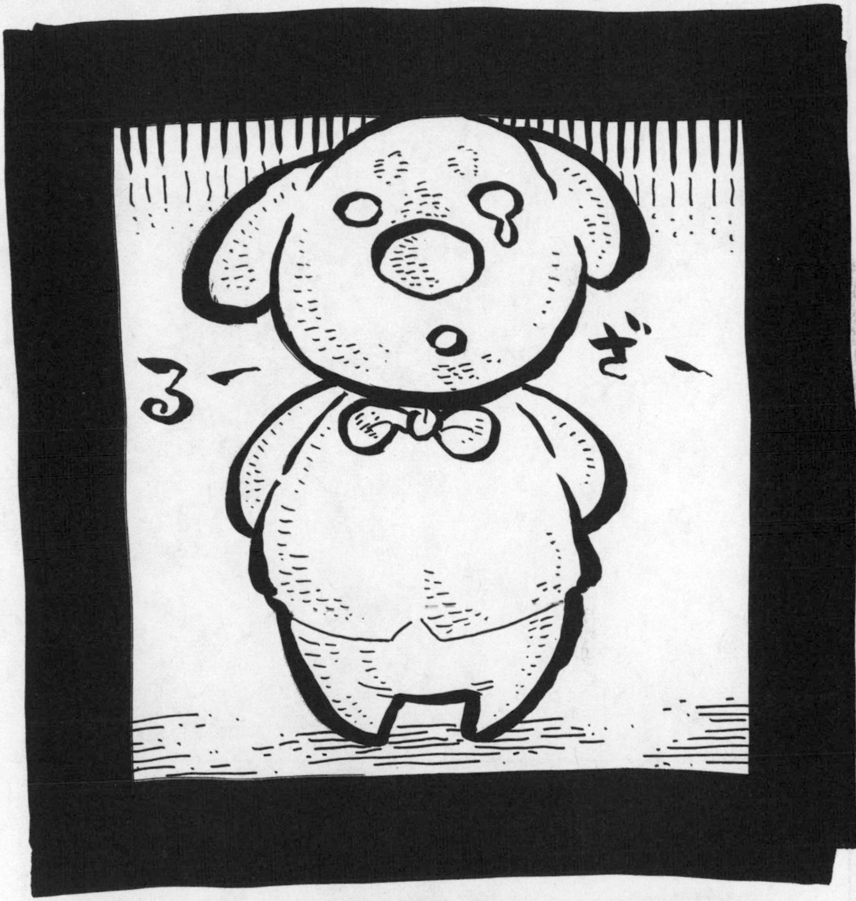

CHAPTER CXCI: FORERUNNERS AND AFTRUNNERS

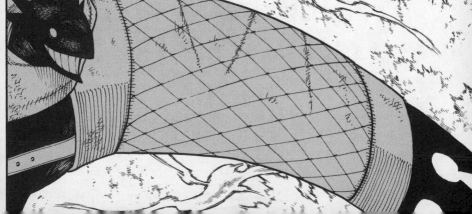

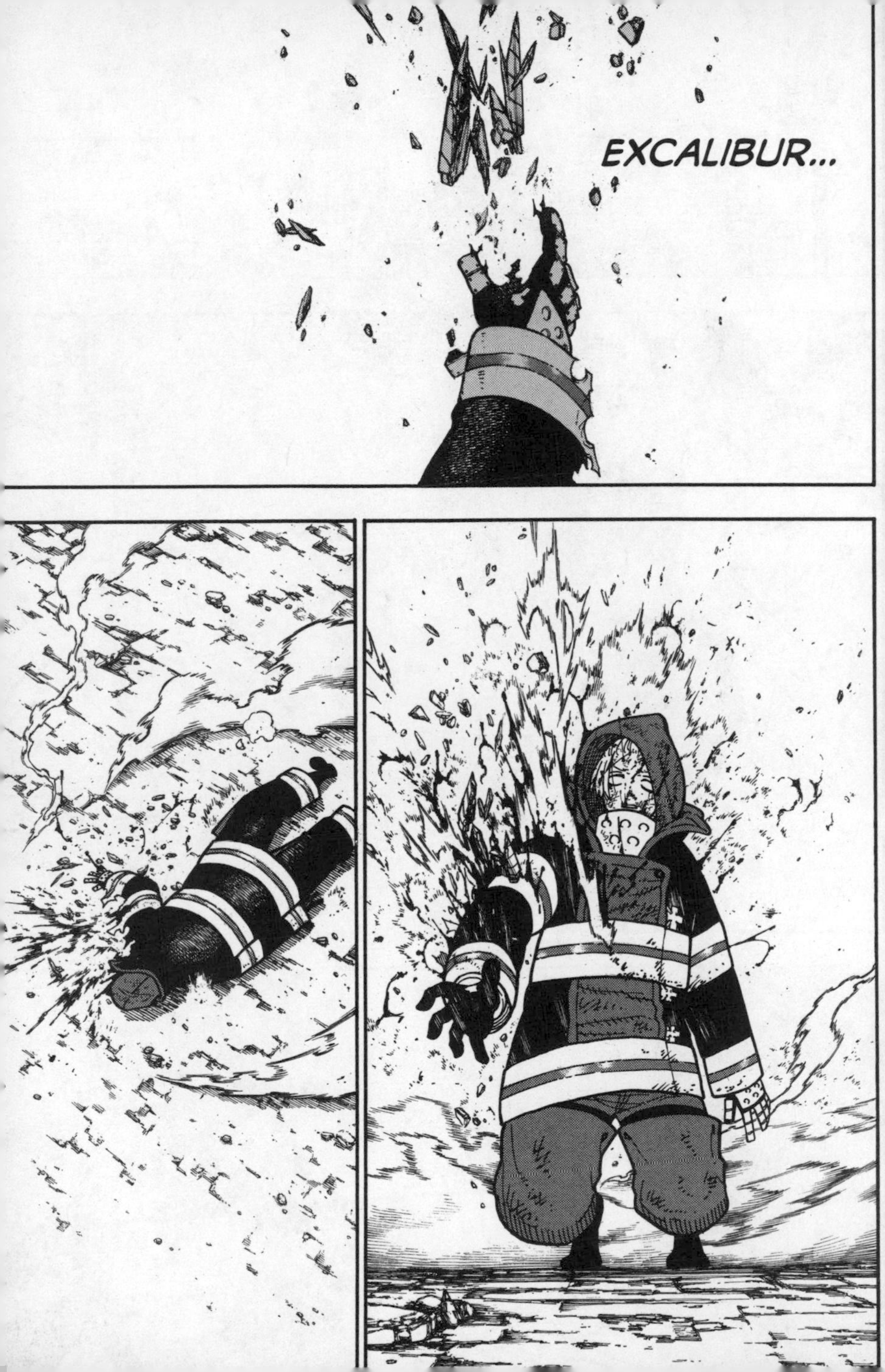
EXCALIBUR...

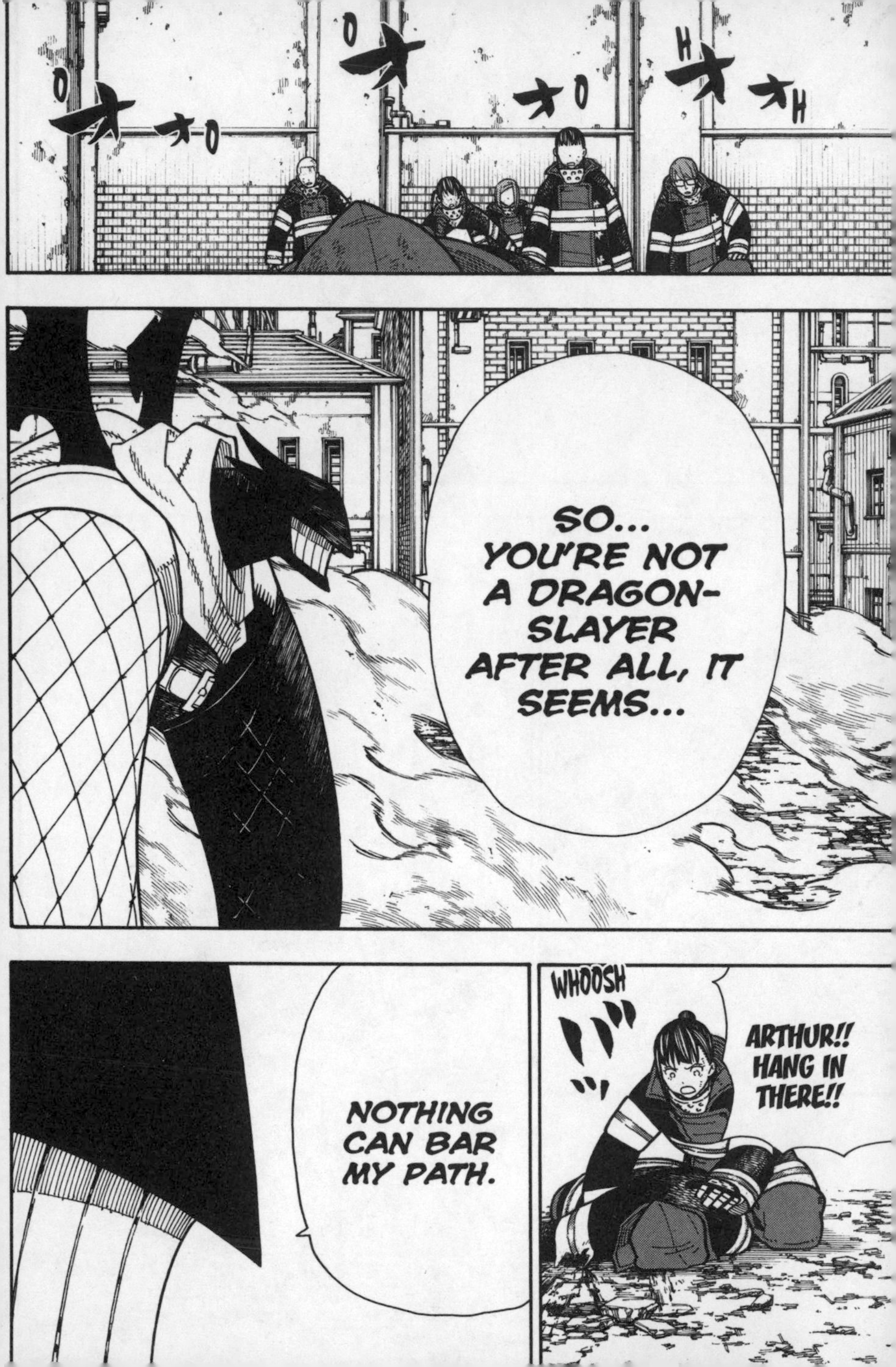
SO... YOU'RE NOT A DRAGON-SLAYER AFTER ALL, IT SEEMS...
WHOOSH
ARTHUR!! HANG IN THERE!!
NOTHING CAN BAR MY PATH.

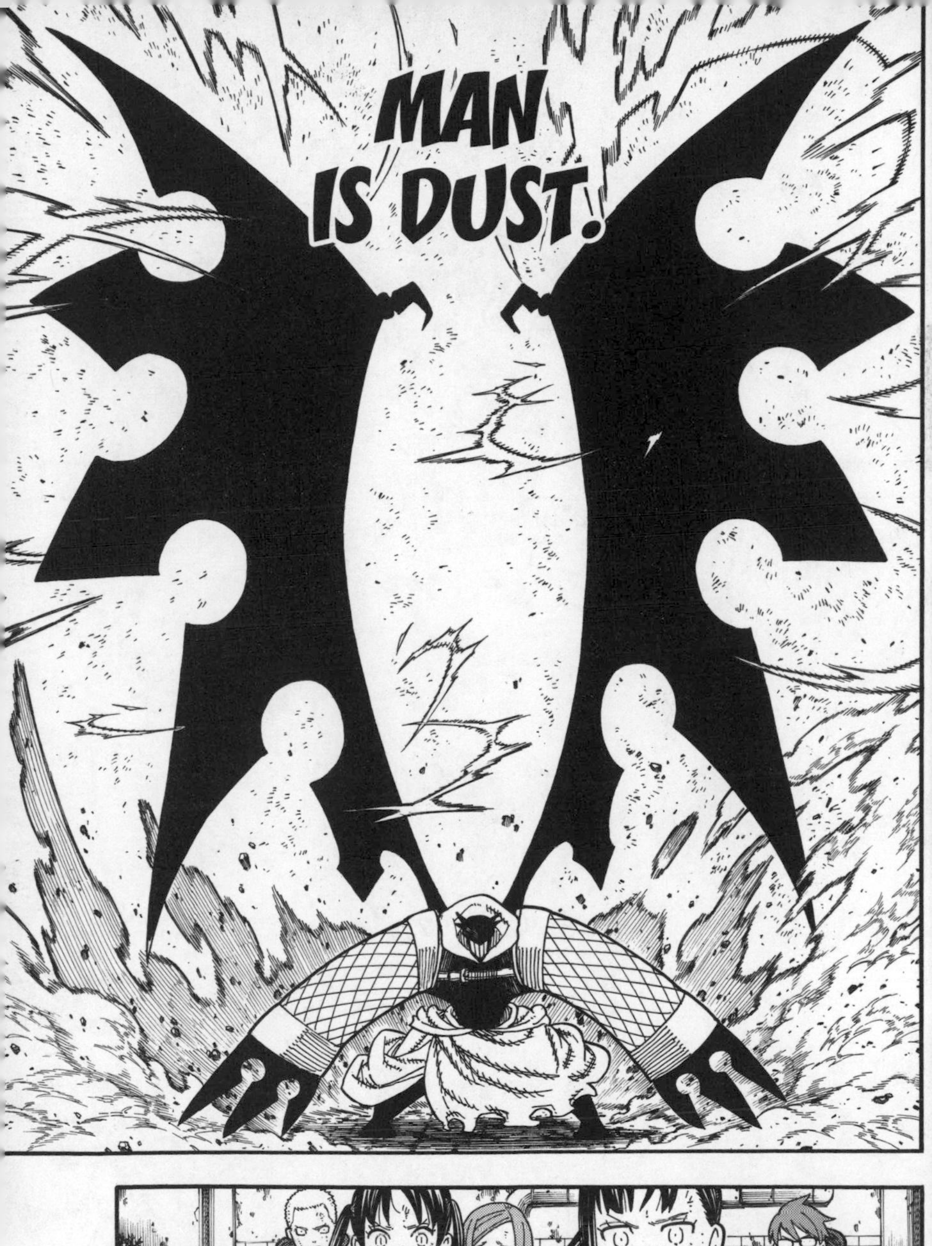
MAN IS DUST!

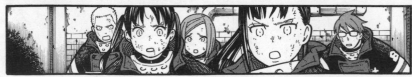

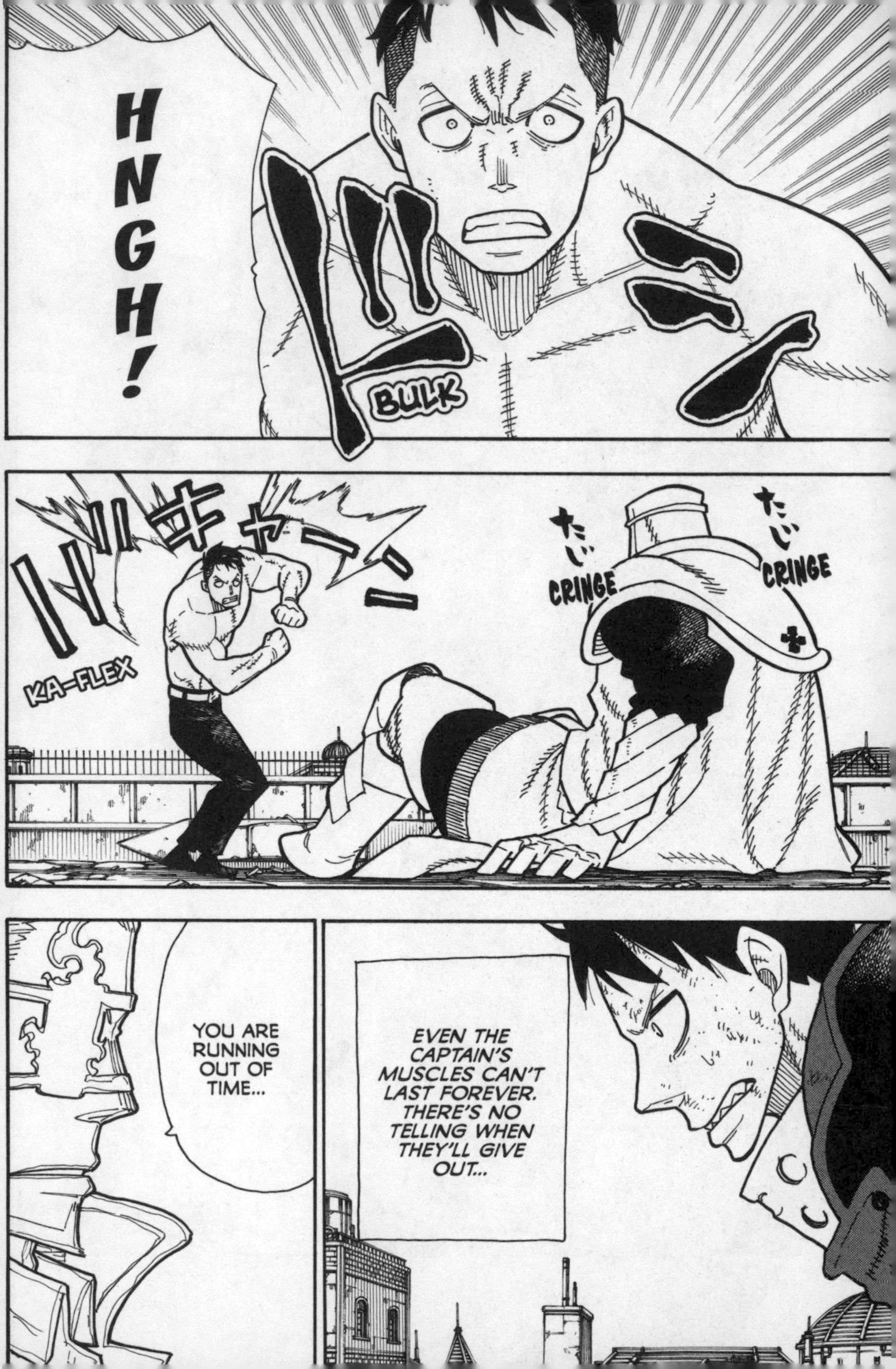
HNGH!
BULK
たじ
CRINGE
たじ
CRINGE
KA-FLEX
EVEN THE CAPTAIN'S MUSCLES CAN'T LAST FOREVER. THERE'S NO TELLING WHEN THEY'LL GIVE OUT...
YOU ARE RUNNING OUT OF TIME...

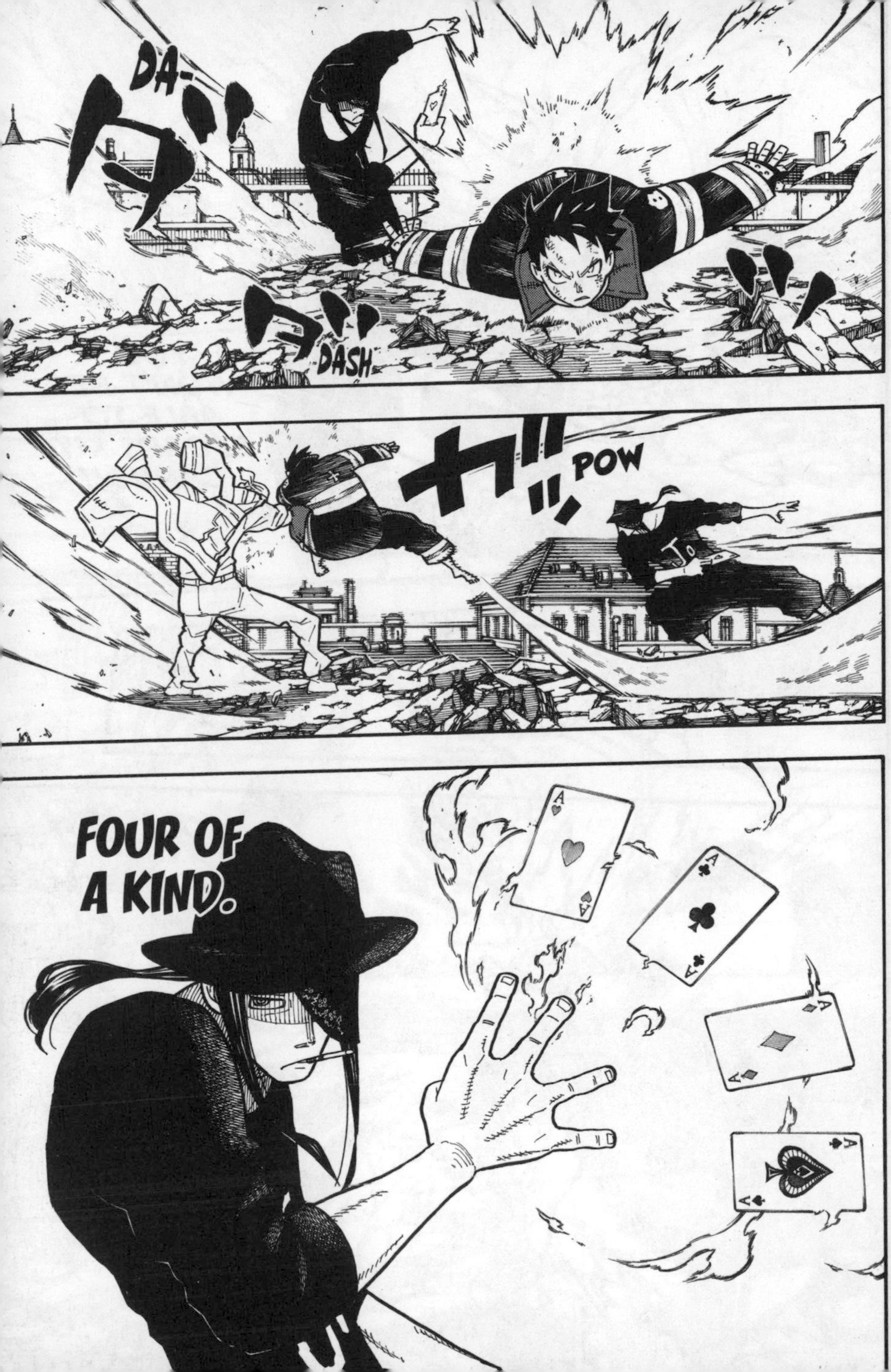
DA-
DASH
POW
FOUR OF A KIND.

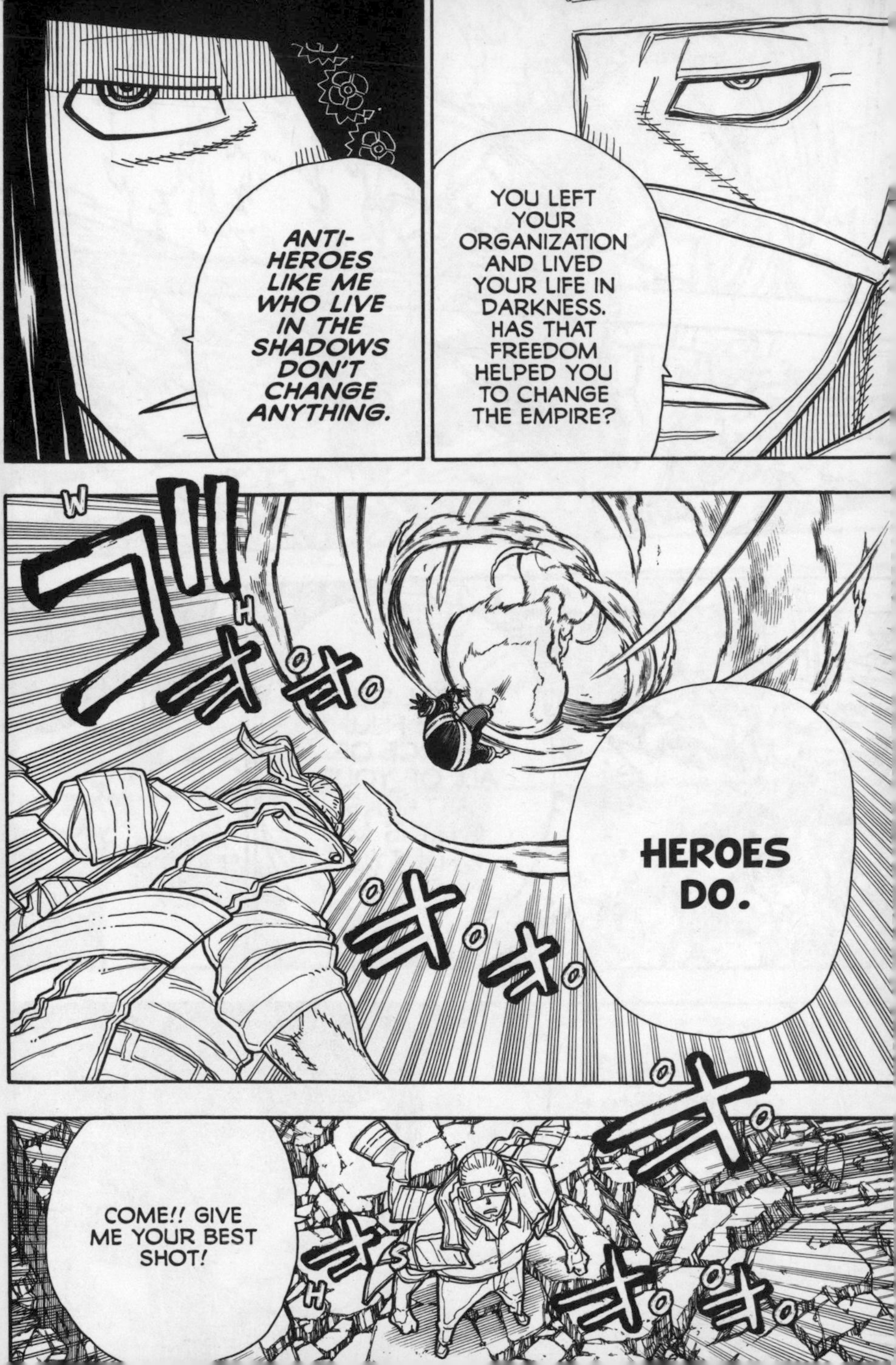
YOU LEFT YOUR ORGANIZATION AND LIVED YOUR LIFE IN DARKNESS. HAS THAT FREEDOM HELPED YOU TO CHANGE THE EMPIRE?
ANTI-HEROES LIKE ME WHO LIVE IN THE SHADOWS DON'T CHANGE ANYTHING.
HEROES DO.
COME!! GIVE ME YOUR BEST SHOT!

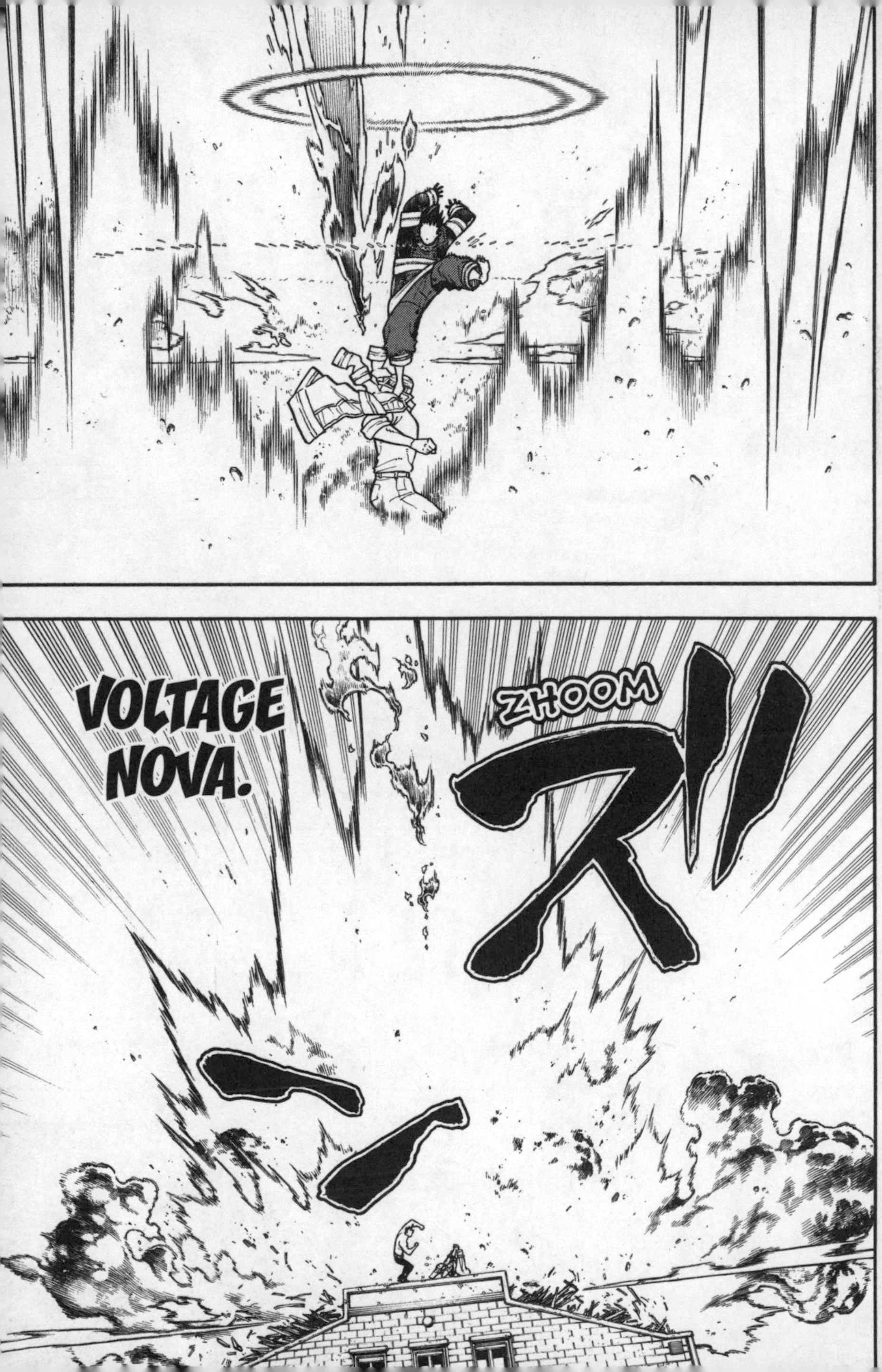

VOLTAGE NOVA.
ZHOOM

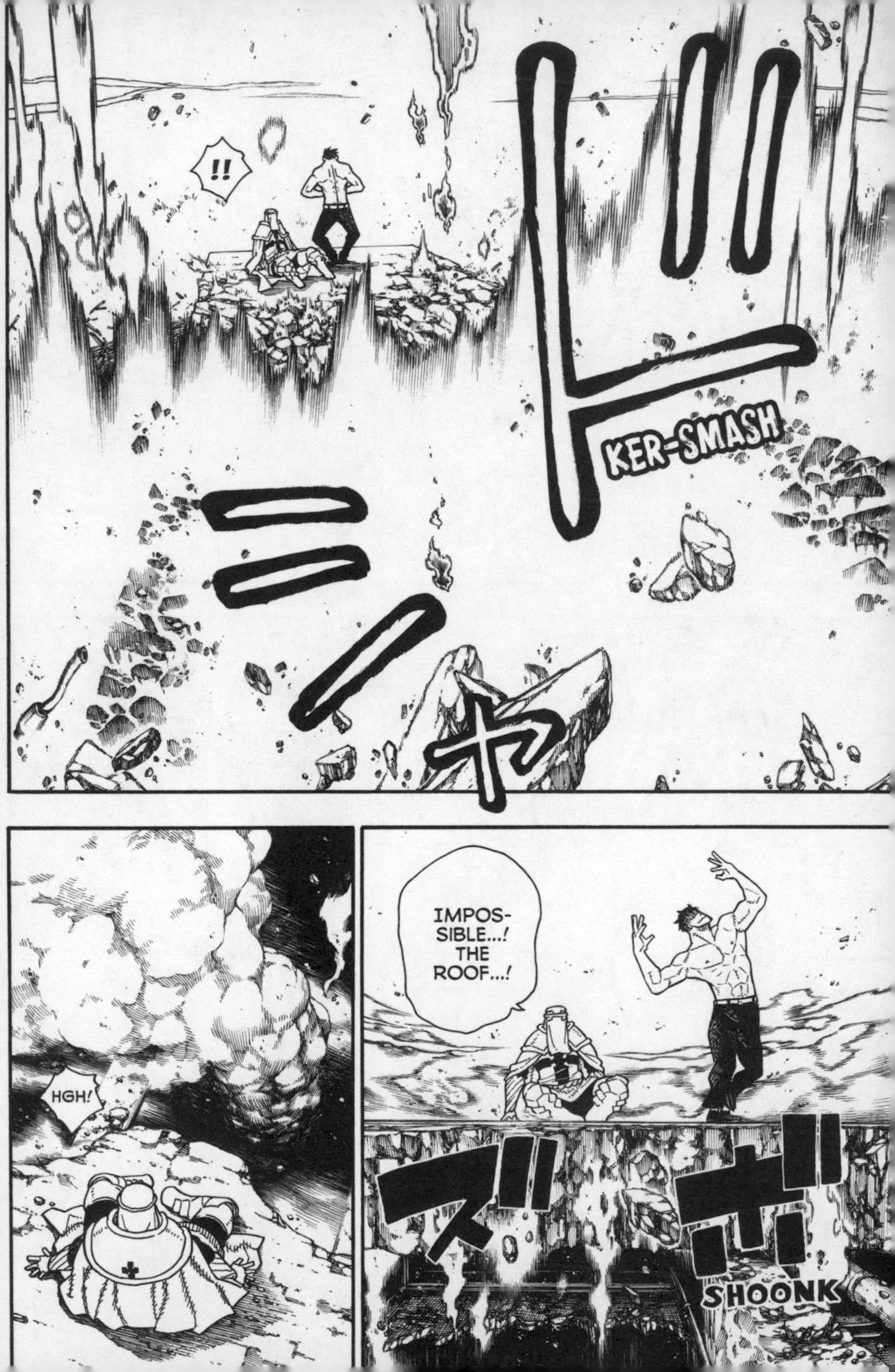
!!
KER-SMASH
IMPOSSIBLE...! THE ROOF...!
SHOONK
HGH!

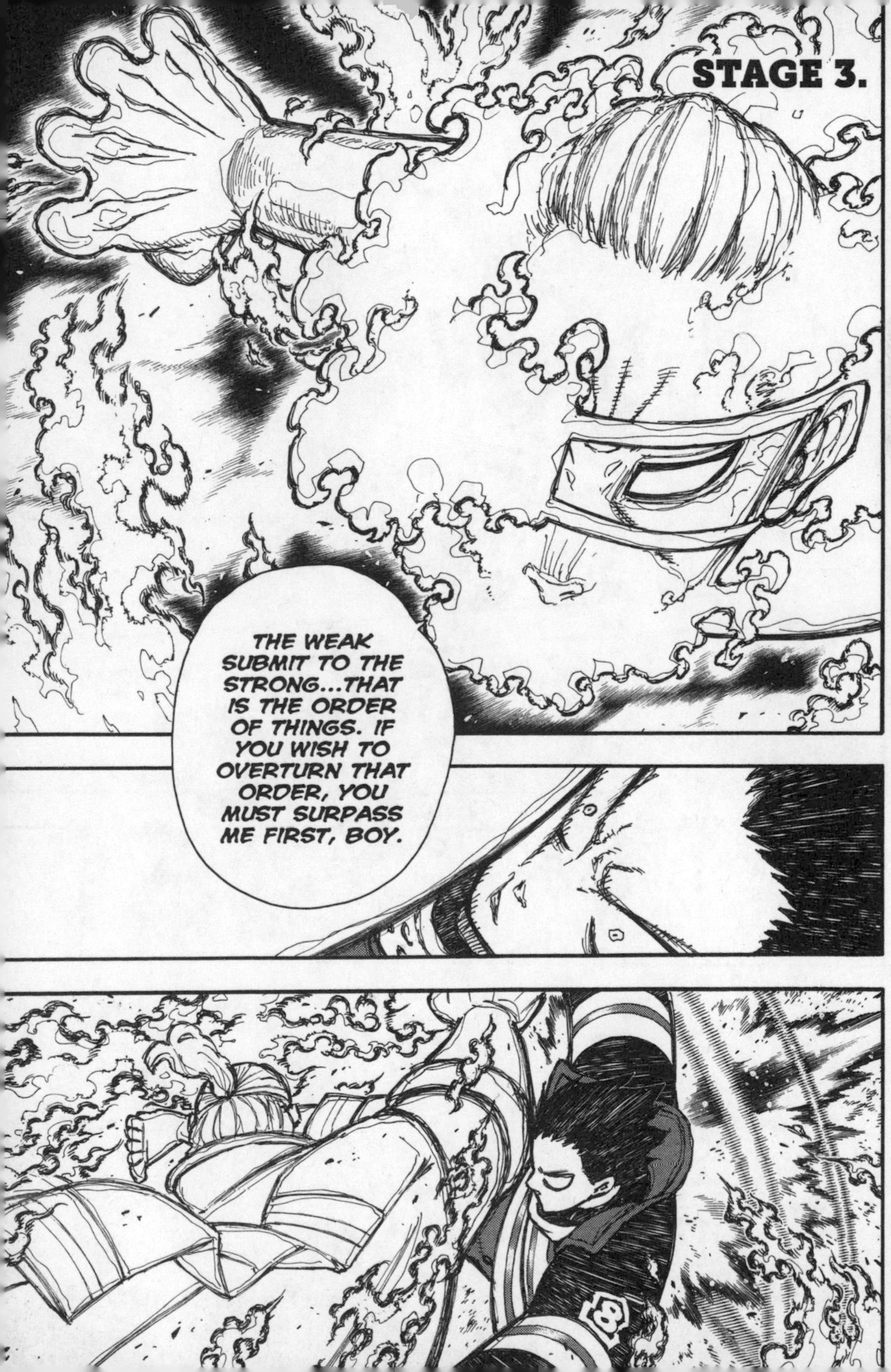
STAGE 3.
THE WEAK SUBMIT TO THE STRONG...THAT IS THE ORDER OF THINGS. IF YOU WISH TO OVERTURN THAT ORDER, YOU MUST SURPASS ME FIRST, BOY.

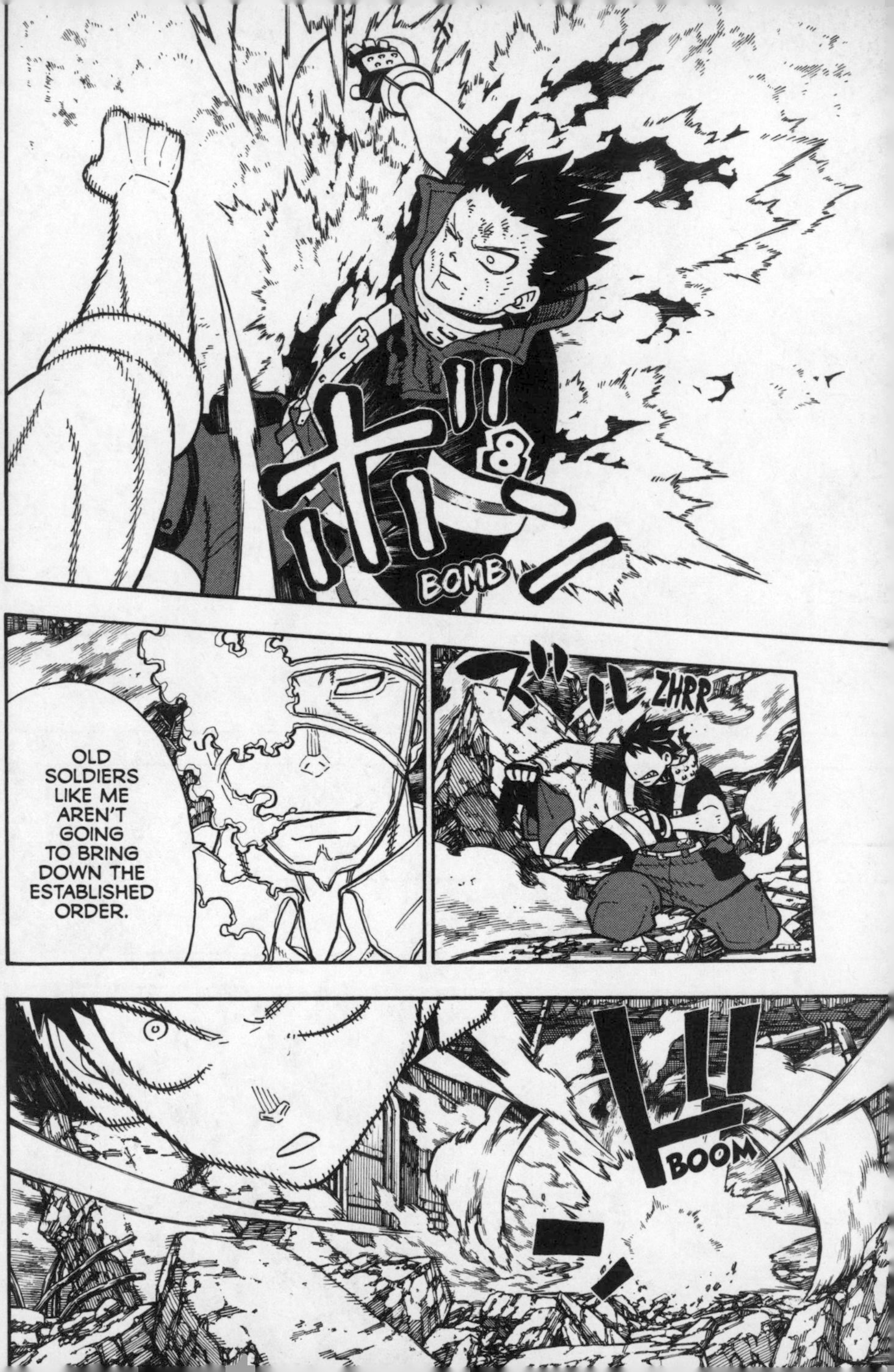
BOMB
ZHRR
OLD SOLDIERS LIKE ME AREN'T GOING TO BRING DOWN THE ESTABLISHED ORDER.
BOOM

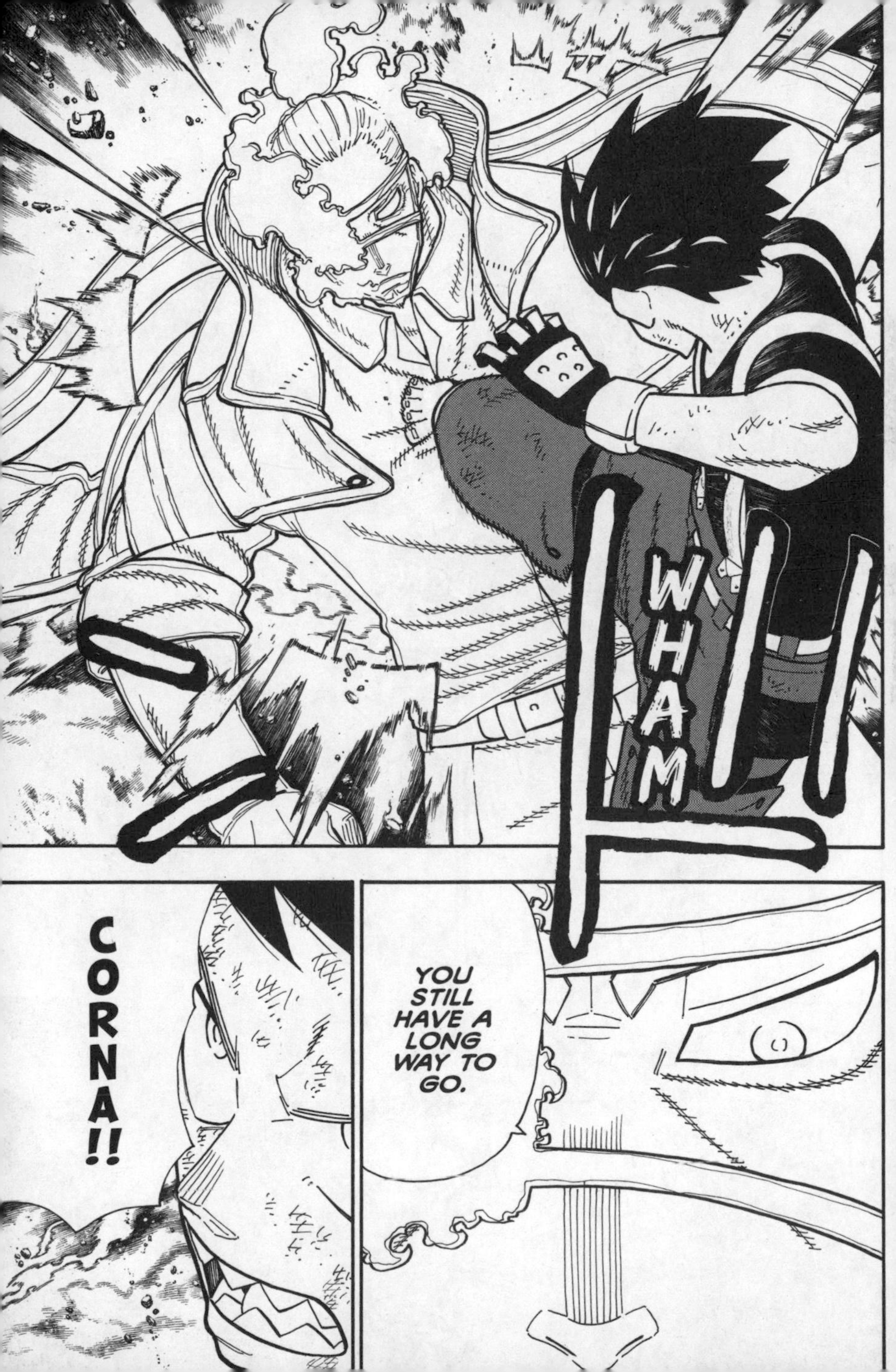
WHAM
YOU STILL HAVE A LONG WAY TO GO.
CORNA!!

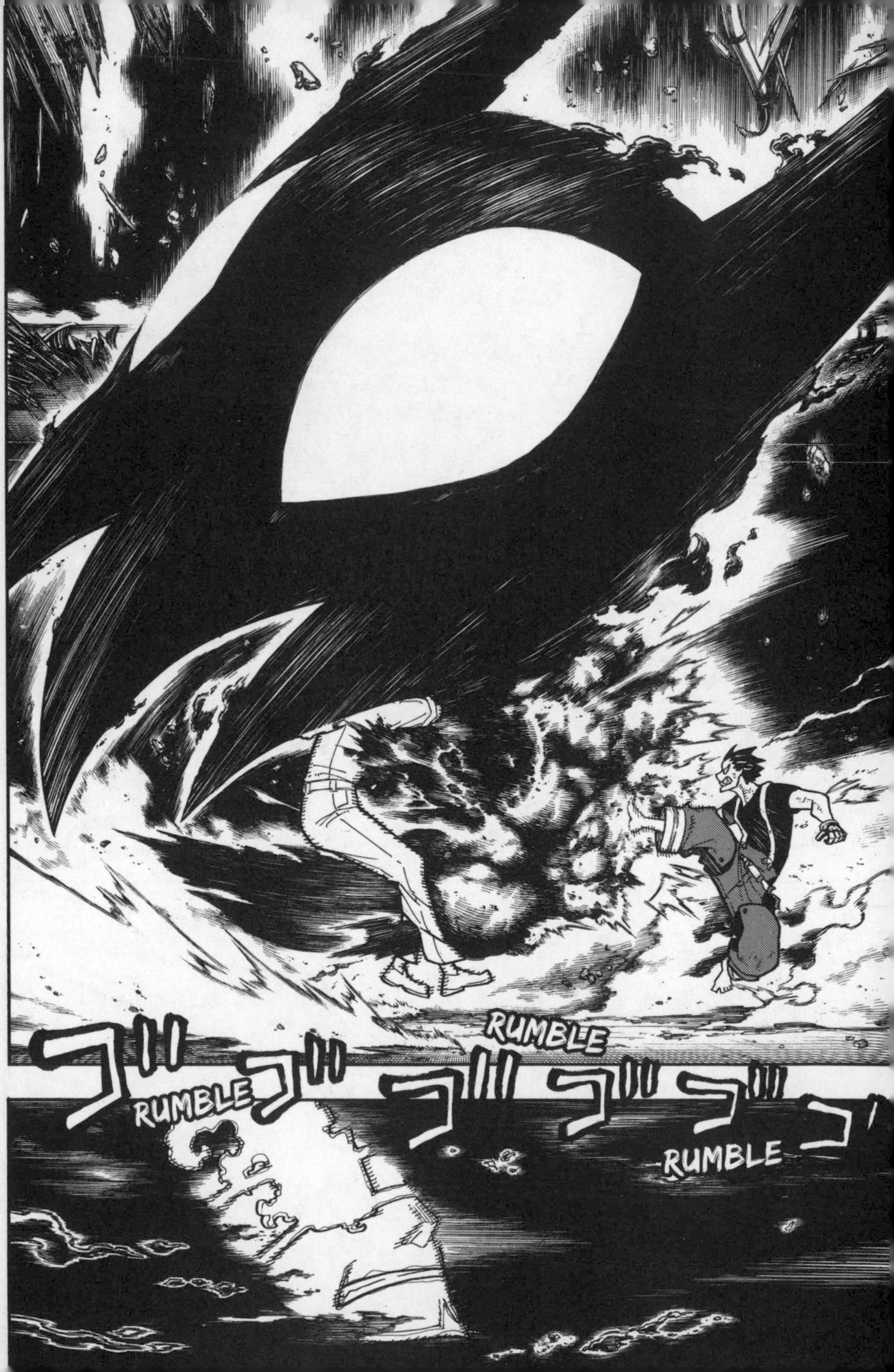
RUMBLE
RUMBLE
RUMBLE

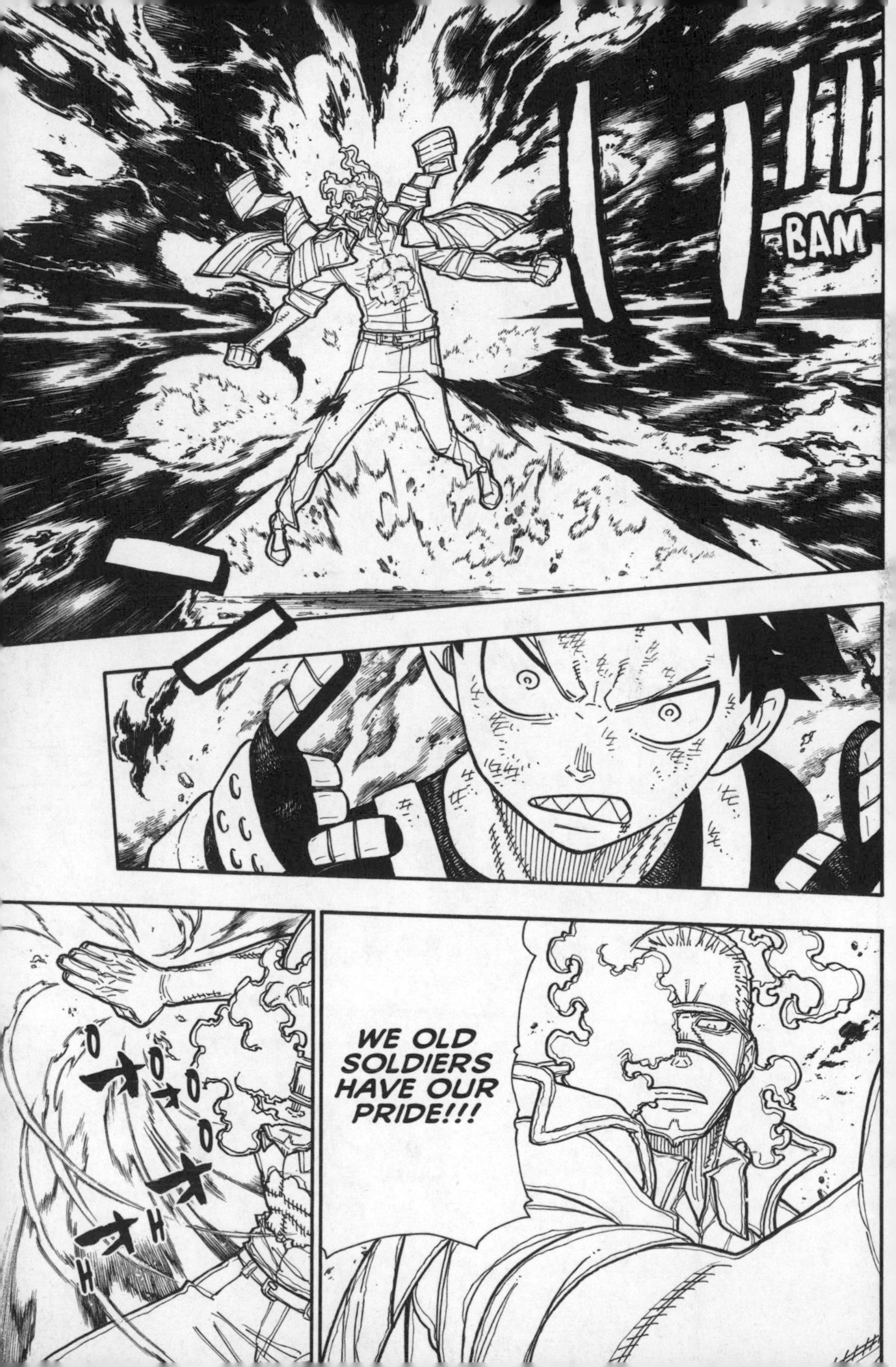
BAM
WE OLD SOLDIERS HAVE OUR PRIDE!!!

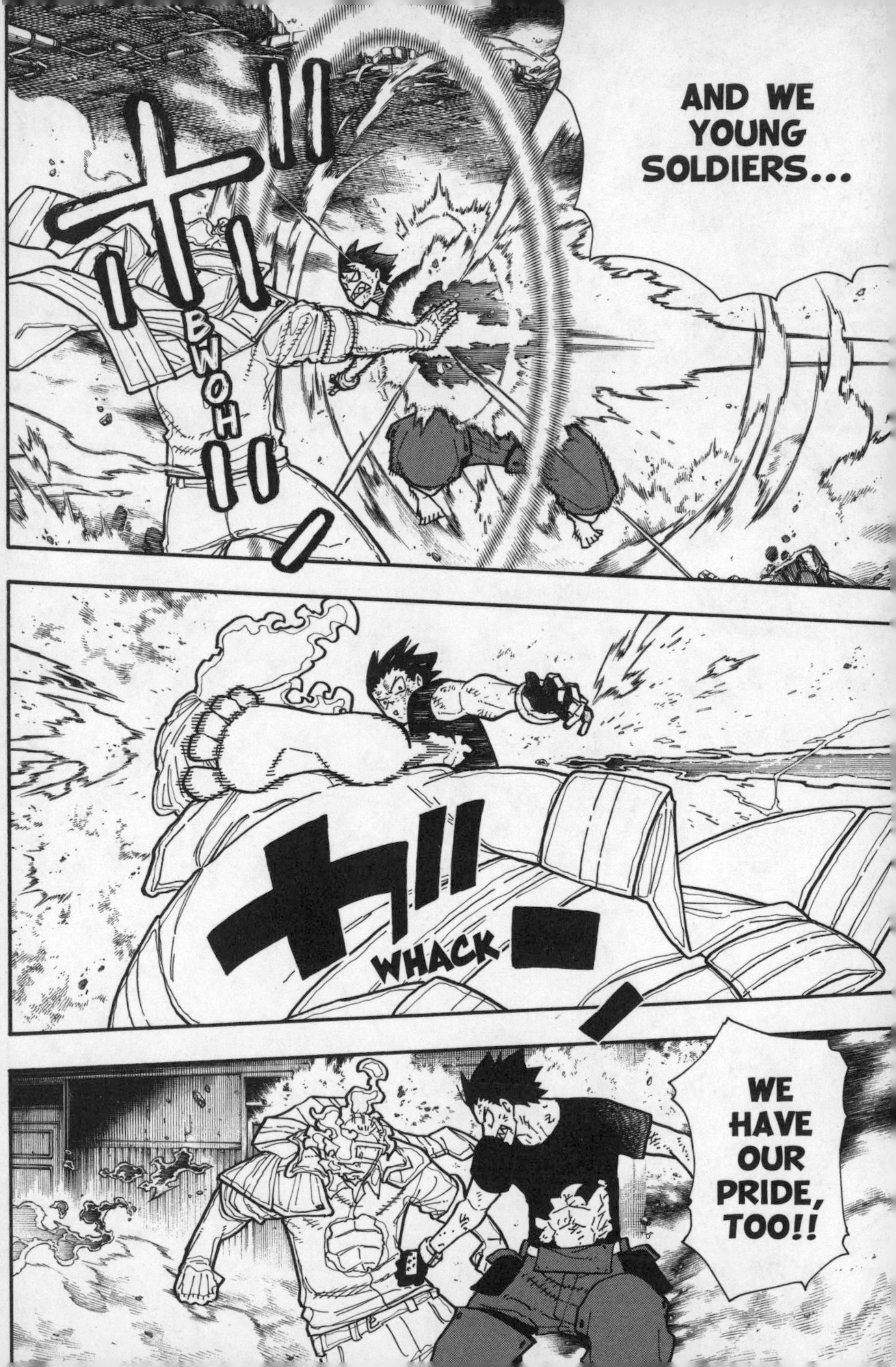
AND WE YOUNG SOLDIERS...
BWOH
WHACK
WE HAVE OUR PRIDE, TOO!!

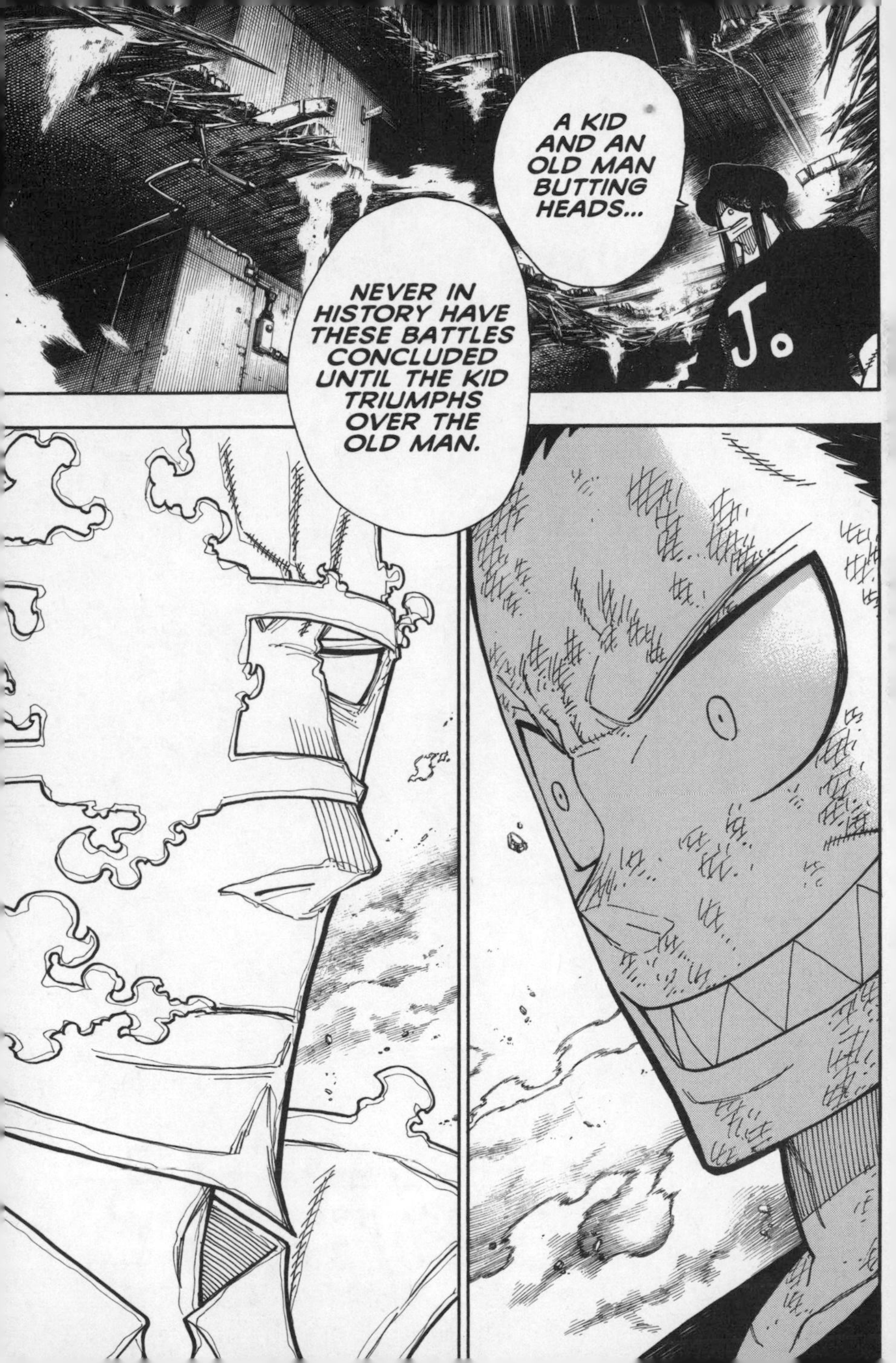
A KID AND AN OLD MAN BUTTING HEADS...
NEVER IN HISTORY HAVE THESE BATTLES CONCLUDED UNTIL THE KID TRIUMPHS OVER THE OLD MAN.

FIRE FORCE

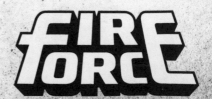

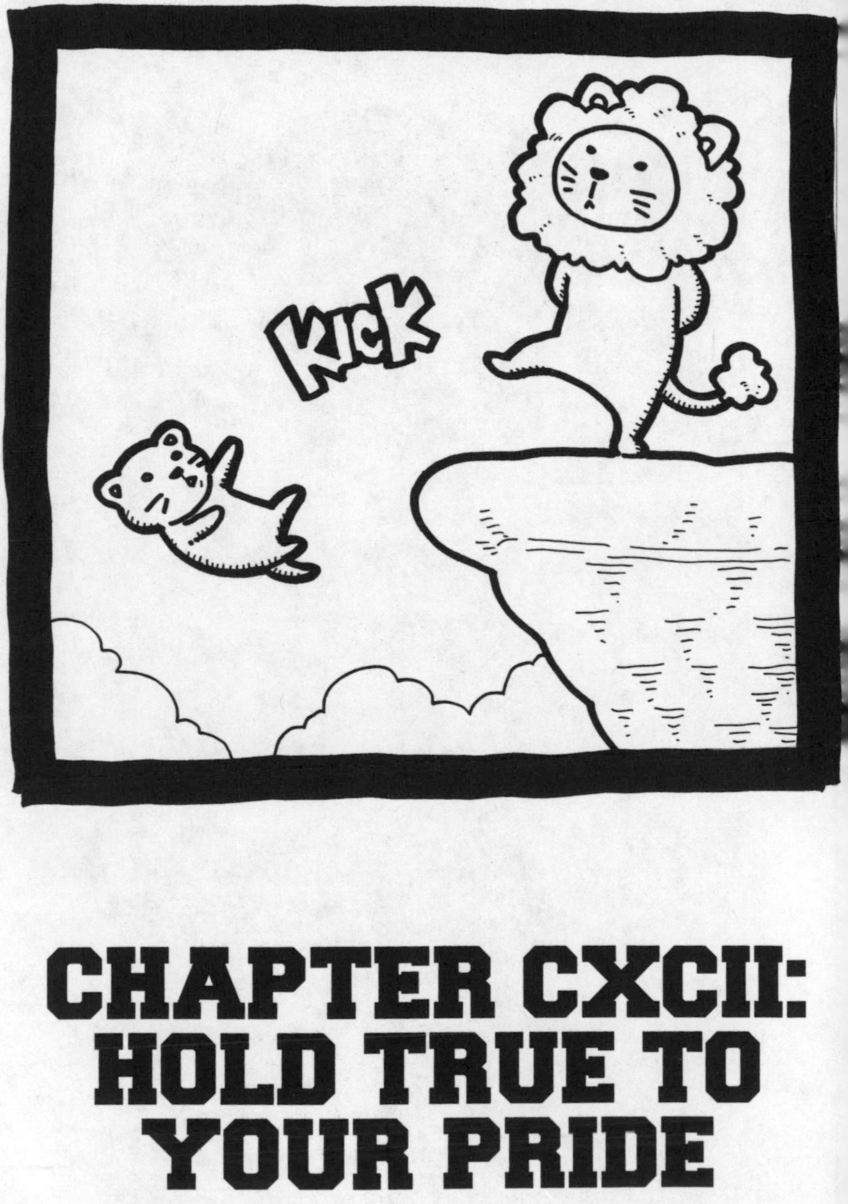
KICK

CHAPTER CXCII: HOLD TRUE TO YOUR PRIDE

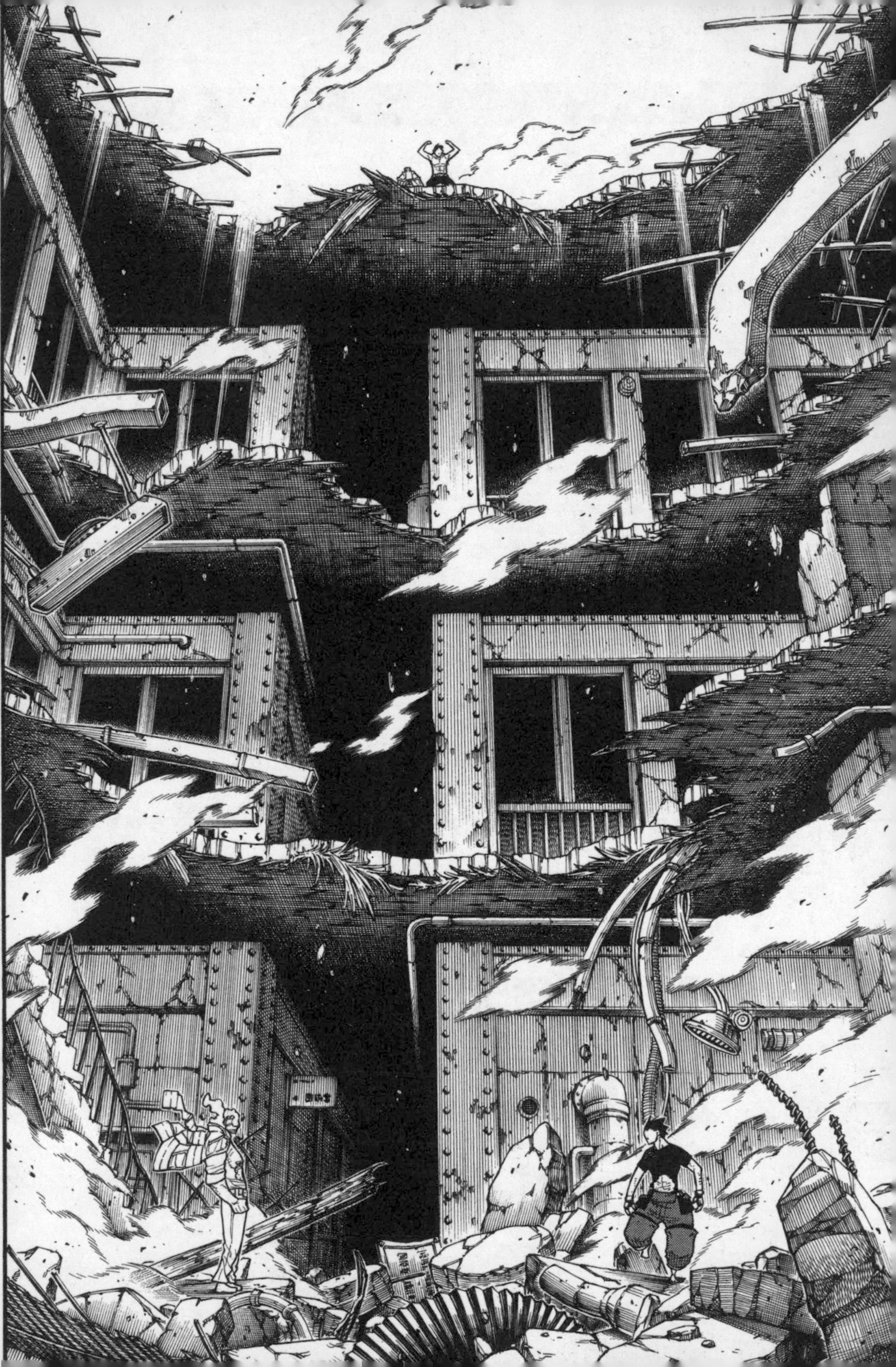

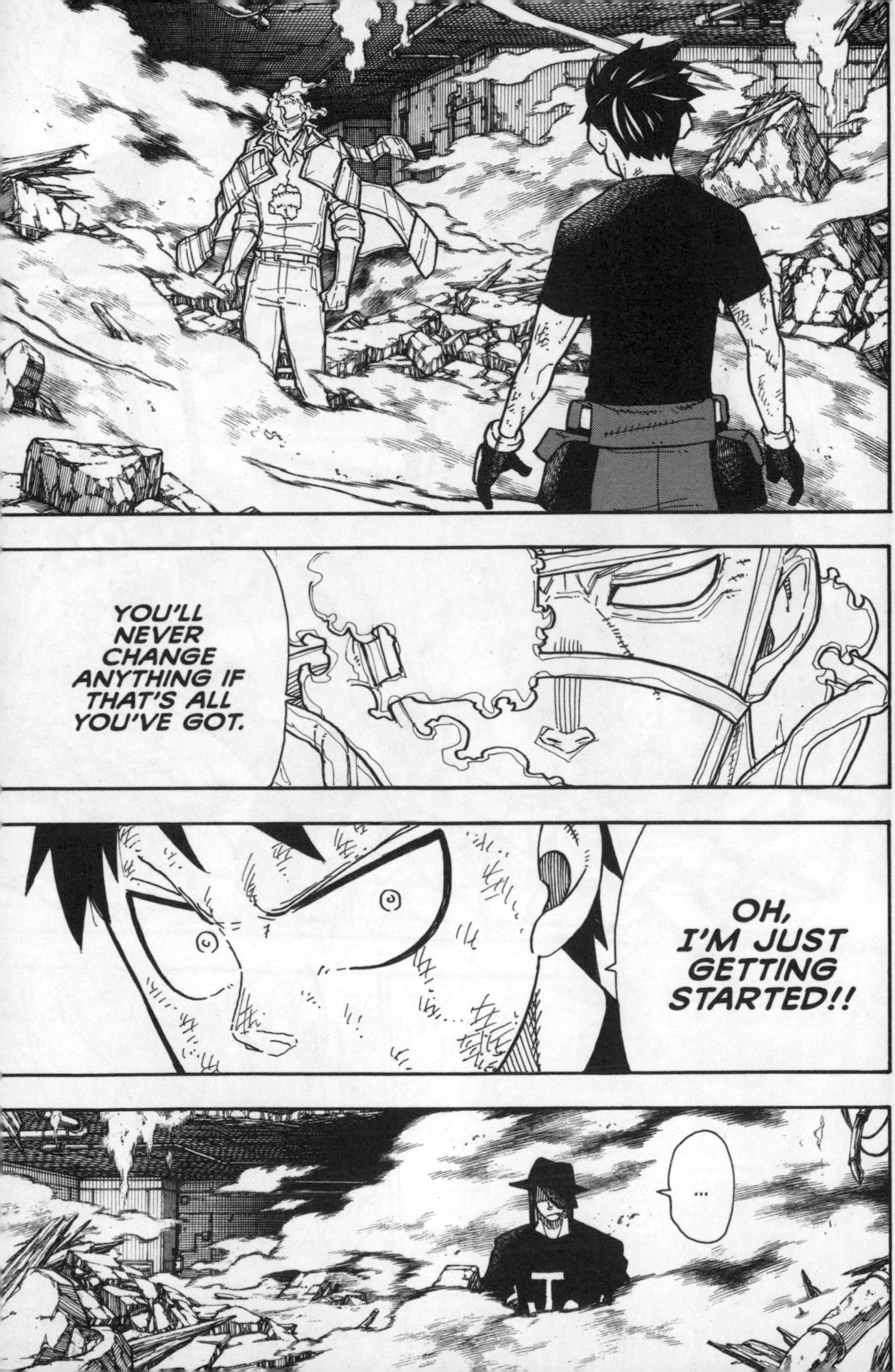
YOU'LL NEVER CHANGE ANYTHING IF THAT'S ALL YOU'VE GOT.
OH, I'M JUST GETTING STARTED!!
...

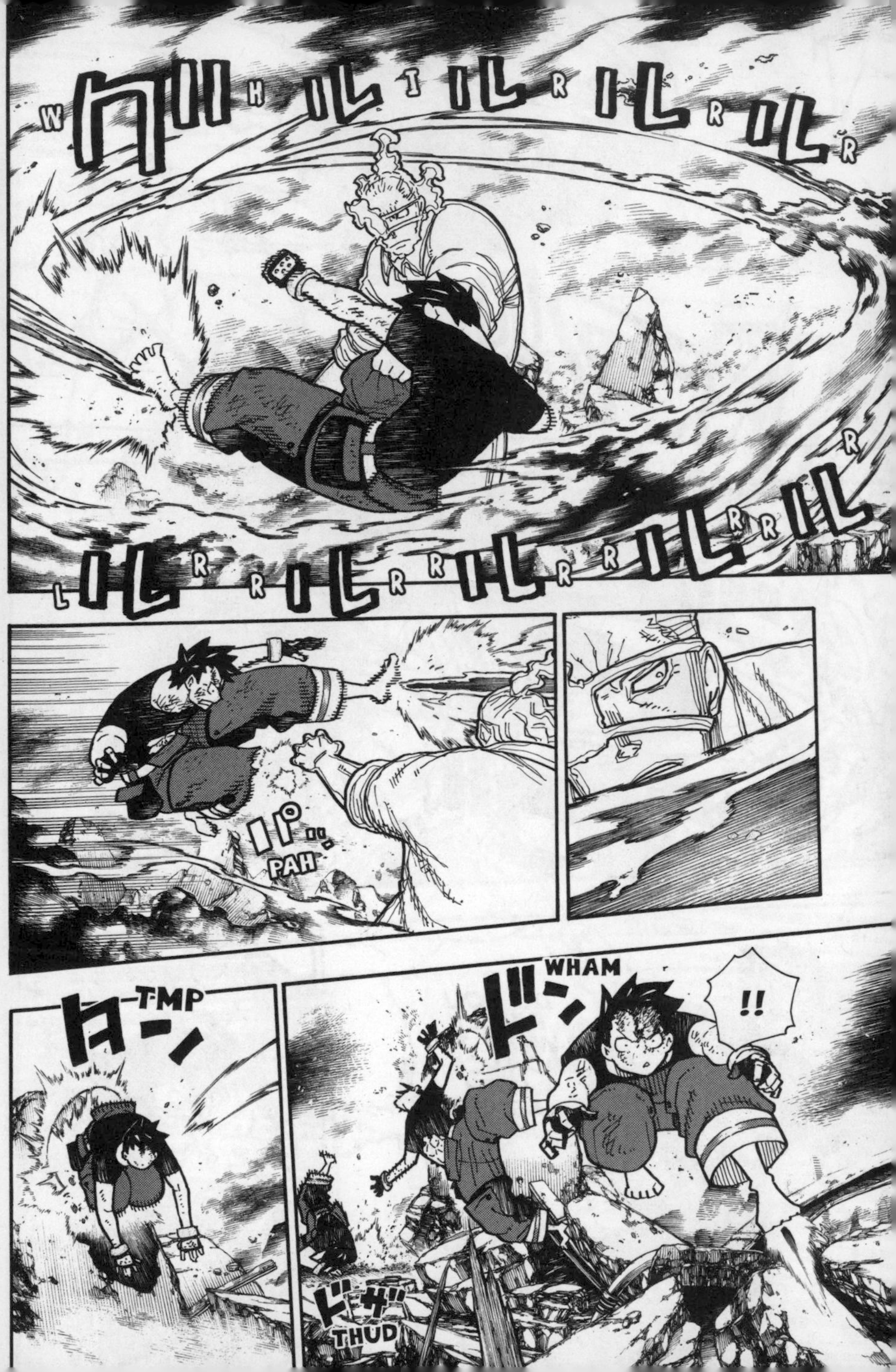
パ
PAH
ドン
WHAM
!!
ドザ
THUD
タン
TMP

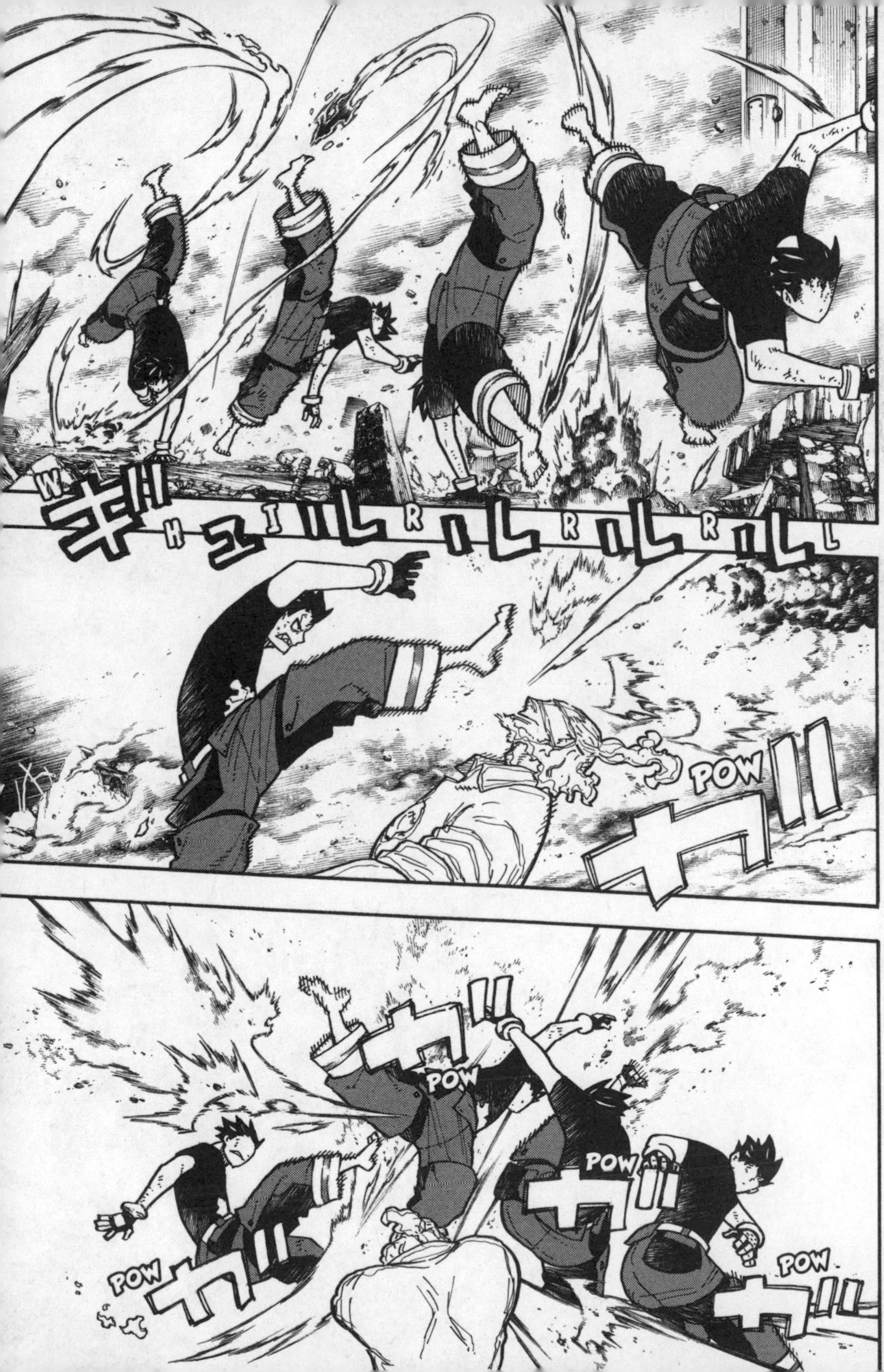
WHIRRRL
POW
POW
POW
POW
POW

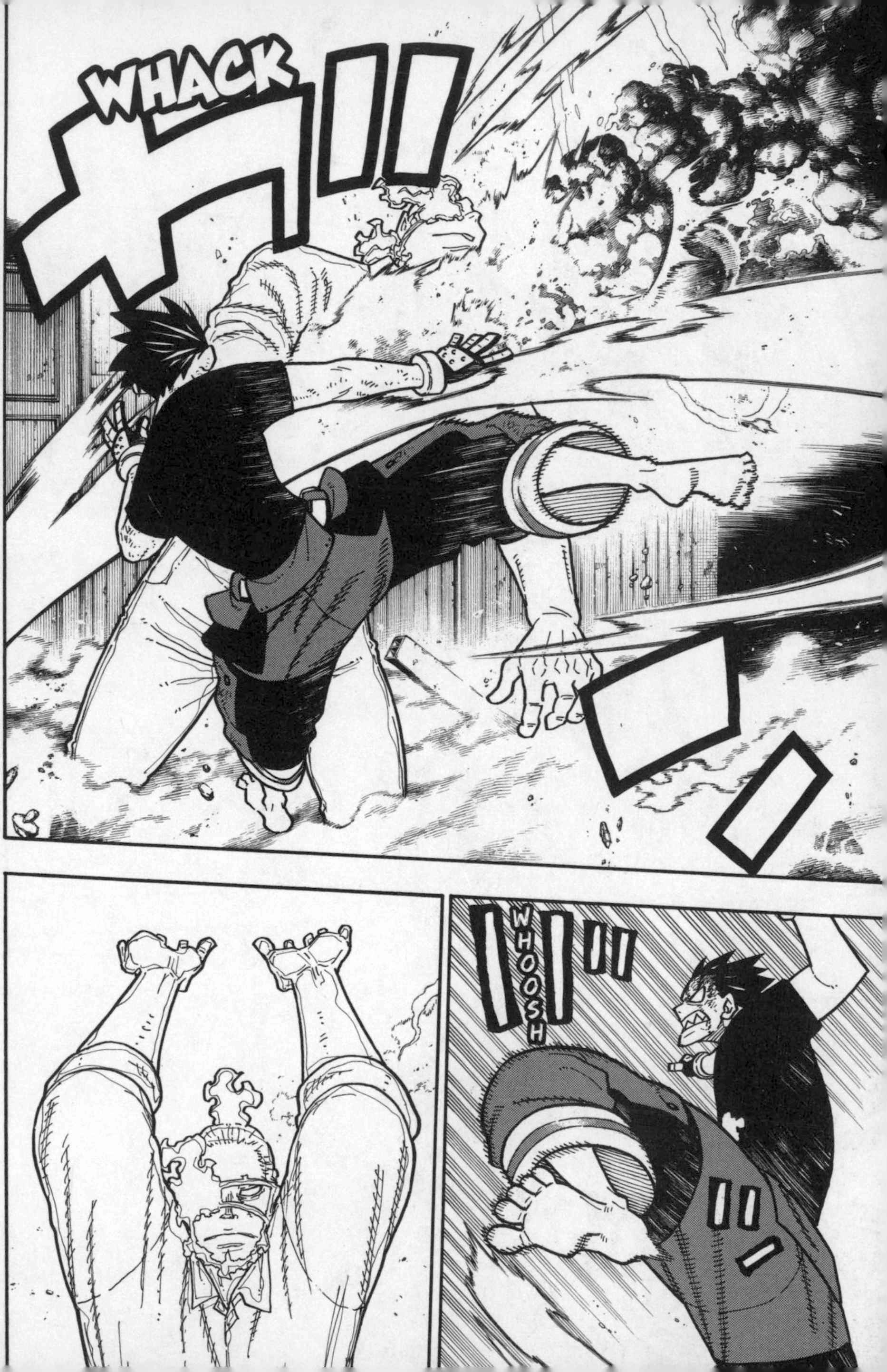
WHACK
WHOOSH

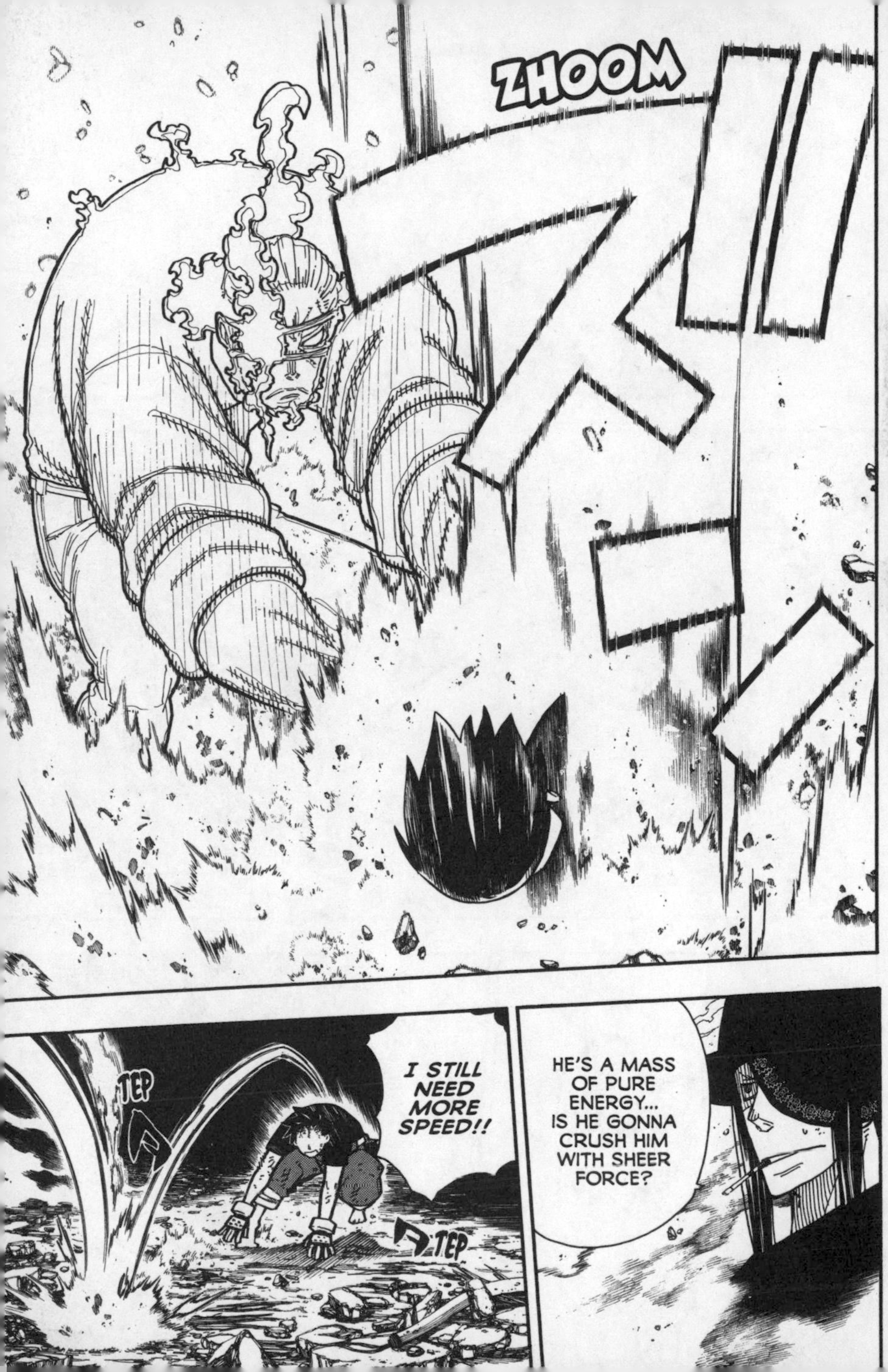
ZHOOM
HE'S A MASS OF PURE ENERGY... IS HE GONNA CRUSH HIM WITH SHEER FORCE?
TEP
I STILL NEED MORE SPEED!!
TEP

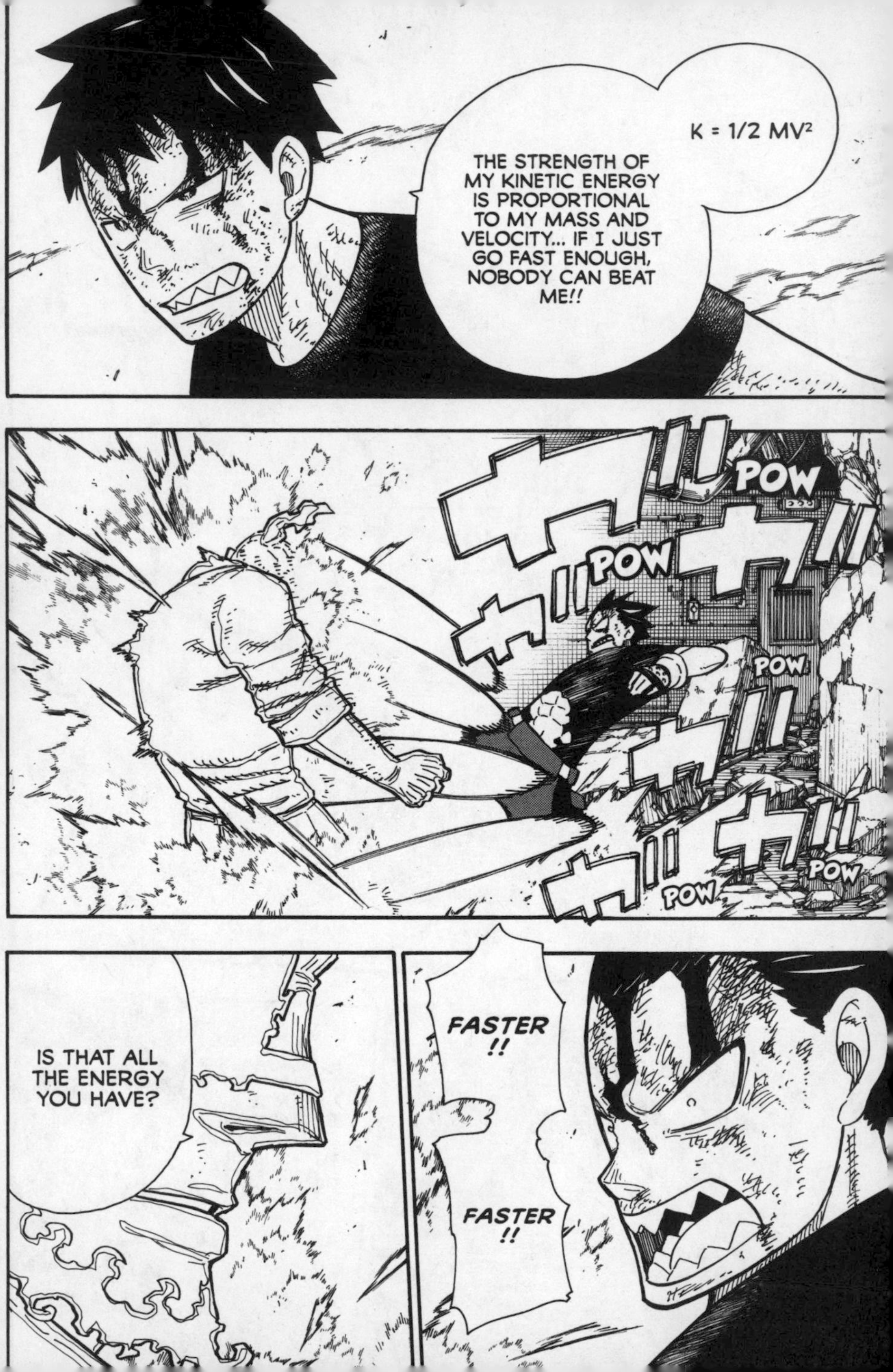
$K = 1/2\ MV^2$
THE STRENGTH OF MY KINETIC ENERGY IS PROPORTIONAL TO MY MASS AND VELOCITY... IF I JUST GO FAST ENOUGH, NOBODY CAN BEAT ME!!
POW
POW
POW
POW
POW
FASTER !!
FASTER !!
IS THAT ALL THE ENERGY YOU HAVE?

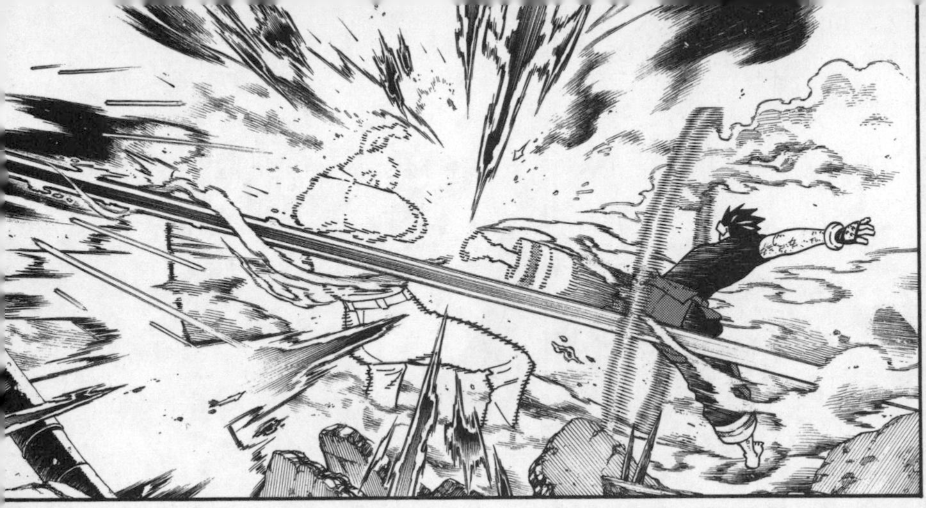
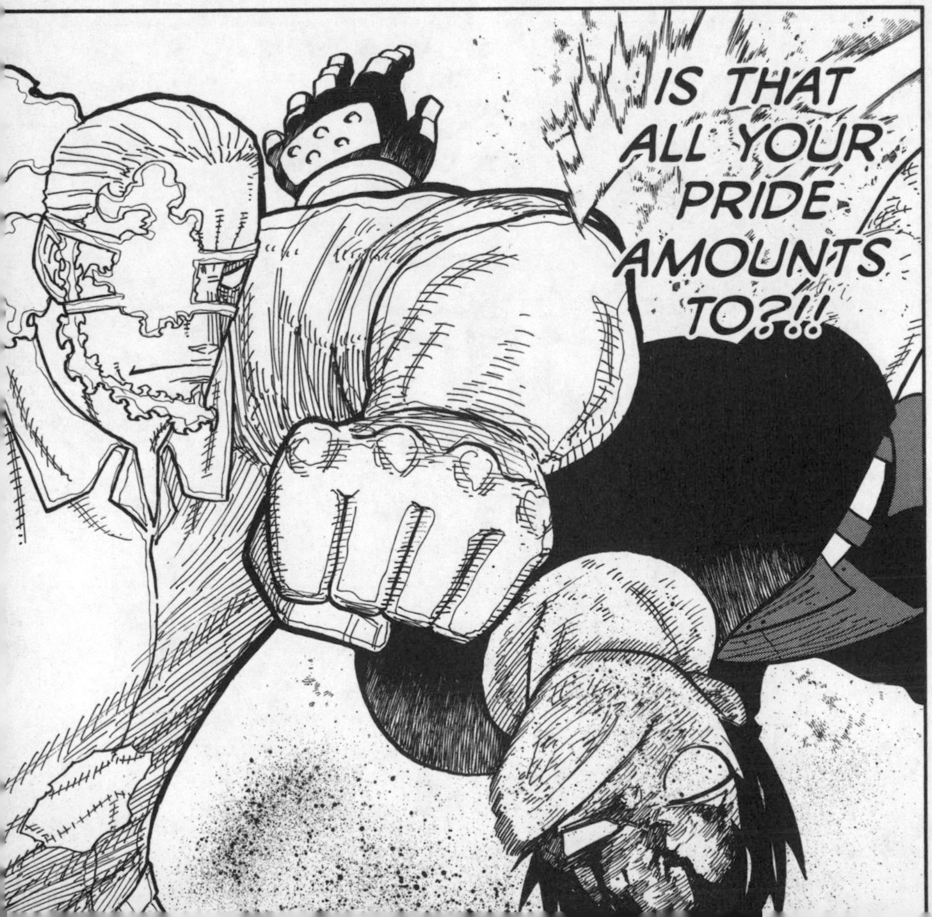
IS THAT ALL YOUR PRIDE AMOUNTS TO?!!

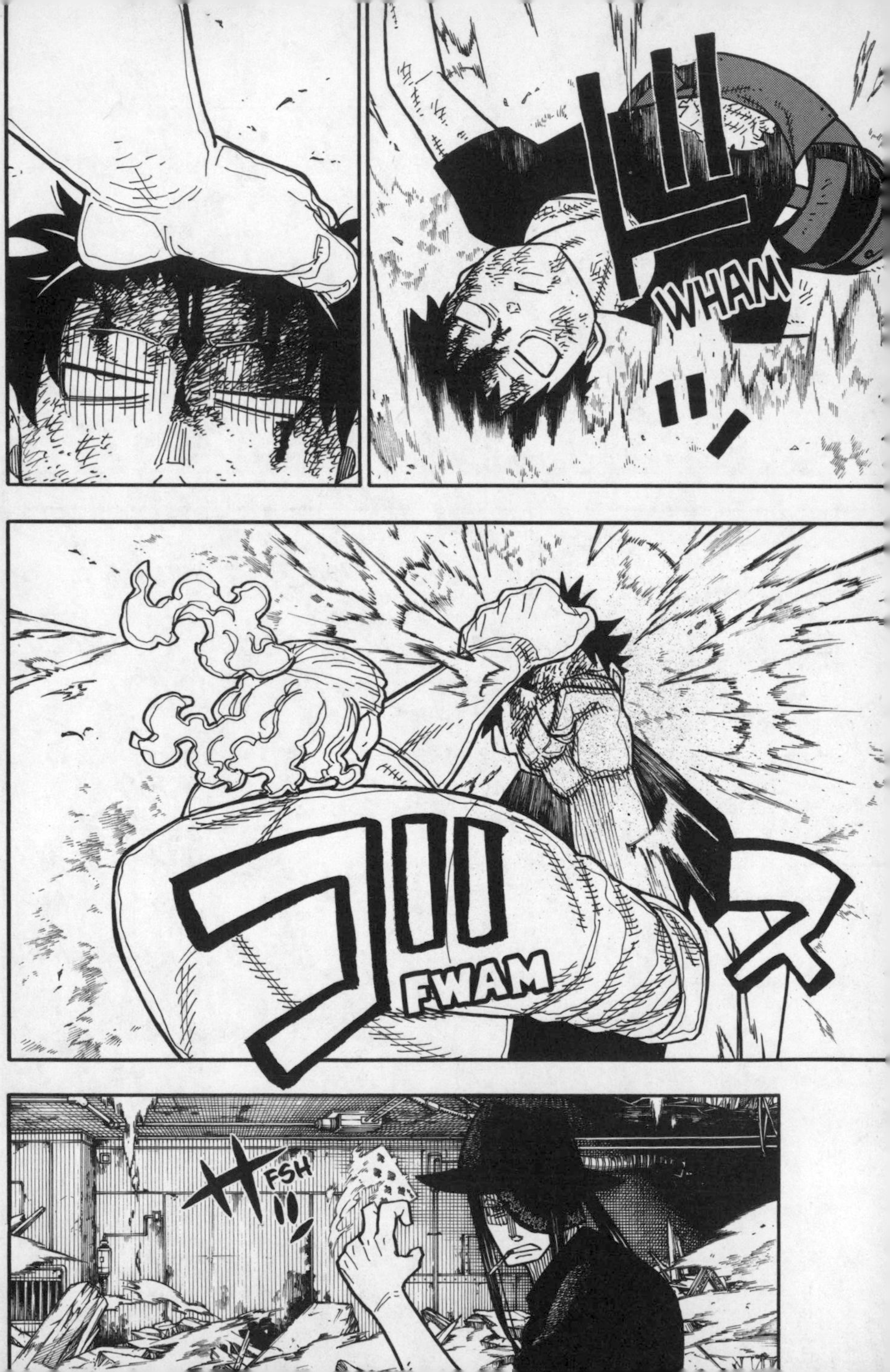
WHAM
FWAM
FSH

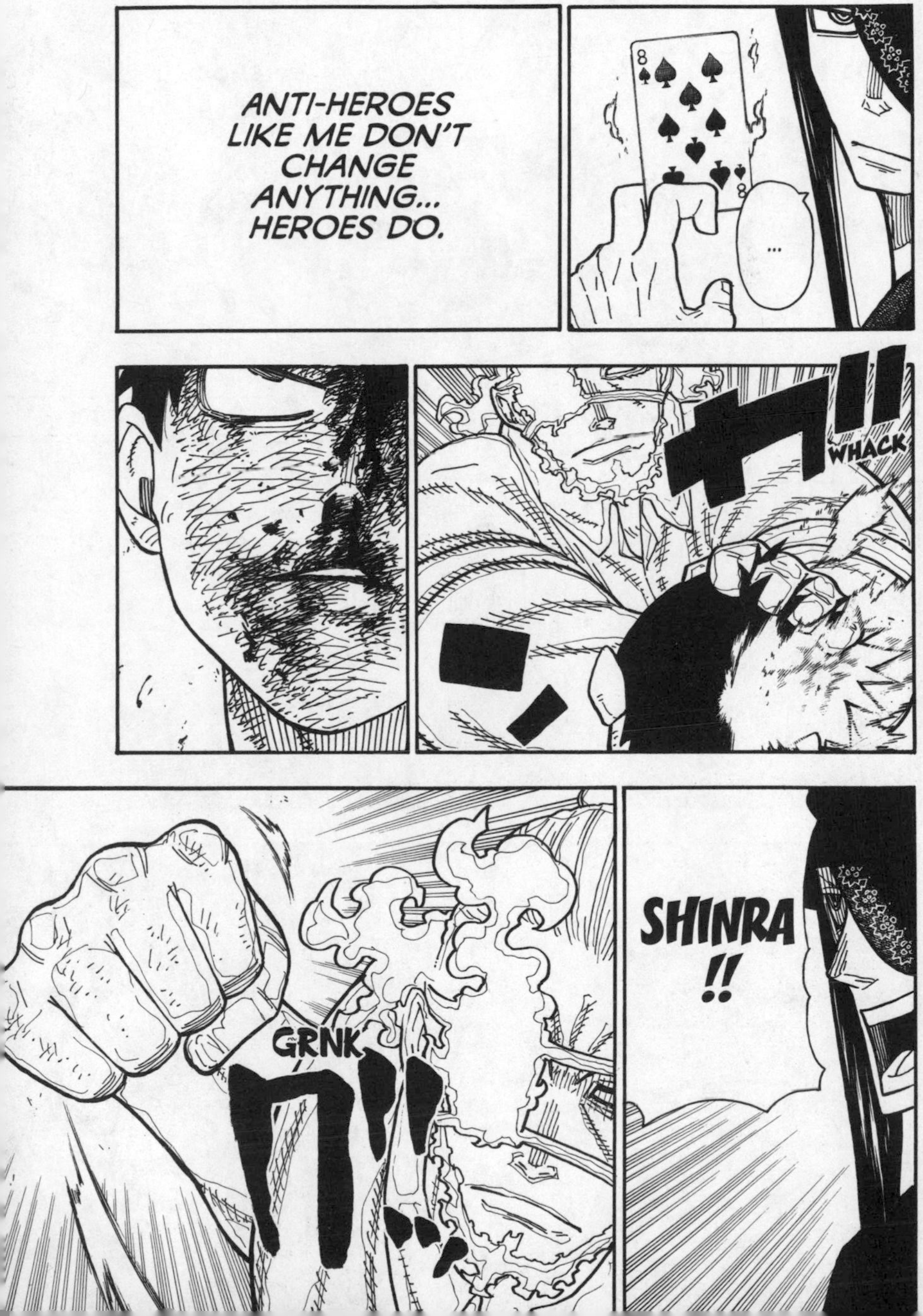
...
ANTI-HEROES LIKE ME DON'T CHANGE ANYTHING... HEROES DO.
WHACK
SHINRA!!
GRNK

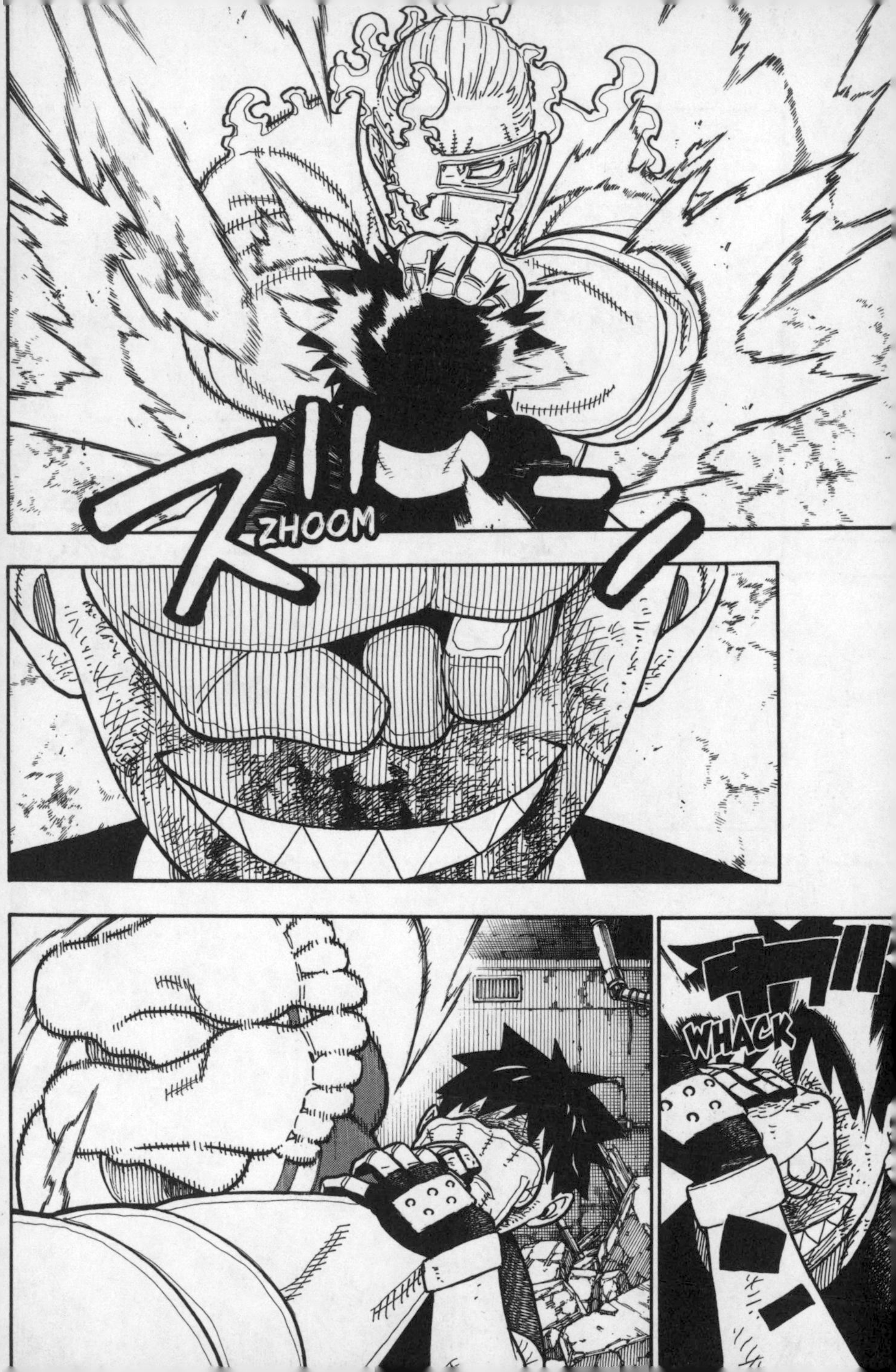

ZHOOM
WHACK

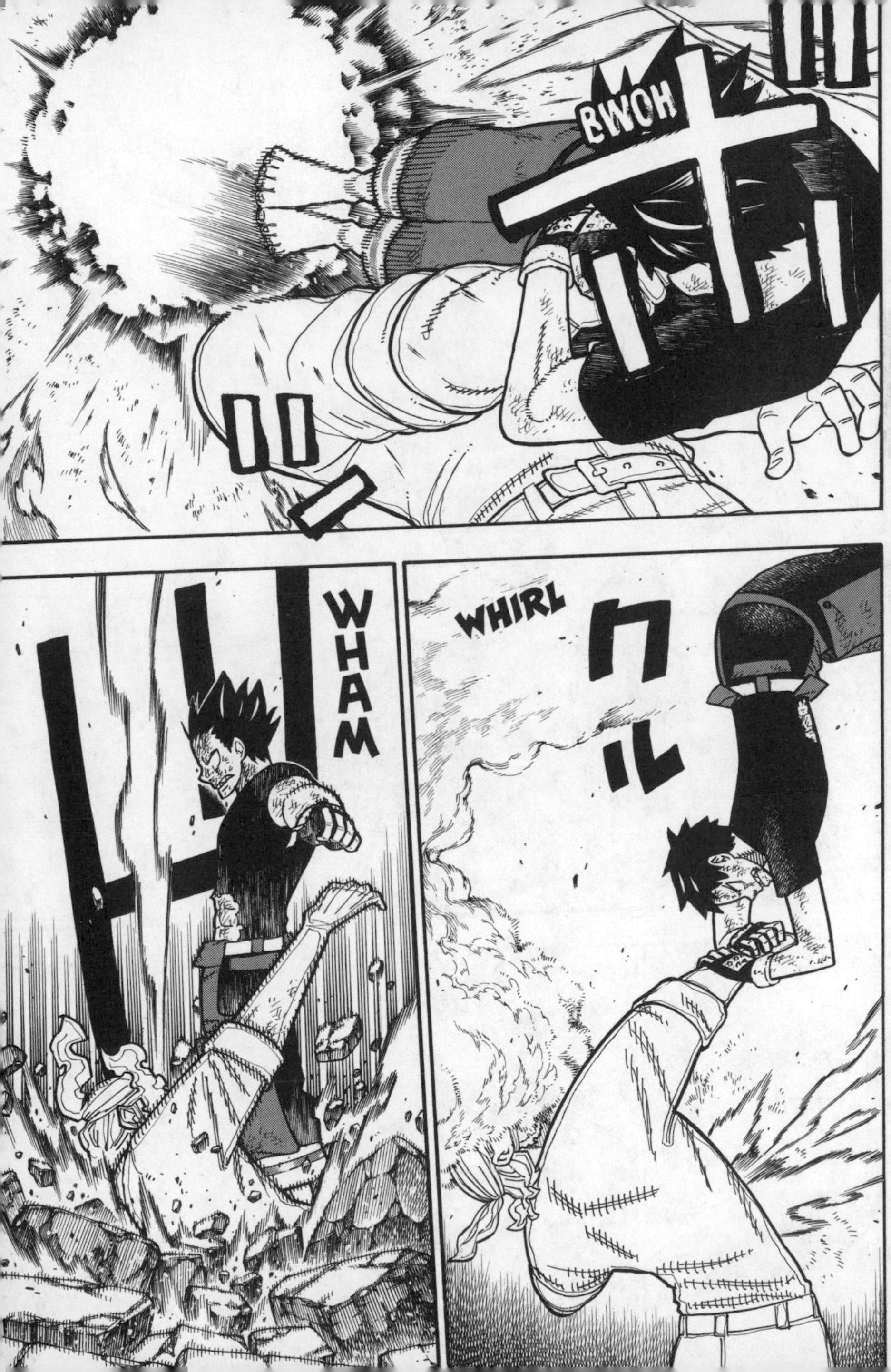
BWOH
WHIRL
クル
WHAM

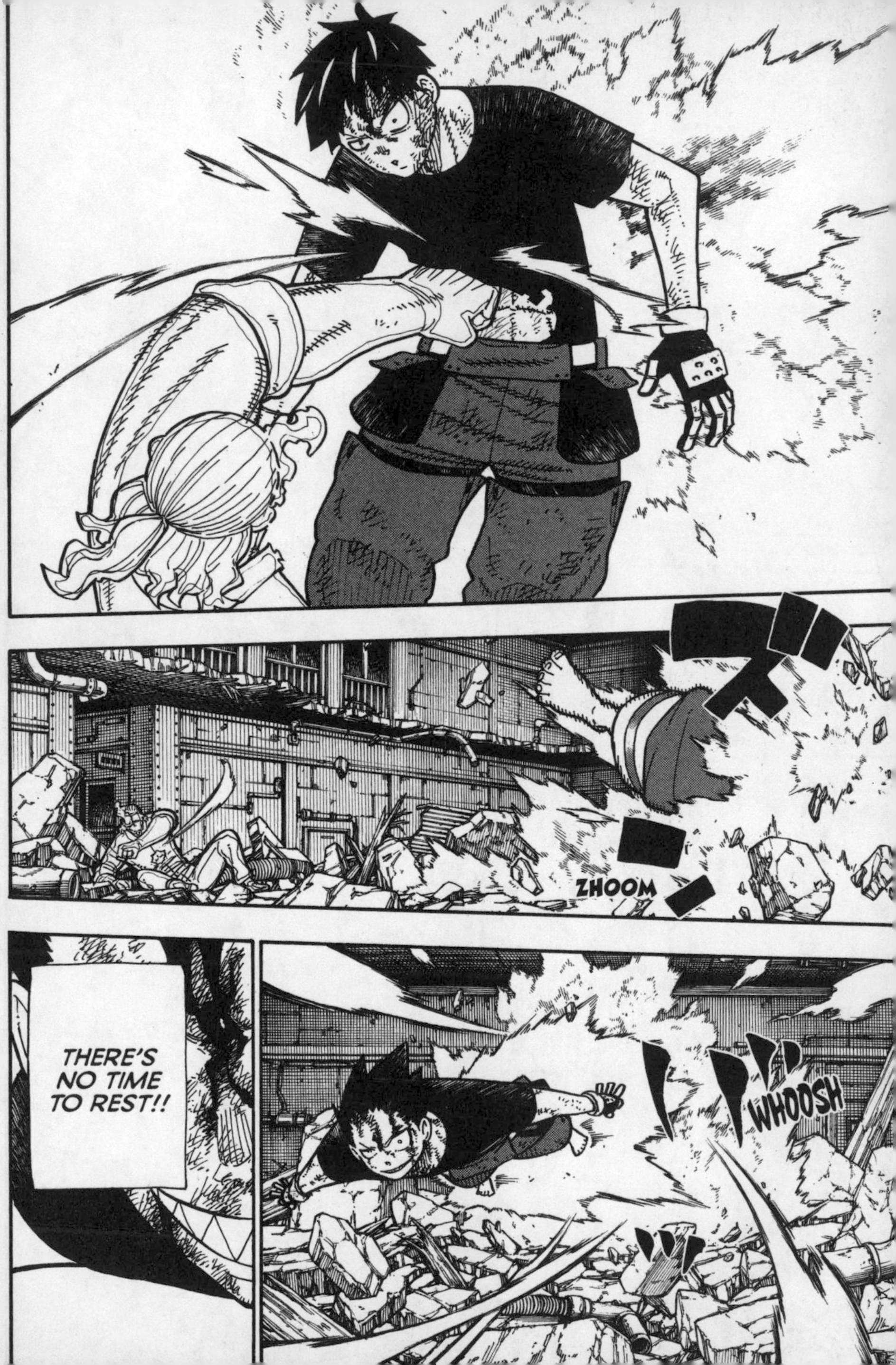
ZHOOM
WHOOSH
THERE'S NO TIME TO REST!!

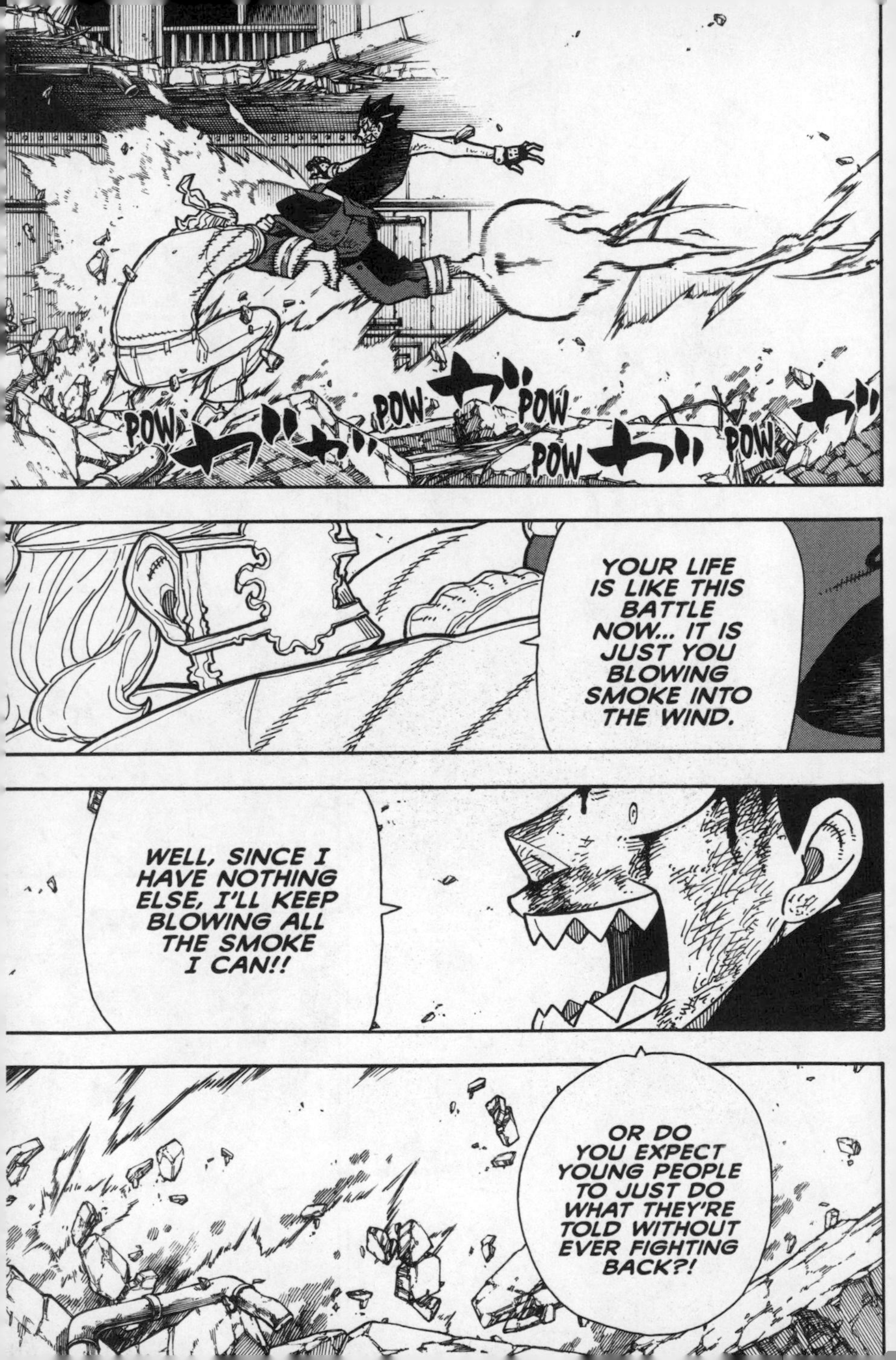
POW
POW
POW
POW
POW
POW
YOUR LIFE IS LIKE THIS BATTLE NOW... IT IS JUST YOU BLOWING SMOKE INTO THE WIND.
WELL, SINCE I HAVE NOTHING ELSE, I'LL KEEP BLOWING ALL THE SMOKE I CAN!!
OR DO YOU EXPECT YOUNG PEOPLE TO JUST DO WHAT THEY'RE TOLD WITHOUT EVER FIGHTING BACK?!

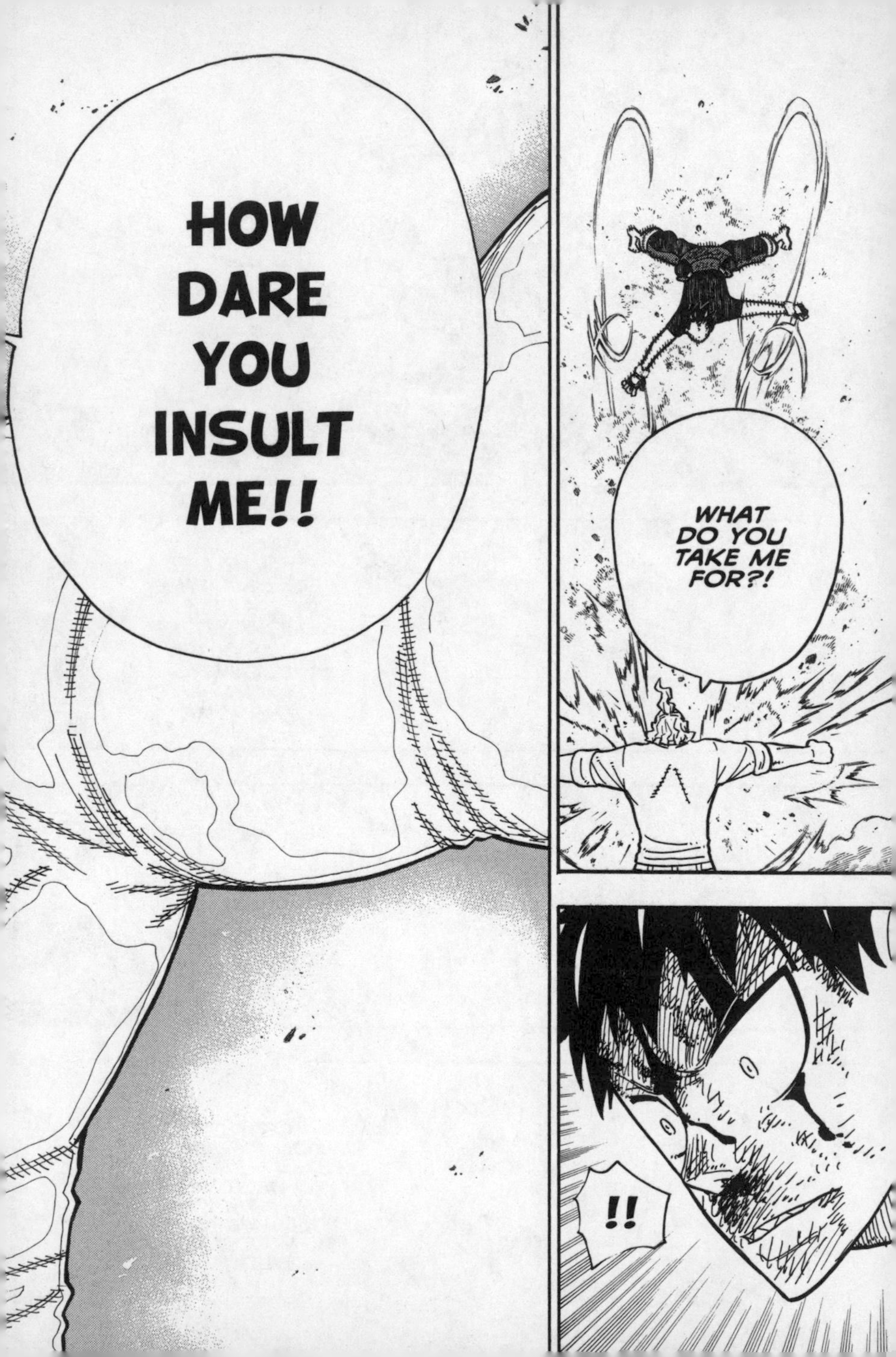
WHAT DO YOU TAKE ME FOR?!
!!
HOW DARE YOU INSULT ME!!

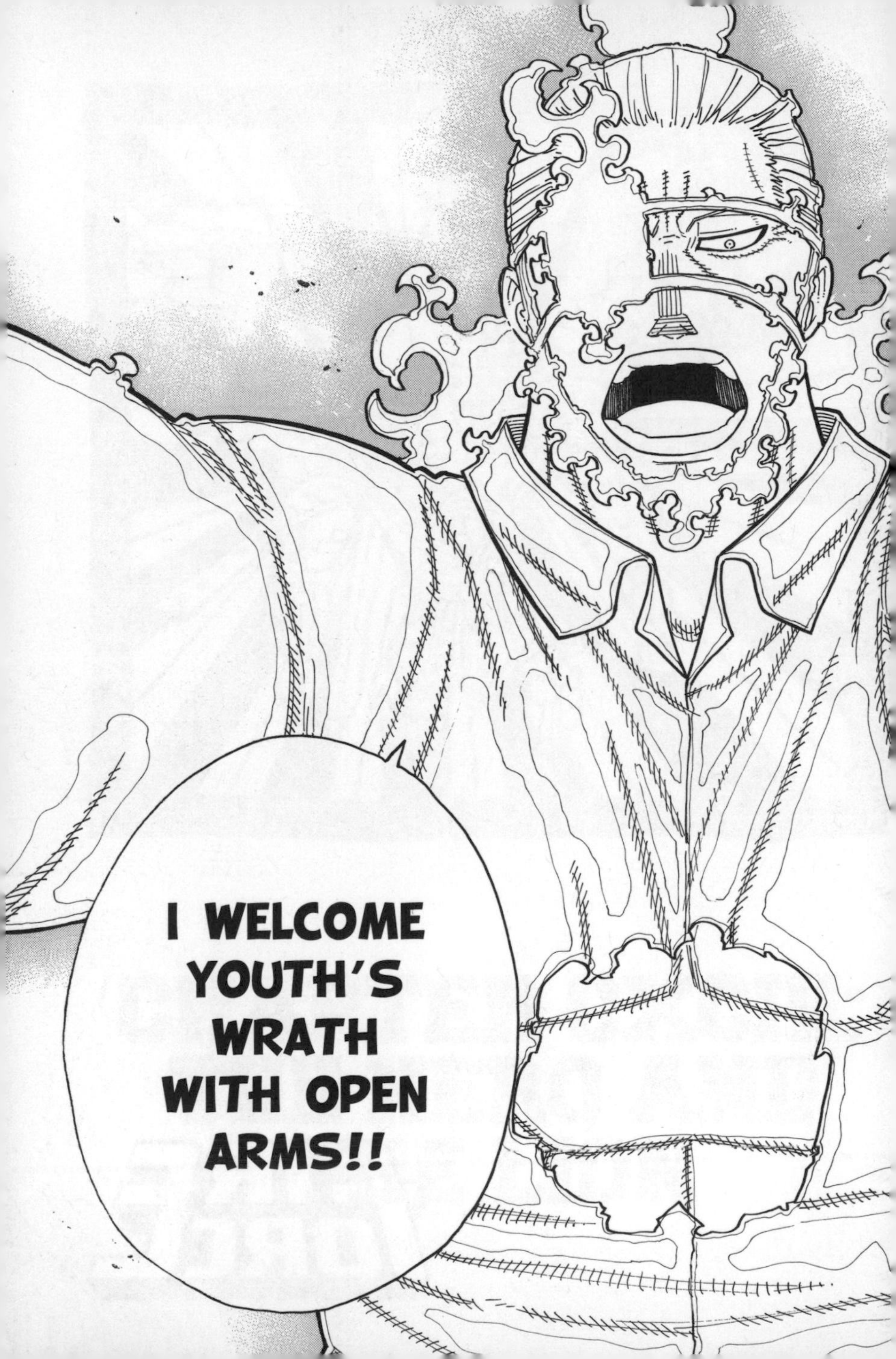
I WELCOME YOUTH'S WRATH WITH OPEN ARMS!!

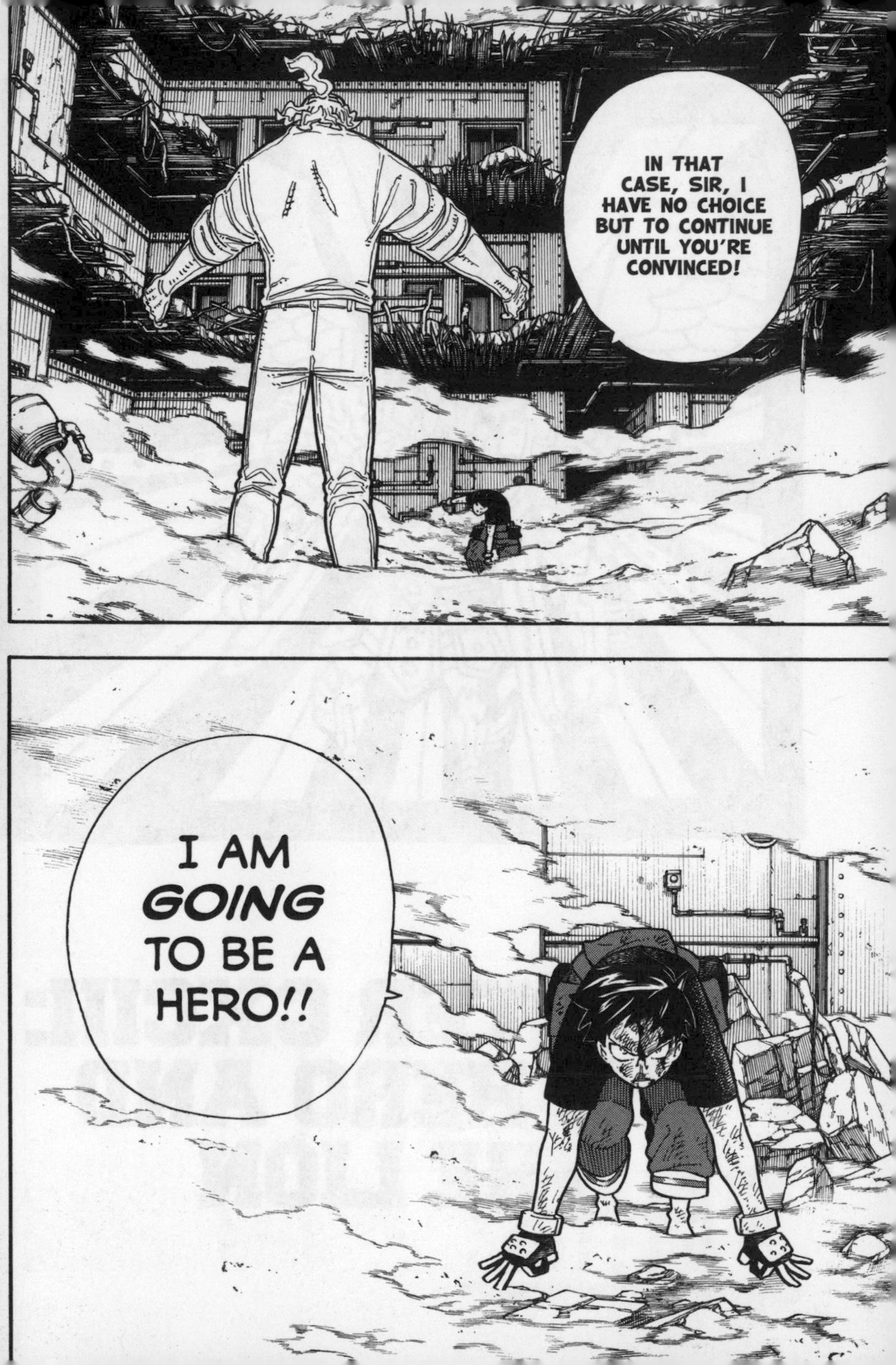
IN THAT CASE, SIR, I HAVE NO CHOICE BUT TO CONTINUE UNTIL YOU'RE CONVINCED!
I AM *GOING* TO BE A HERO!!

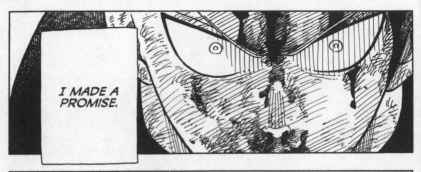

I MADE A PROMISE.

I PROMISED I WOULD BECOME A HERO...

...AND PROTECT MOM AND SHŌ...

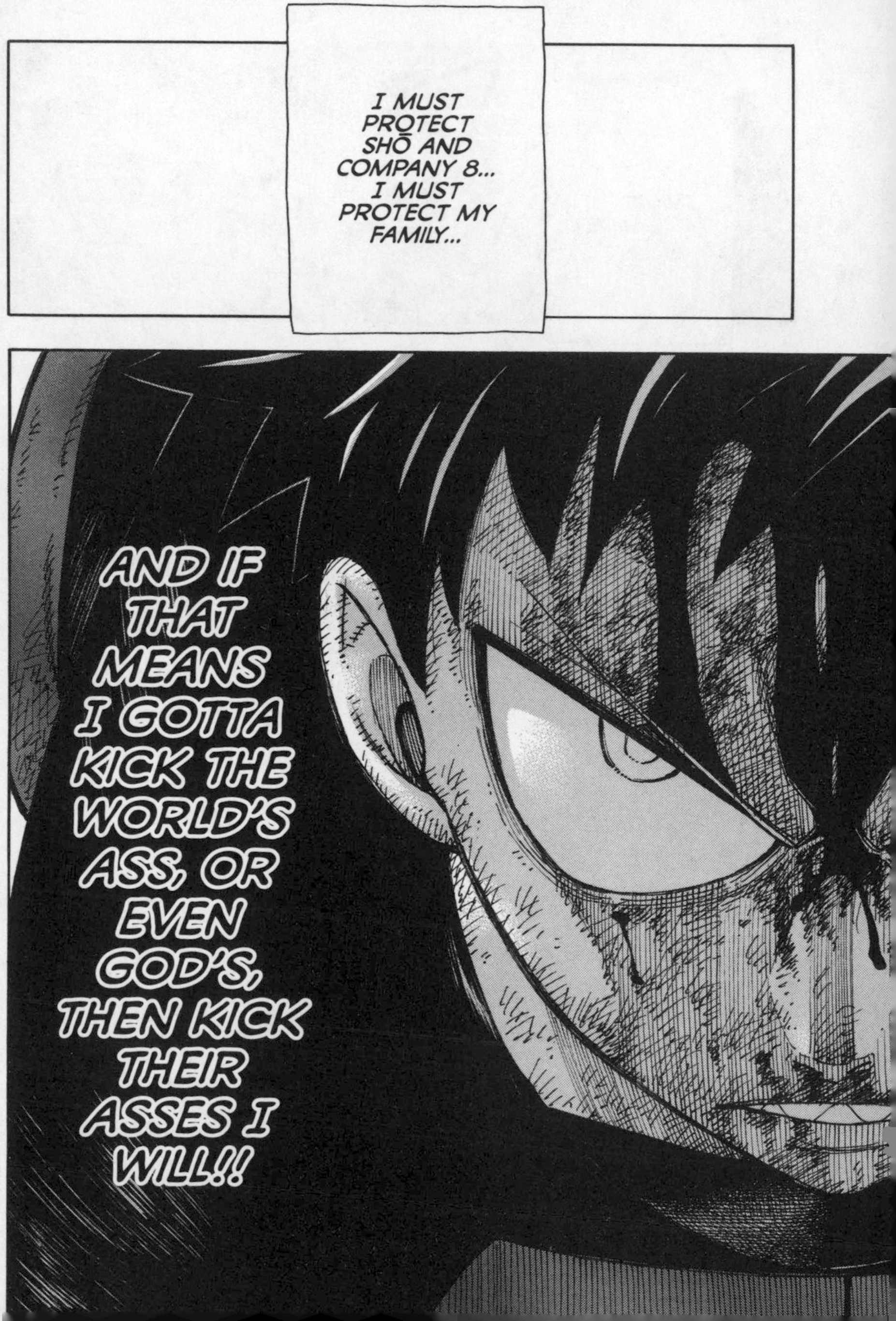
I MUST PROTECT SHŌ AND COMPANY 8... I MUST PROTECT MY FAMILY...
AND IF THAT MEANS I GOTTA KICK THE WORLD'S ASS, OR EVEN GOD'S, THEN KICK THEIR ASSES I WILL!!

CLACK

CLACK

CLACK

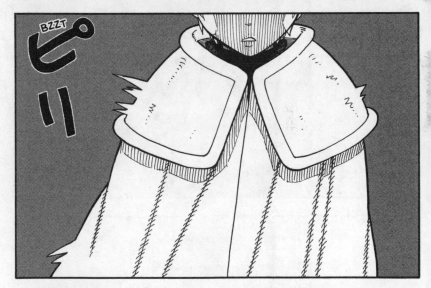

BZZT

IS SOME-
THING THE
MATTER,
COMMAND-
ER?

...

133

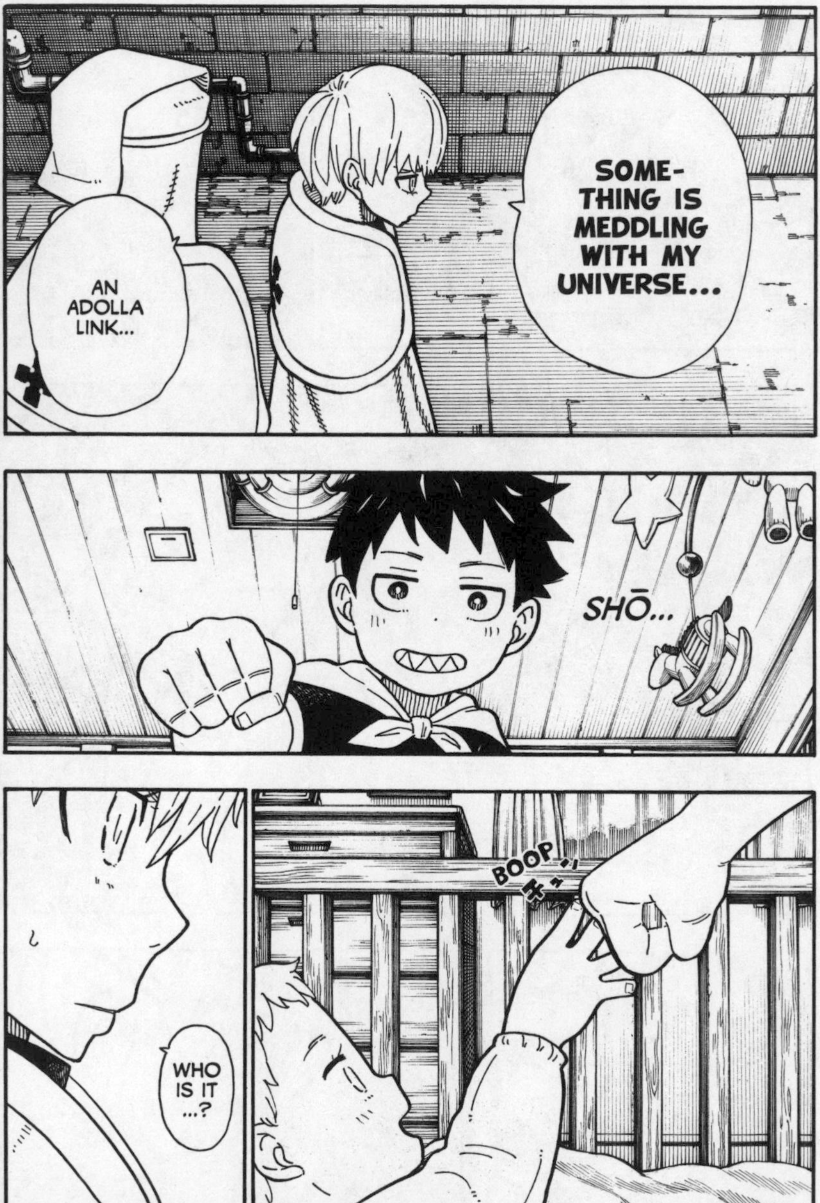
SOME-THING IS MEDDLING WITH MY UNIVERSE...
AN ADOLLA LINK...
SHŌ...
BOOP
WHO IS IT ...?

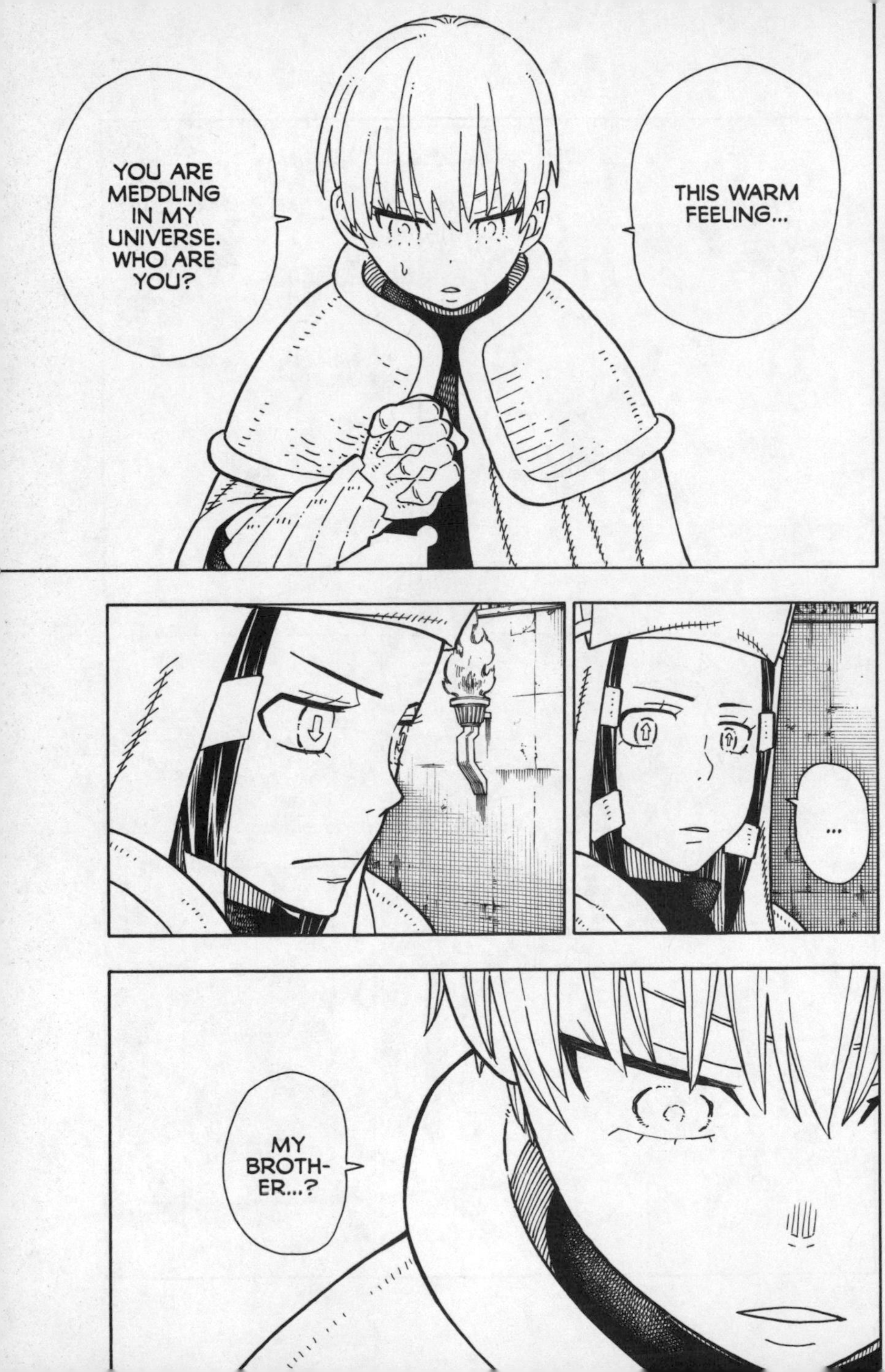
THIS WARM FEELING...
YOU ARE MEDDLING IN MY UNIVERSE. WHO ARE YOU?
...
MY BROTH-ER...?

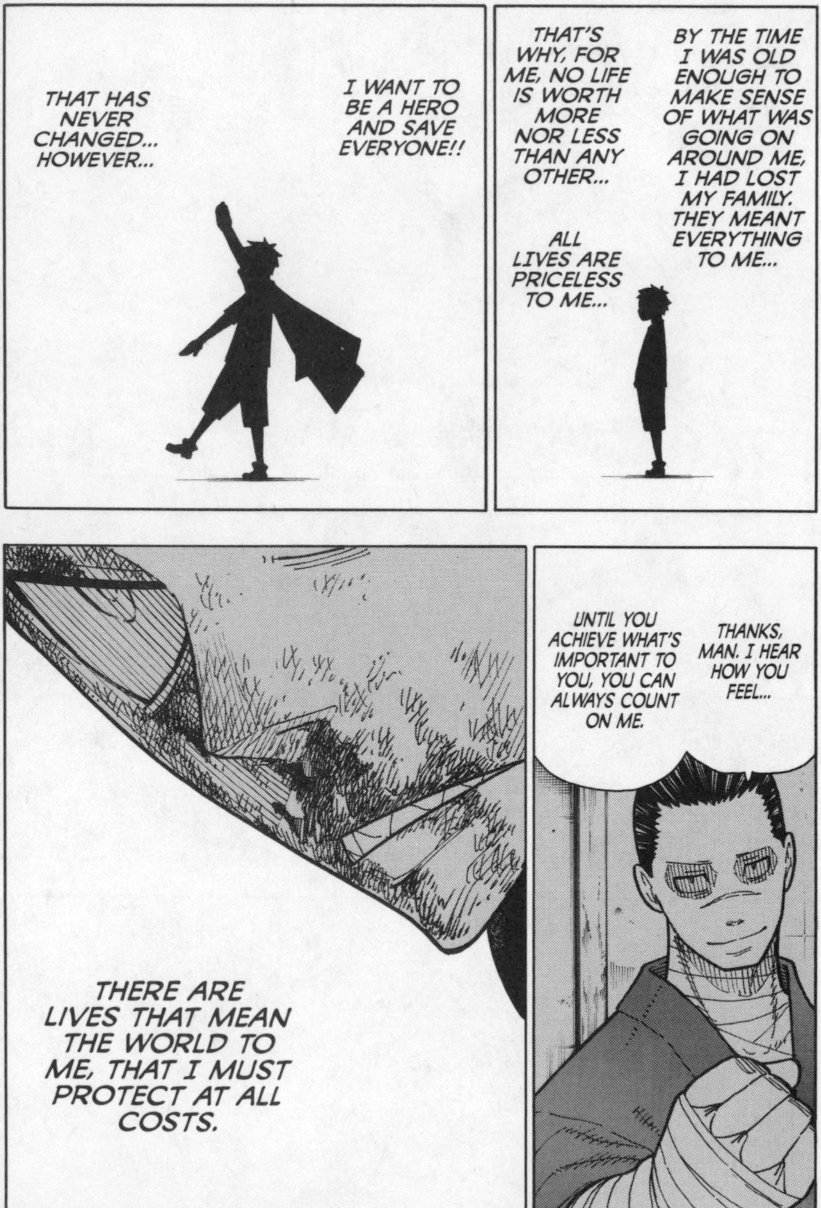
BY THE TIME I WAS OLD ENOUGH TO MAKE SENSE OF WHAT WAS GOING ON AROUND ME, I HAD LOST MY FAMILY. THEY MEANT EVERYTHING TO ME...
THAT'S WHY, FOR ME, NO LIFE IS WORTH MORE NOR LESS THAN ANY OTHER...
ALL LIVES ARE PRICELESS TO ME...
I WANT TO BE A HERO AND SAVE EVERYONE!!
THAT HAS NEVER CHANGED... HOWEVER...
THANKS, MAN. I HEAR HOW YOU FEEL...
UNTIL YOU ACHIEVE WHAT'S IMPORTANT TO YOU, YOU CAN ALWAYS COUNT ON ME.
THERE ARE LIVES THAT MEAN THE WORLD TO ME, THAT I MUST PROTECT AT ALL COSTS.

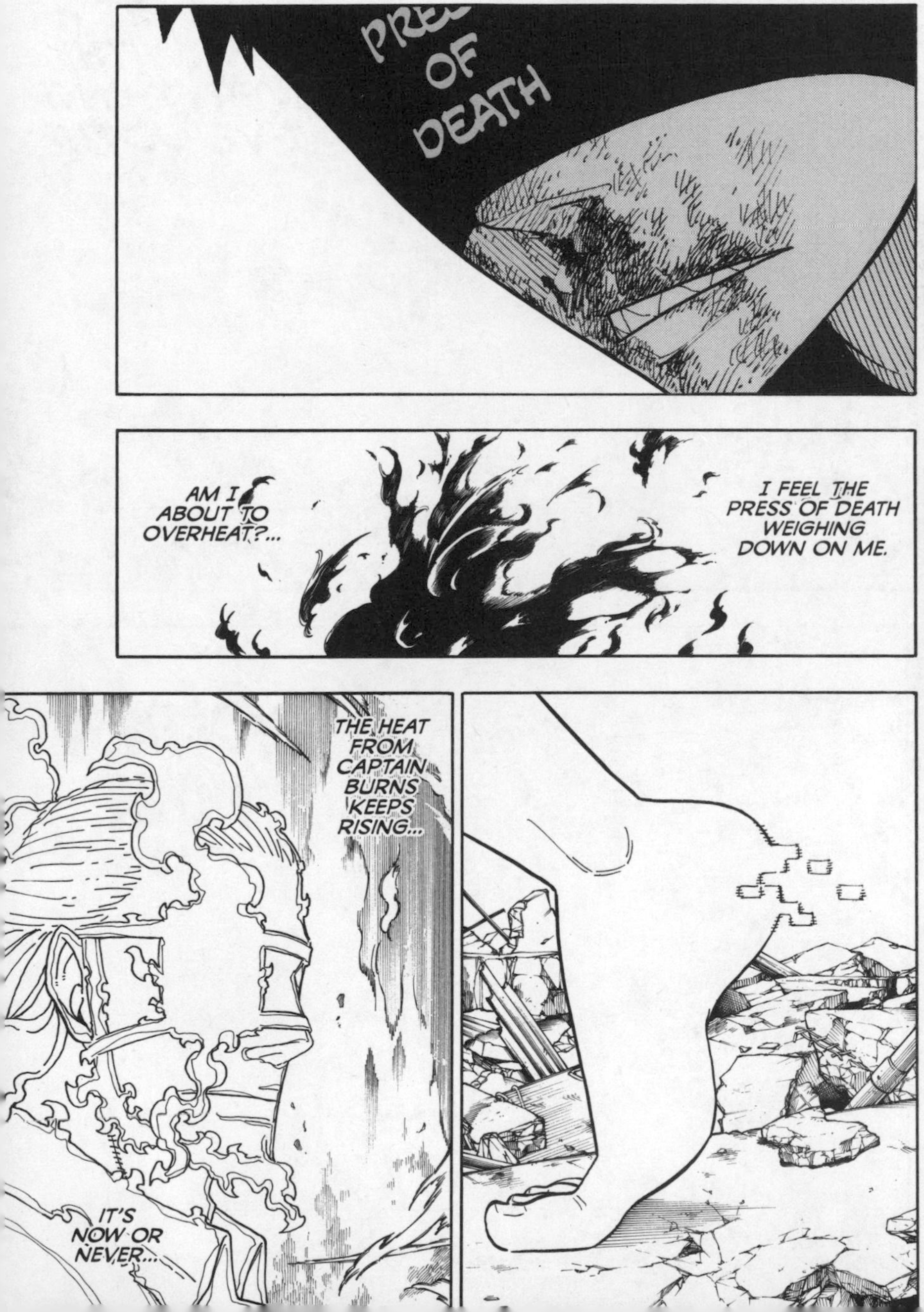
PRE
OF DEATH
I FEEL THE PRESS OF DEATH WEIGHING DOWN ON ME.
AM I ABOUT TO OVERHEAT?...
THE HEAT FROM CAPTAIN BURNS KEEPS RISING...
IT'S NOW OR NEVER...

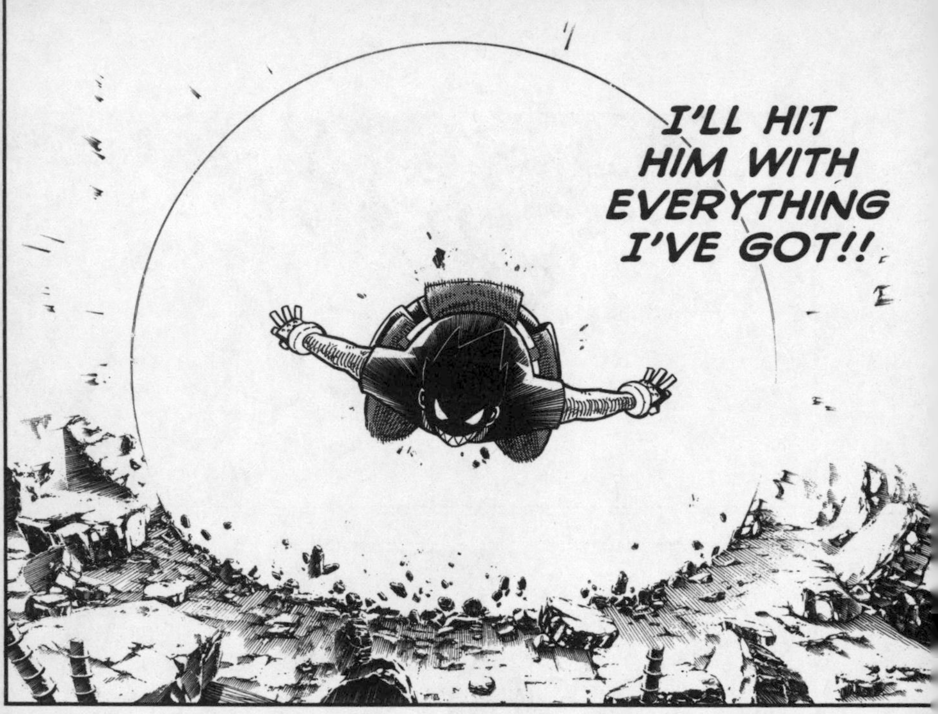
I'LL HIT HIM WITH EVERYTHING I'VE GOT!!
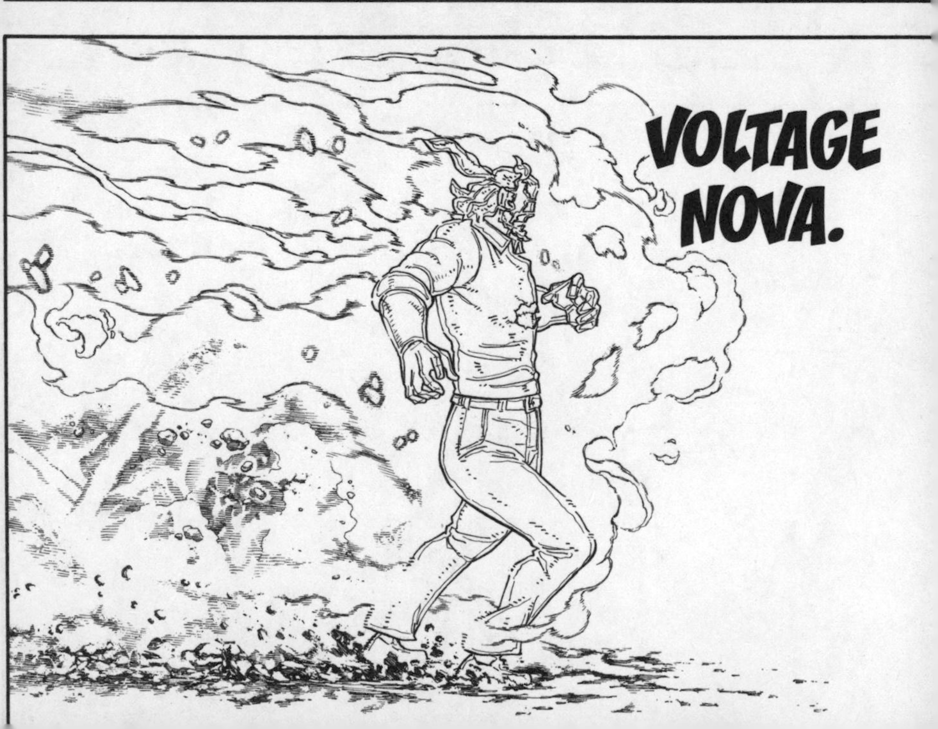
VOLTAGE NOVA.

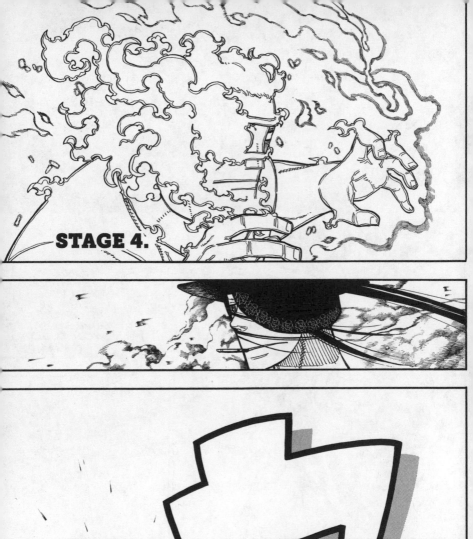

STAGE 4.

FLASH

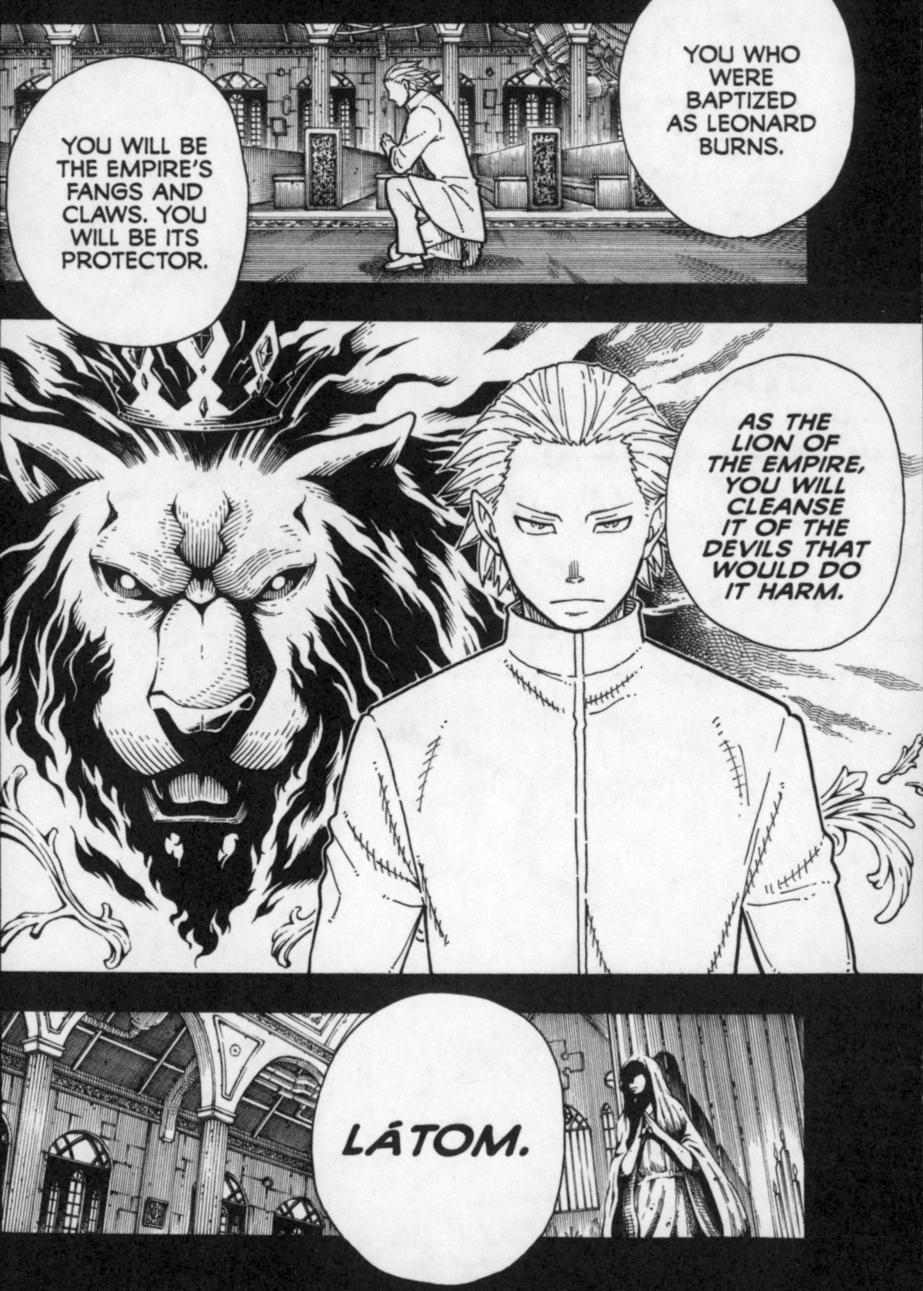
YOU WHO WERE BAPTIZED AS LEONARD BURNS.
YOU WILL BE THE EMPIRE'S FANGS AND CLAWS. YOU WILL BE ITS PROTECTOR.
AS THE LION OF THE EMPIRE, YOU WILL CLEANSE IT OF THE DEVILS THAT WOULD DO IT HARM.
LÁTOM.

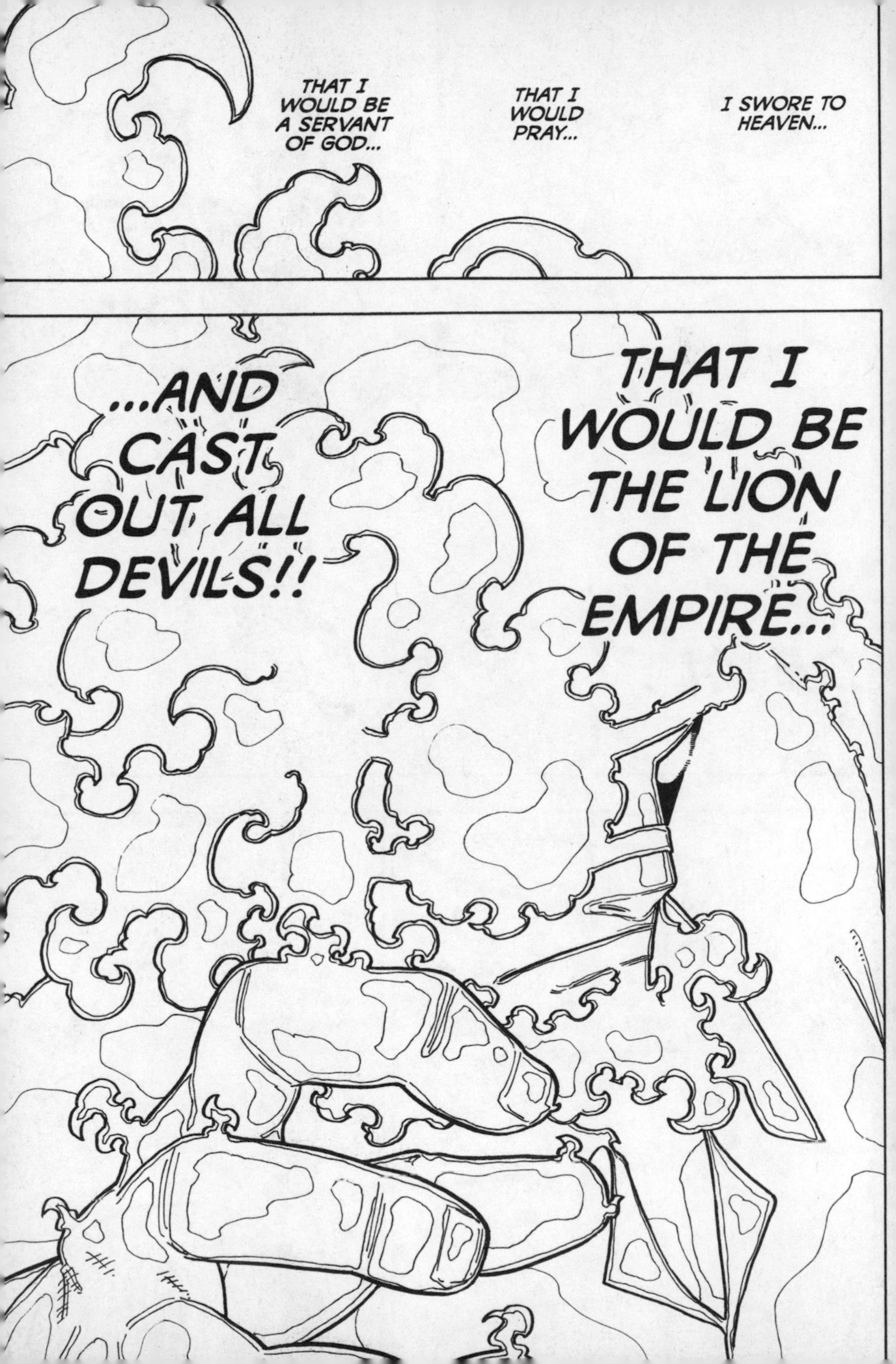
I SWORE TO HEAVEN...
THAT I WOULD PRAY...
THAT I WOULD BE A SERVANT OF GOD...
THAT I WOULD BE THE LION OF THE EMPIRE...
...AND CAST OUT ALL DEVILS!!

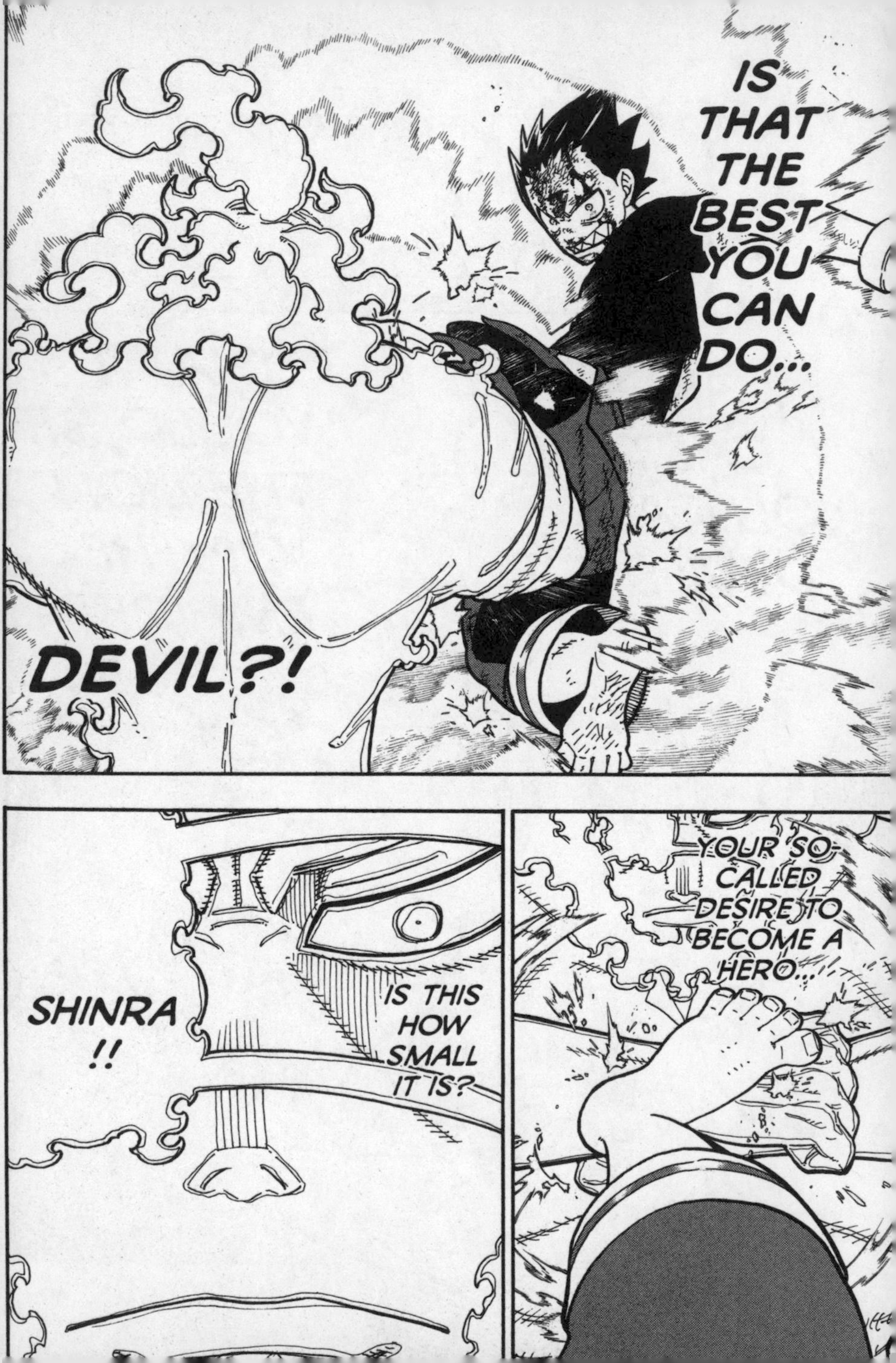
IS THAT THE BEST YOU CAN DO...
DEVIL?!
YOUR SO-CALLED DESIRE TO BECOME A HERO...
IS THIS HOW SMALL IT IS?
SHINRA!!

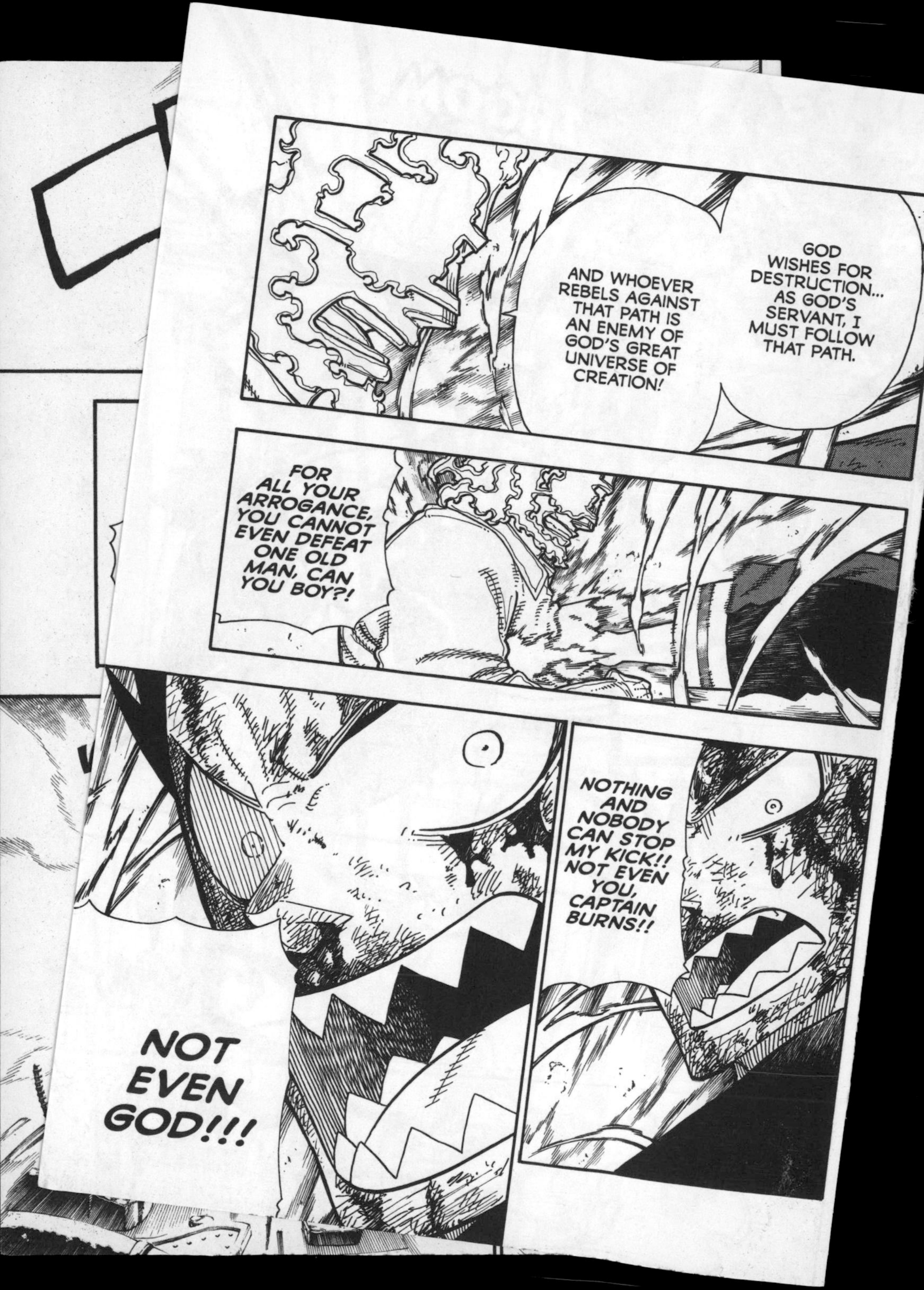
GOD WISHES FOR DESTRUCTION... AS GOD'S SERVANT, I MUST FOLLOW THAT PATH.
AND WHOEVER REBELS AGAINST THAT PATH IS AN ENEMY OF GOD'S GREAT UNIVERSE OF CREATION!
FOR ALL YOUR ARROGANCE, YOU CANNOT EVEN DEFEAT ONE OLD MAN, CAN YOU BOY?!
NOTHING AND NOBODY CAN STOP MY KICK!! NOT EVEN YOU, CAPTAIN BURNS!!
NOT EVEN GOD!!!

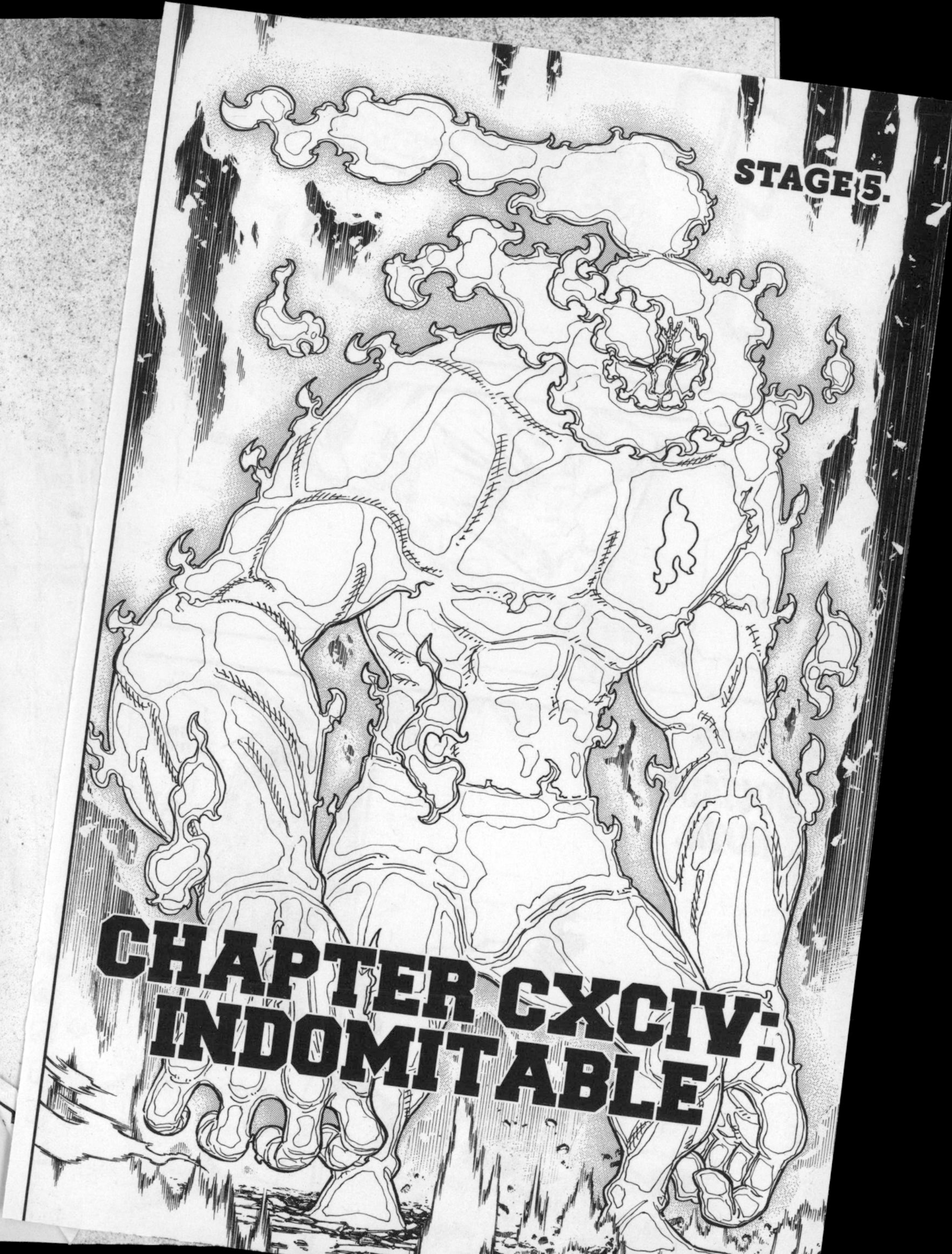
STAGE 5.
CHAPTER CXCIV:
INDOMITABLE

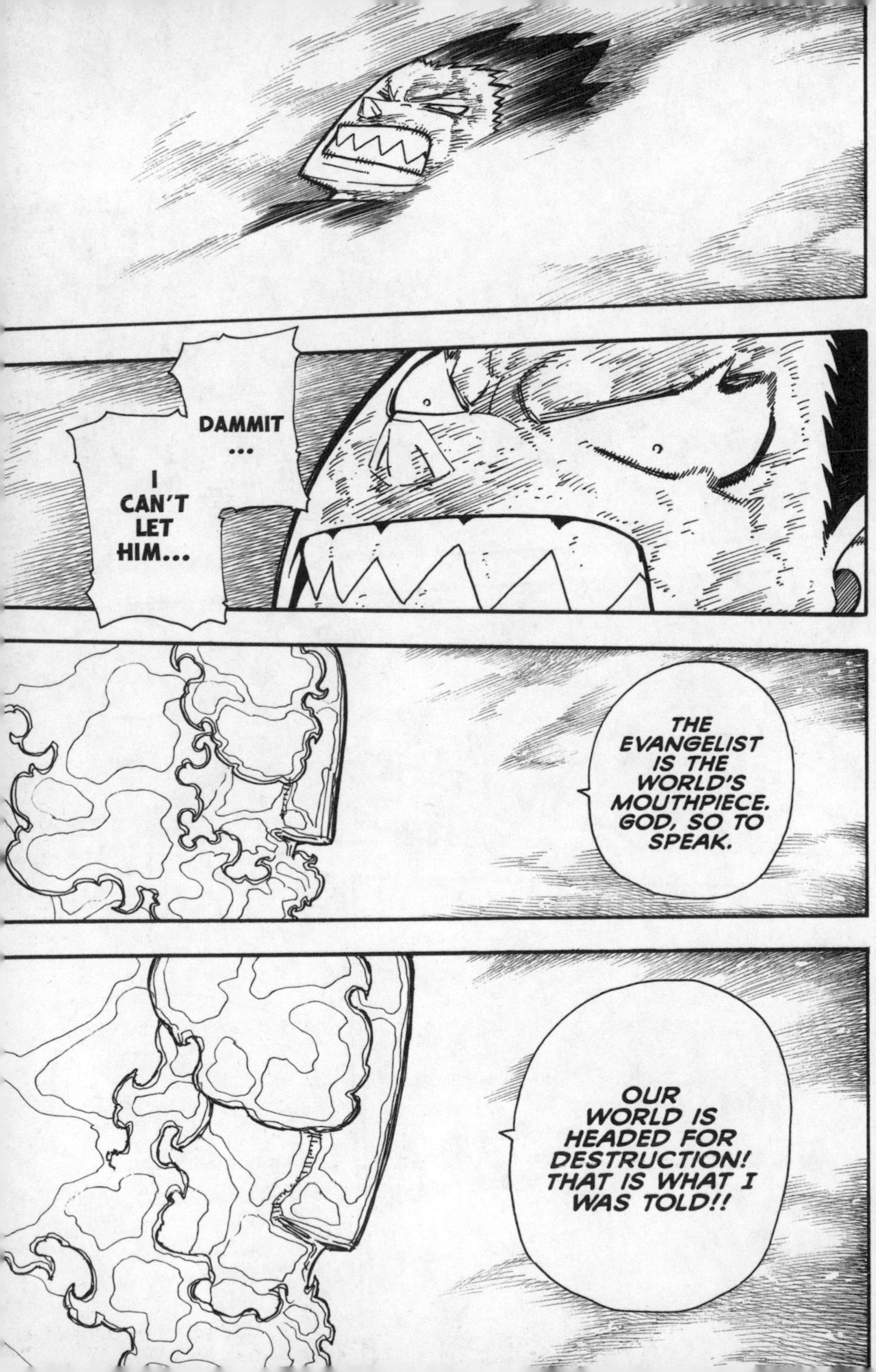
DAMMIT ...
I CAN'T LET HIM...
THE EVANGELIST IS THE WORLD'S MOUTHPIECE. GOD, SO TO SPEAK.
OUR WORLD IS HEADED FOR DESTRUCTION! THAT IS WHAT I WAS TOLD!!

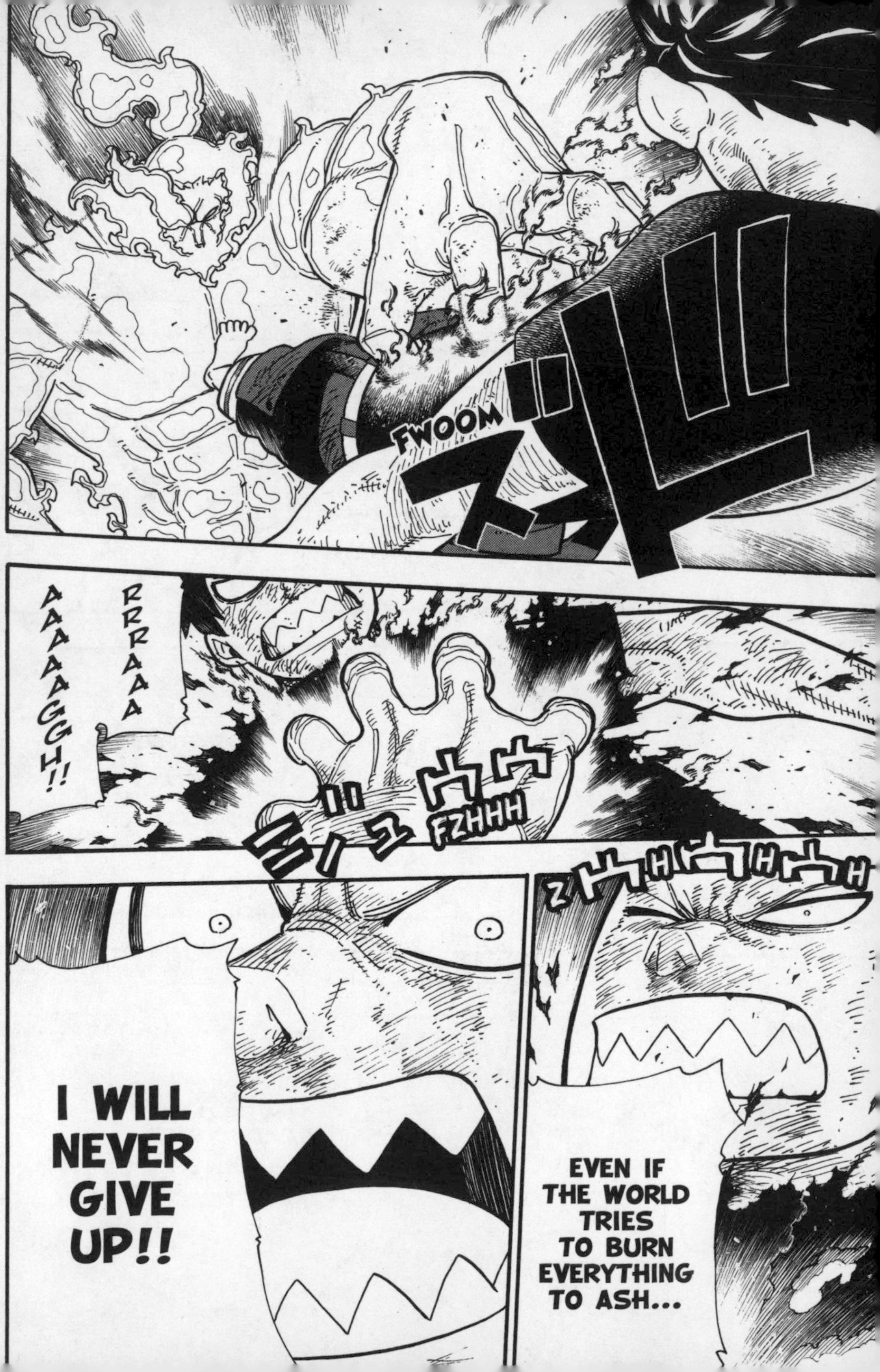
FWOOM
RRRAAA
AAAAAGGGH!!
FZHHH
EVEN IF THE WORLD TRIES TO BURN EVERYTHING TO ASH...
I WILL NEVER GIVE UP!!

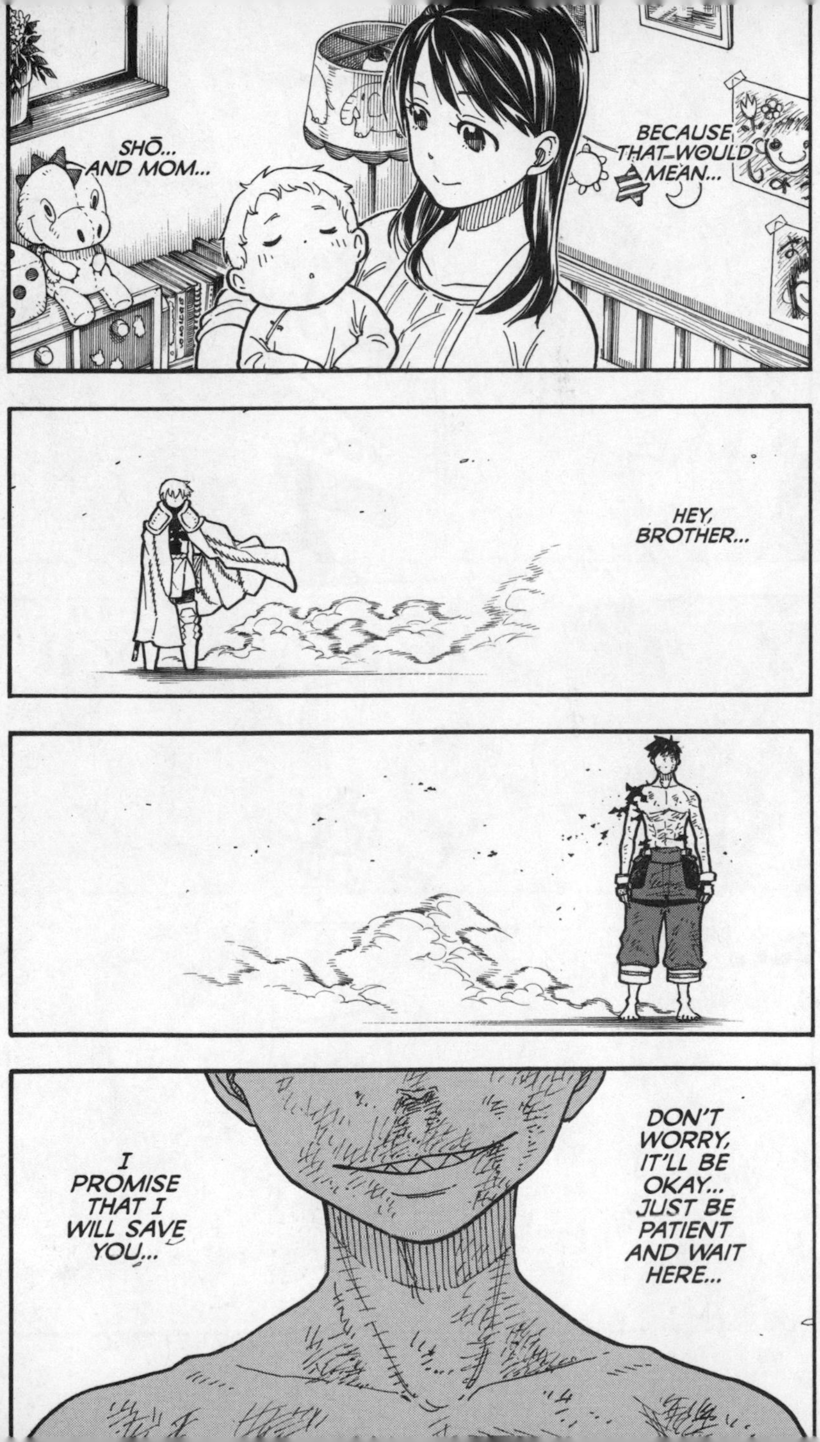
BECAUSE THAT WOULD MEAN...
SHŌ... AND MOM...
HEY, BROTHER...
DON'T WORRY, IT'LL BE OKAY... JUST BE PATIENT AND WAIT HERE...
I PROMISE THAT I WILL SAVE YOU...

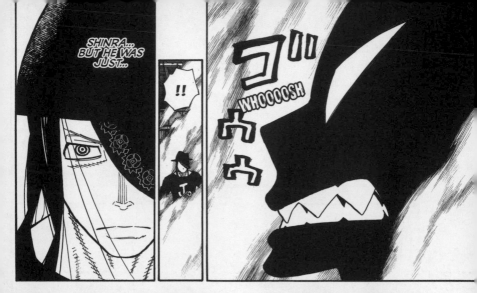

SHINRA...
BUT HE WAS
JUST...

!!

WHOOOOSH

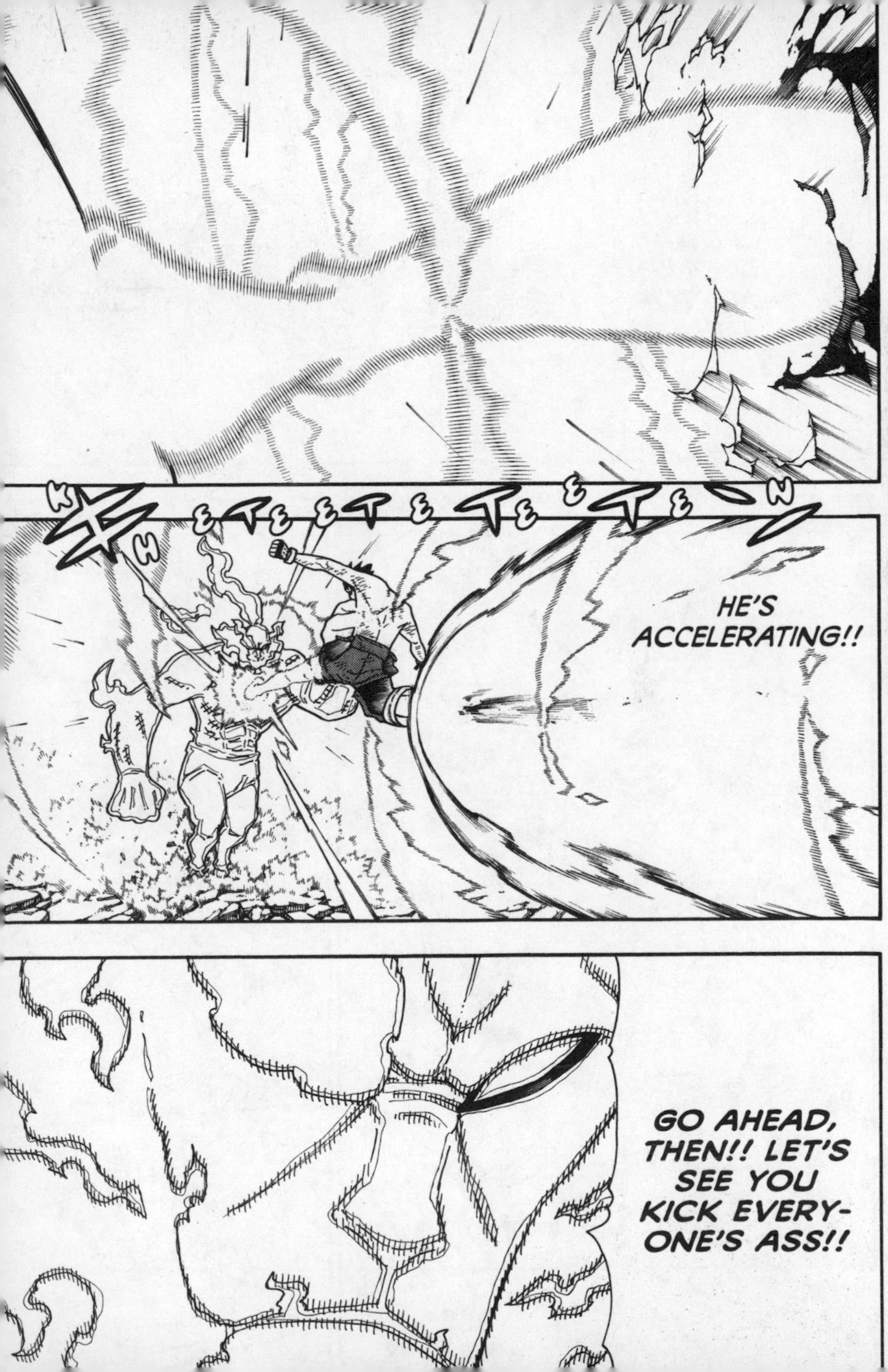
HE'S ACCELERATING!!
GO AHEAD, THEN!! LET'S SEE YOU KICK EVERY-ONE'S ASS!!

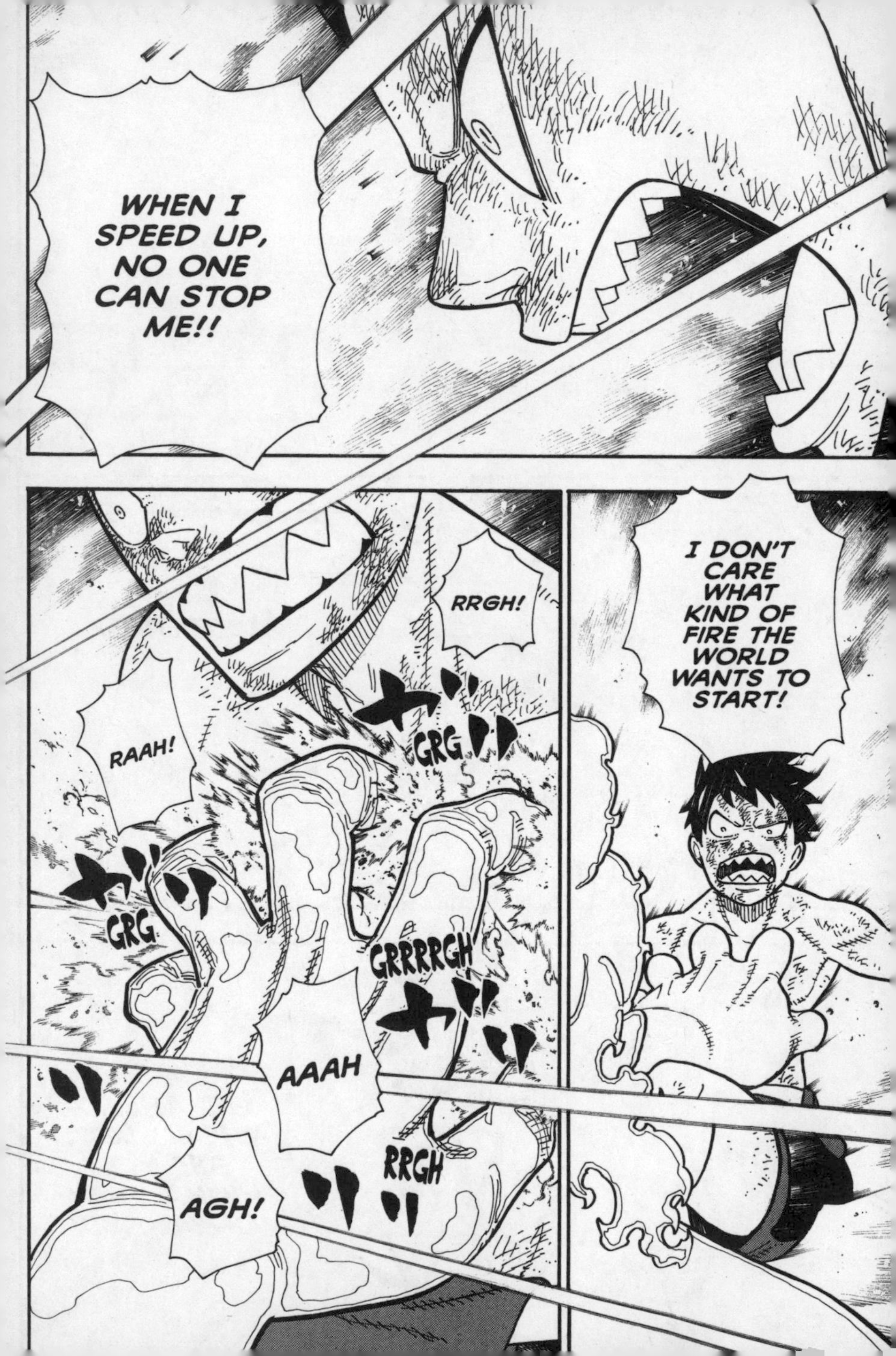
WHEN I SPEED UP, NO ONE CAN STOP ME!!
I DON'T CARE WHAT KIND OF FIRE THE WORLD WANTS TO START!
RRGH!
GRG
RAAH!
GRG
GRRRRGH
AAAH
RRGH
AGH!

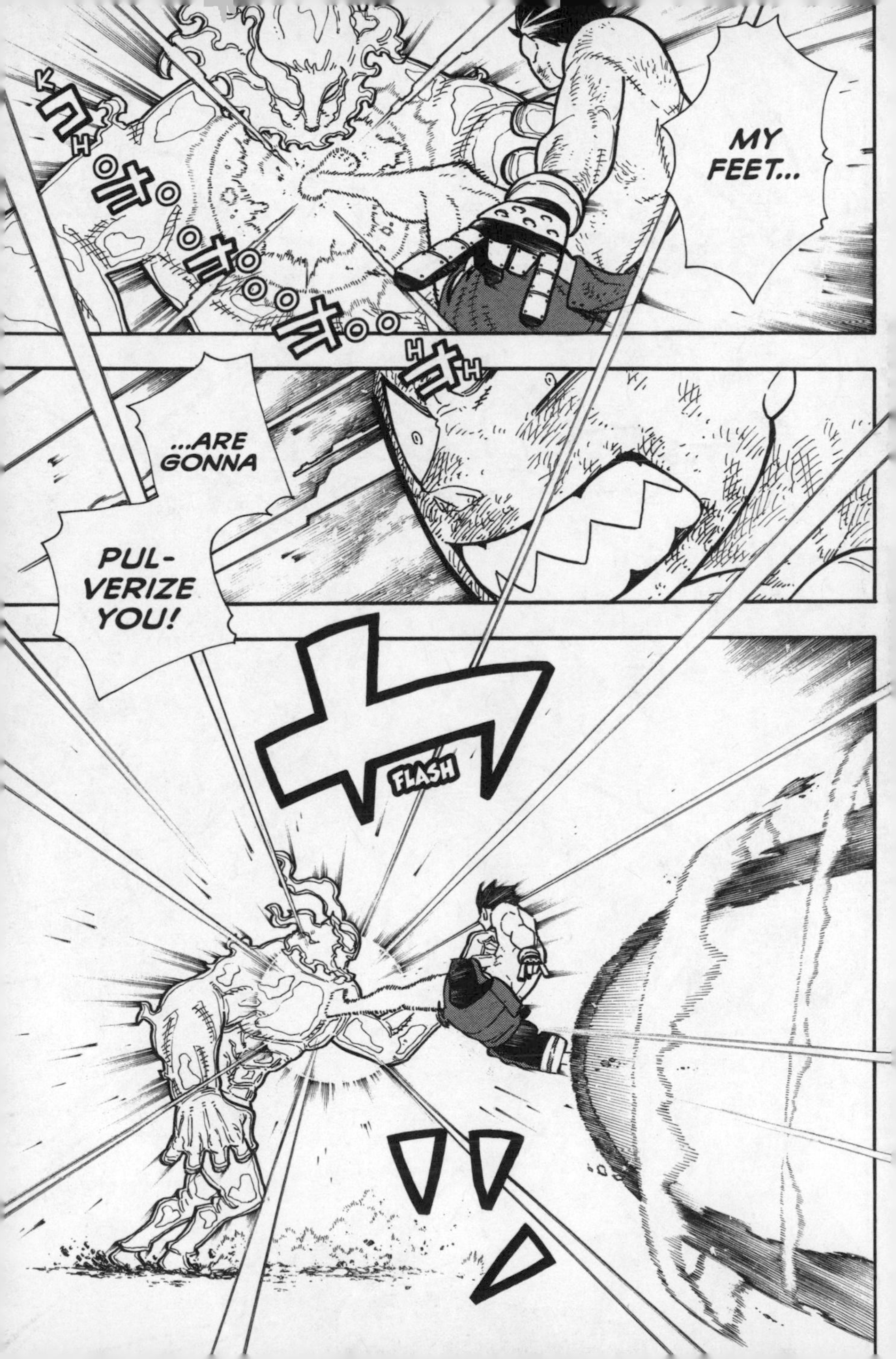
MY FEET...
...ARE GONNA
PUL-VERIZE YOU!
FLASH

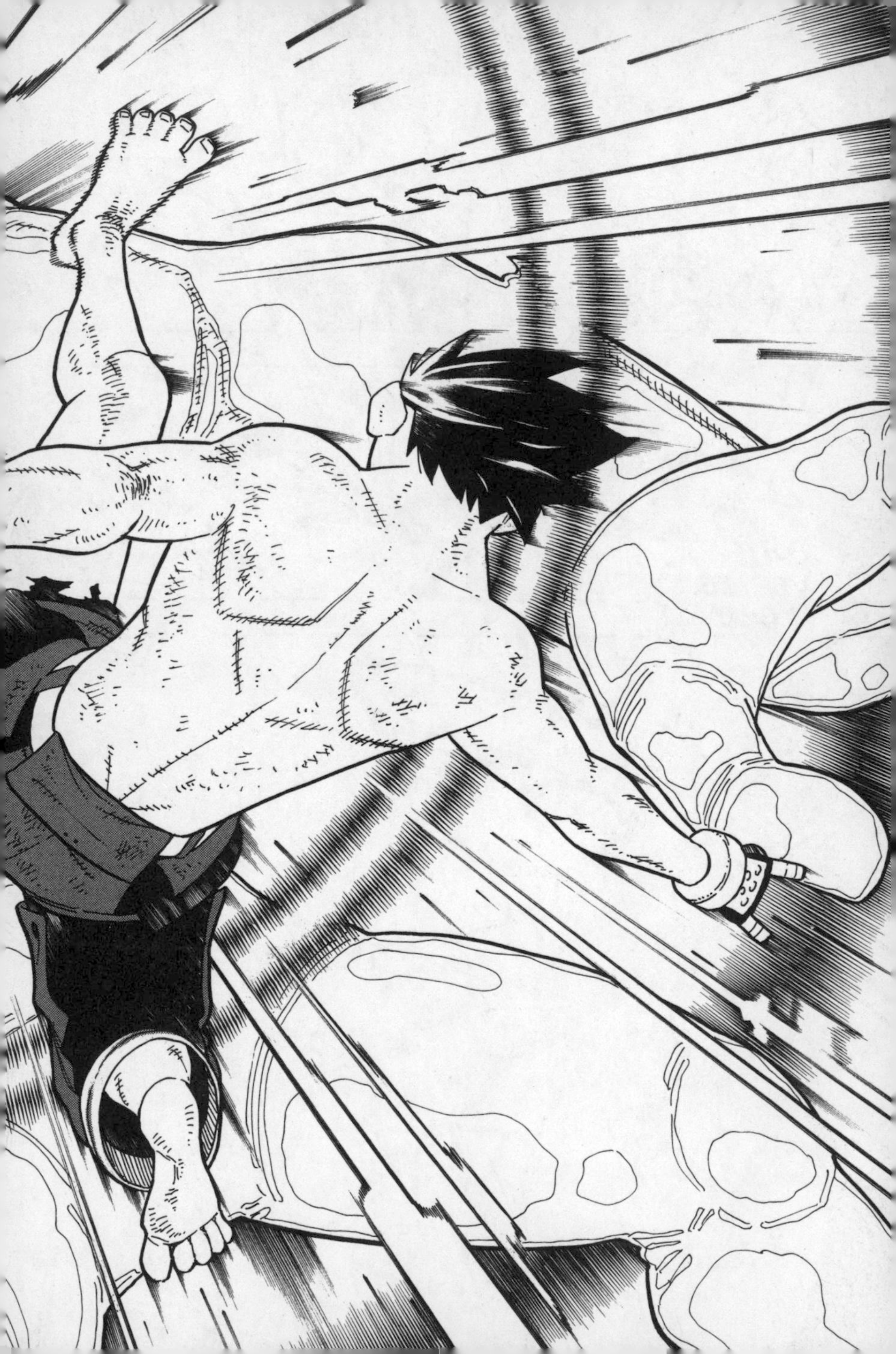

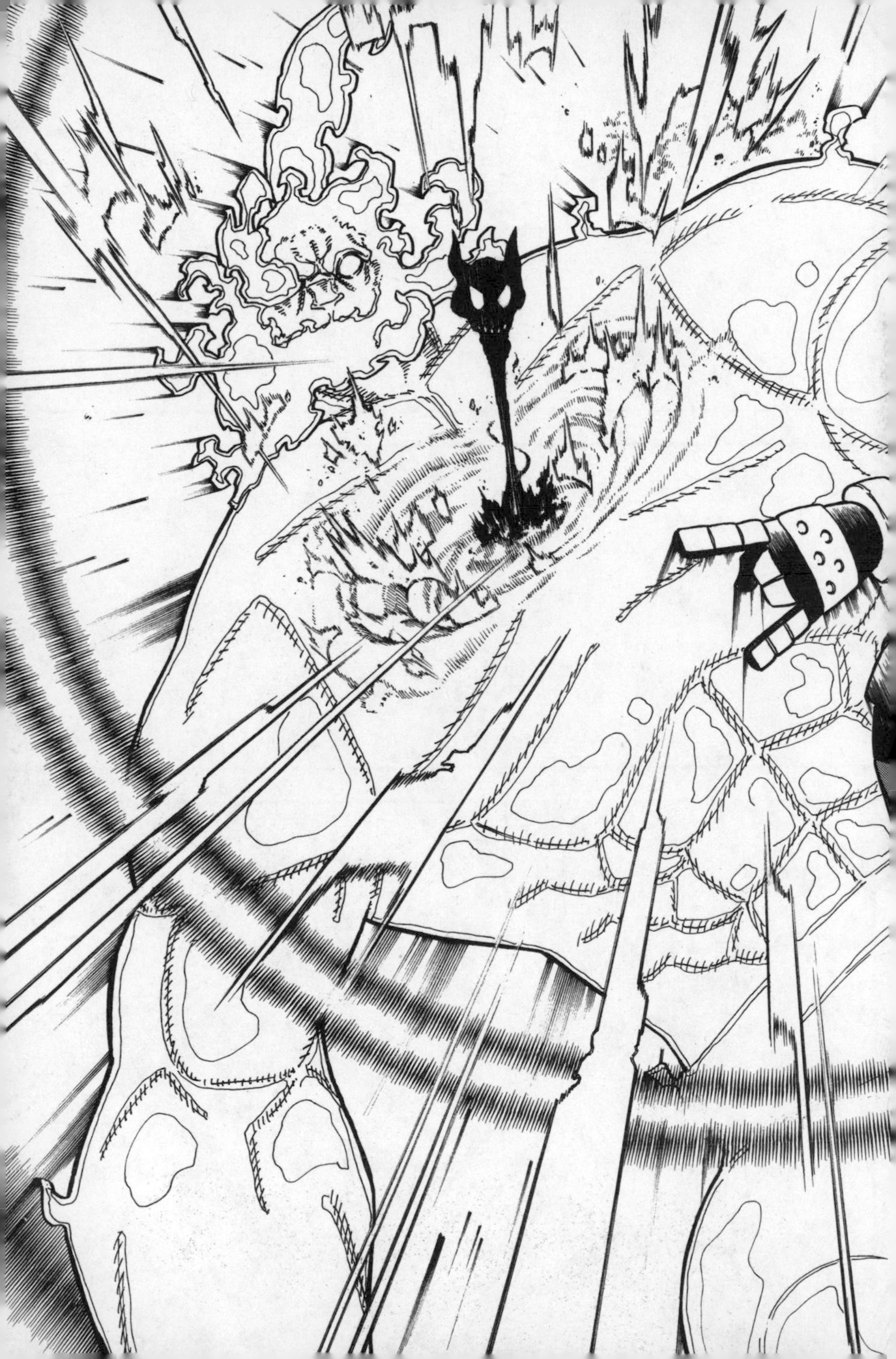

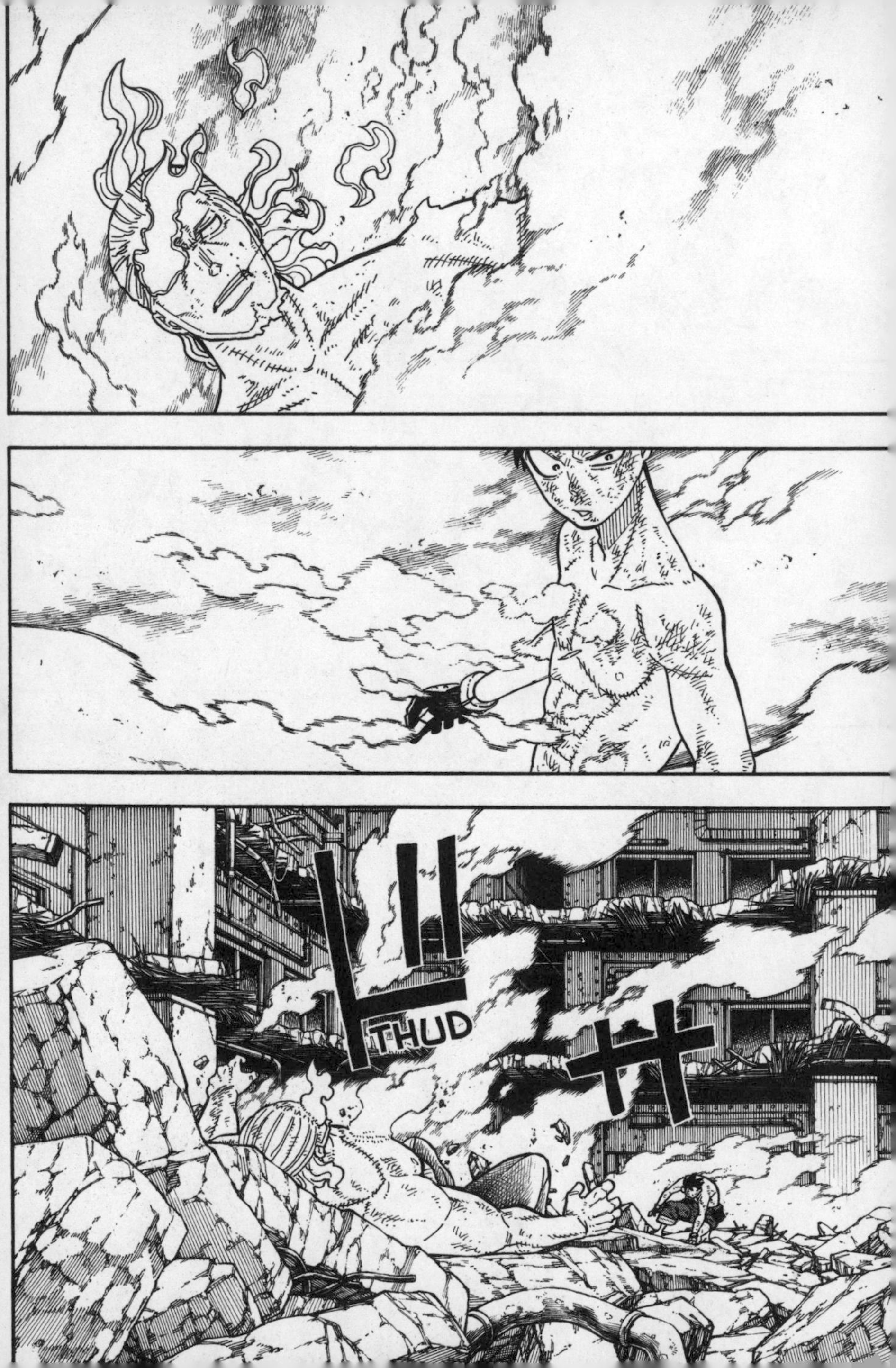
THUD

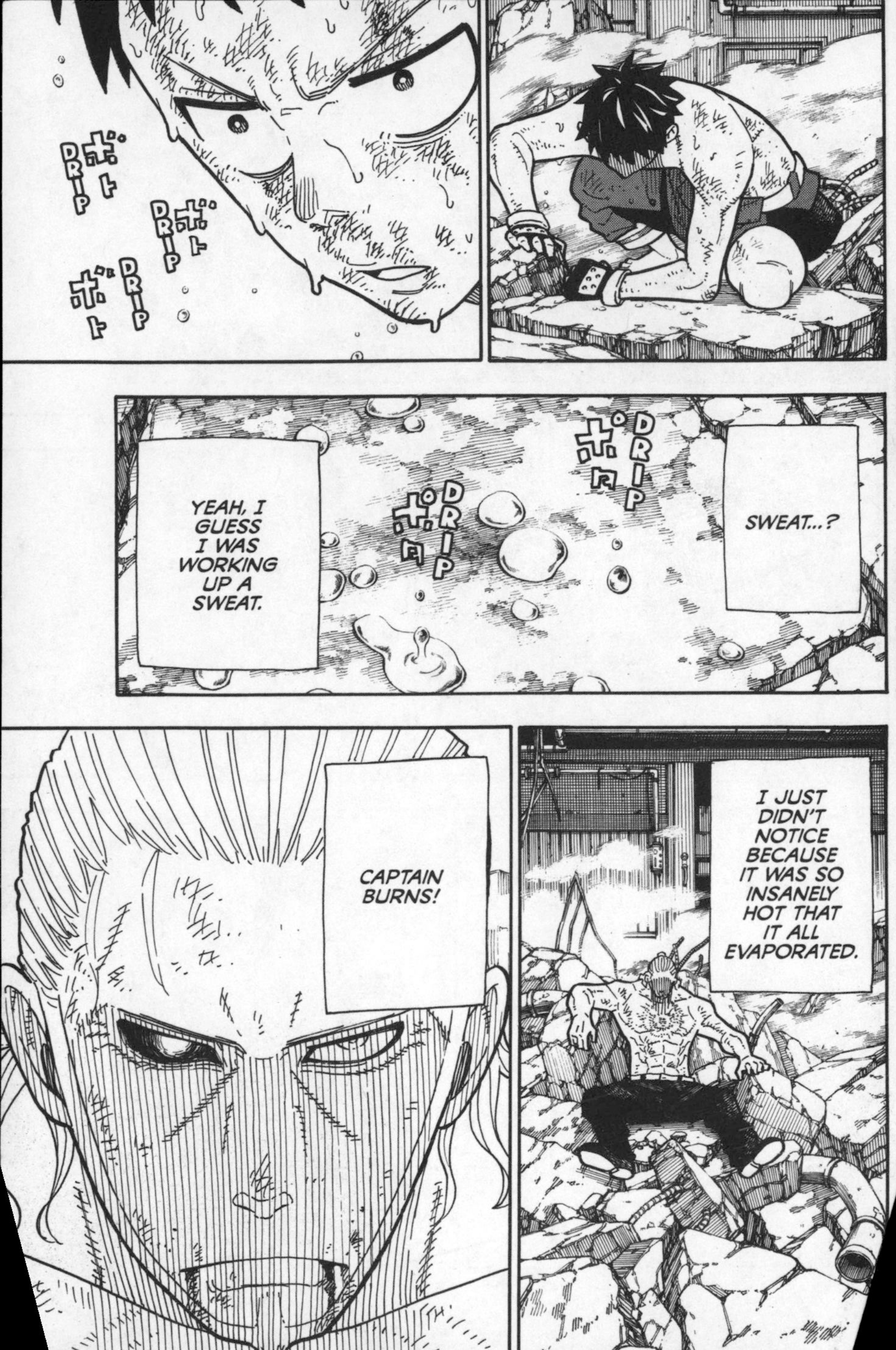

DRIP
DRIP
DRIP
SWEAT...?
DRIP
DRIP
YEAH, I GUESS I WAS WORKING UP A SWEAT.
I JUST DIDN'T NOTICE BECAUSE IT WAS SO INSANELY HOT THAT IT ALL EVAPORATED.
CAPTAIN BURNS!

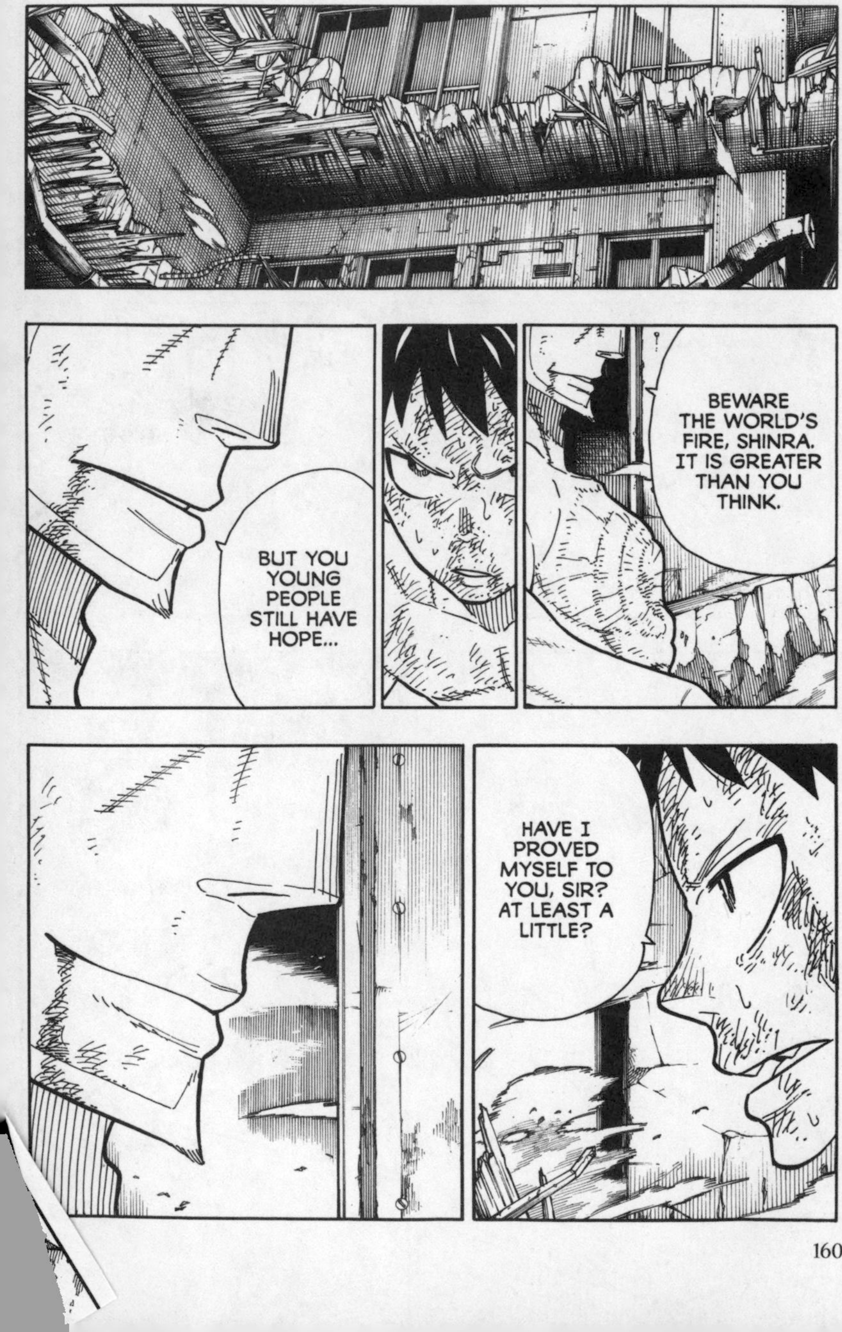
BEWARE THE WORLD'S FIRE, SHINRA. IT IS GREATER THAN YOU THINK.
BUT YOU YOUNG PEOPLE STILL HAVE HOPE...
HAVE I PROVED MYSELF TO YOU, SIR? AT LEAST A LITTLE?

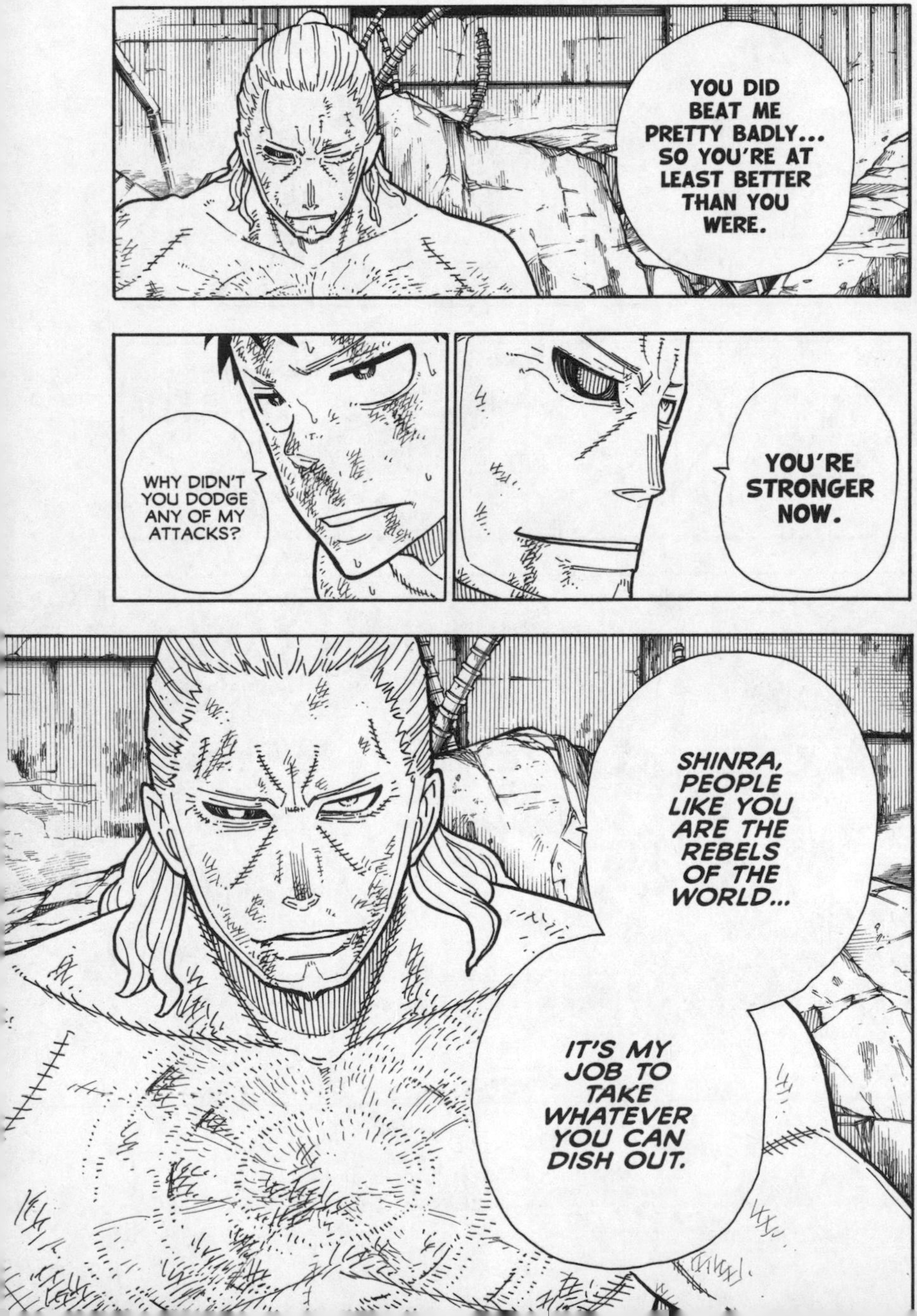
YOU DID BEAT ME PRETTY BADLY... SO YOU'RE AT LEAST BETTER THAN YOU WERE.
YOU'RE STRONGER NOW.
WHY DIDN'T YOU DODGE ANY OF MY ATTACKS?
SHINRA, PEOPLE LIKE YOU ARE THE REBELS OF THE WORLD...
IT'S MY JOB TO TAKE WHATEVER YOU CAN DISH OUT.

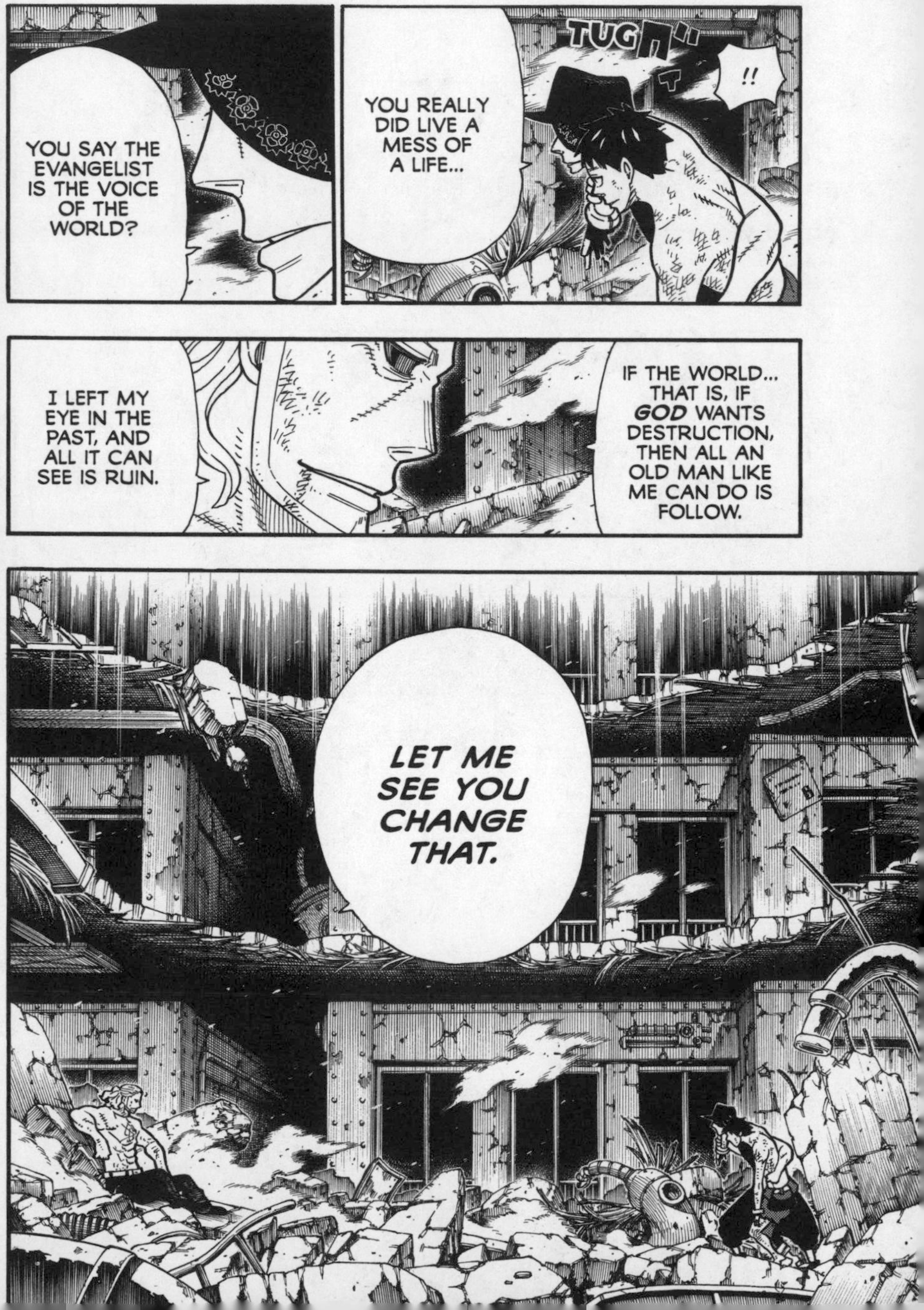
TUG
!!
YOU REALLY DID LIVE A MESS OF A LIFE...
YOU SAY THE EVANGELIST IS THE VOICE OF THE WORLD?
IF THE WORLD... THAT IS, IF *GOD* WANTS DESTRUCTION, THEN ALL AN OLD MAN LIKE ME CAN DO IS FOLLOW.
I LEFT MY EYE IN THE PAST, AND ALL IT CAN SEE IS RUIN.
LET ME SEE YOU CHANGE THAT.

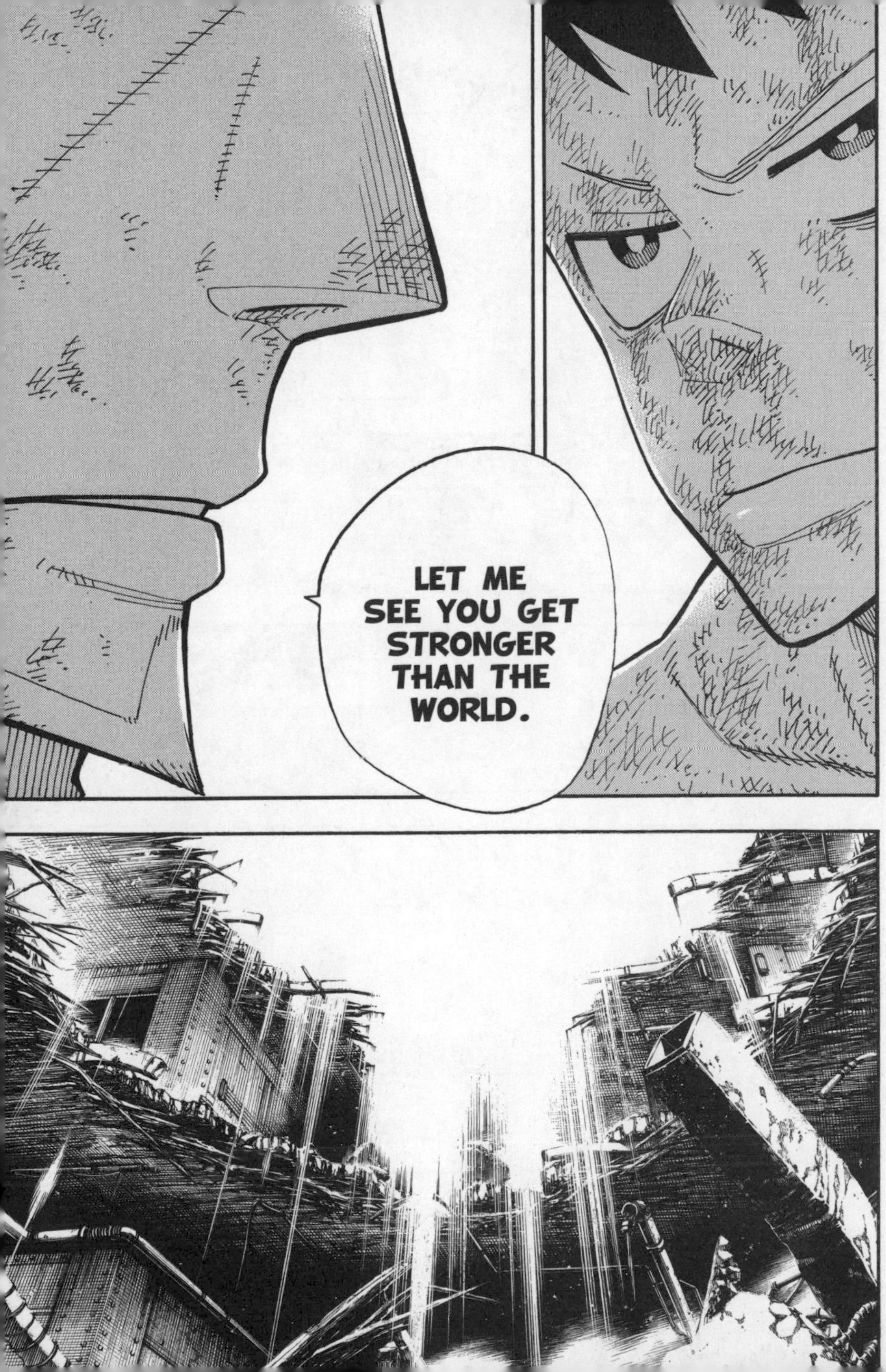
LET ME SEE YOU GET STRONGER THAN THE WORLD.

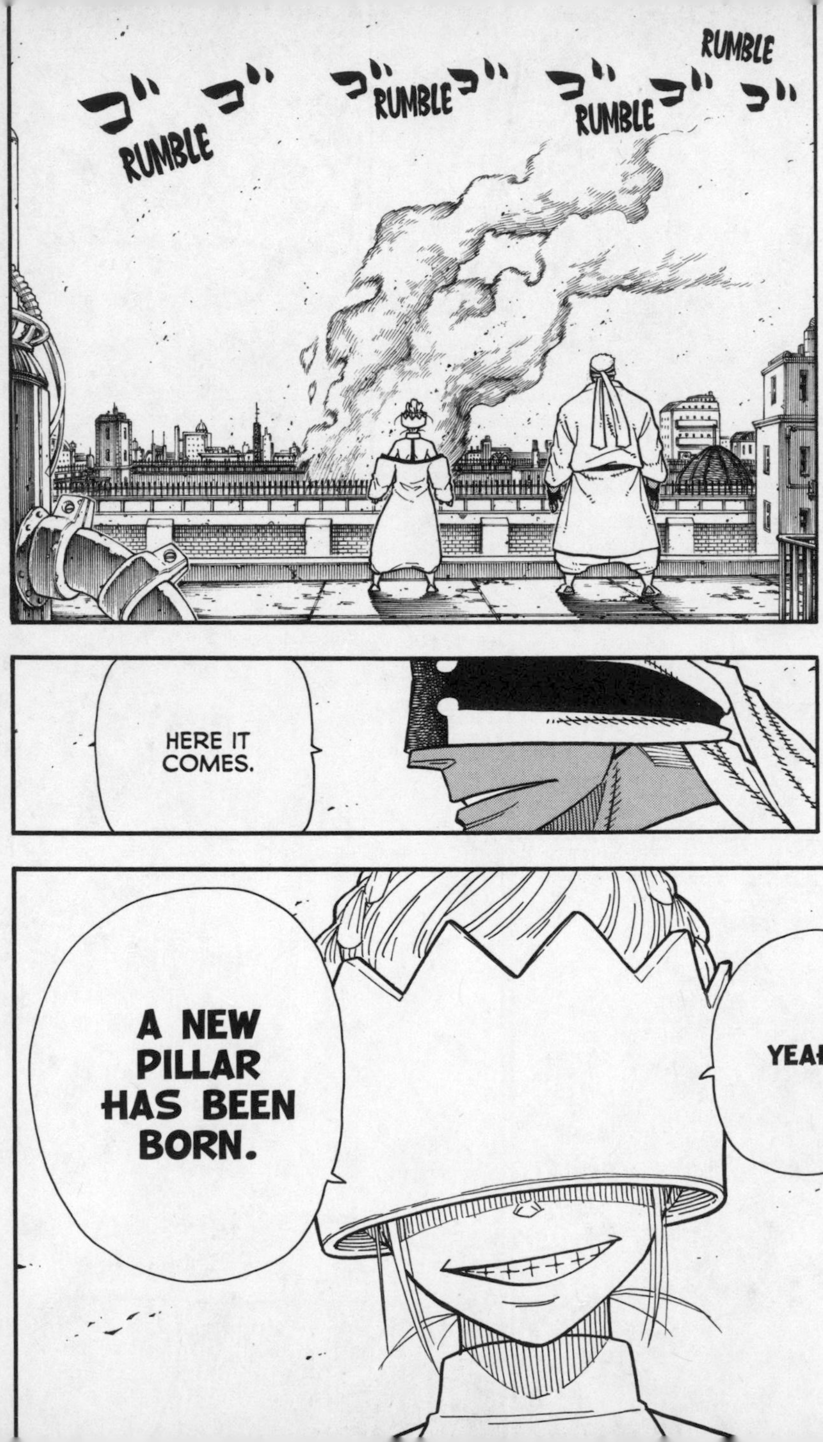
ゴ ゴ
RUMBLE
ゴ ゴ
RUMBLE
ゴ ゴ
RUMBLE
ゴ ゴ
RUMBLE
HERE IT COMES.
YEAH.
A NEW PILLAR HAS BEEN BORN.

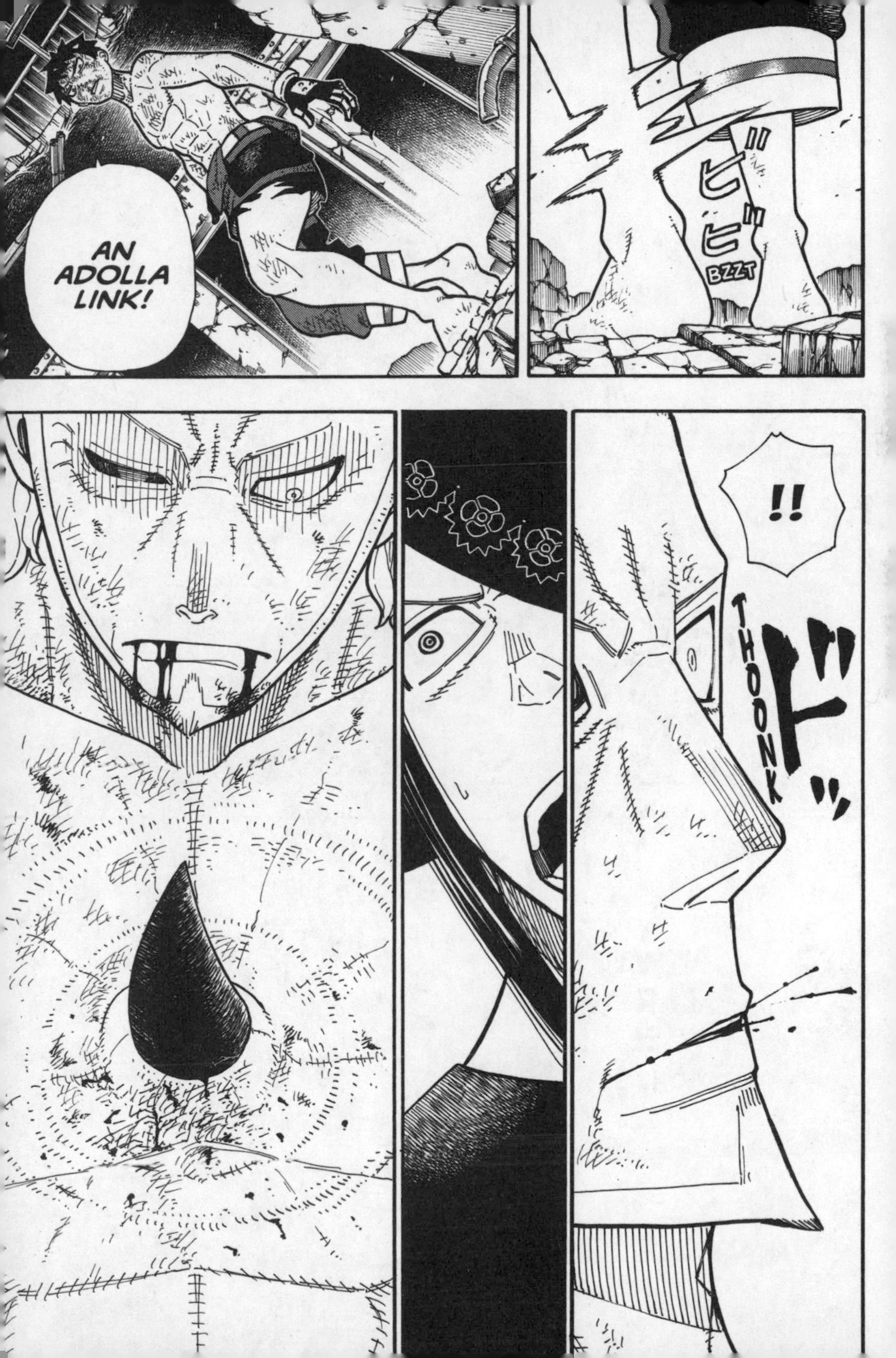
ビビ
BZZT
AN ADOLLA LINK!
!!
ドッ
THOONK

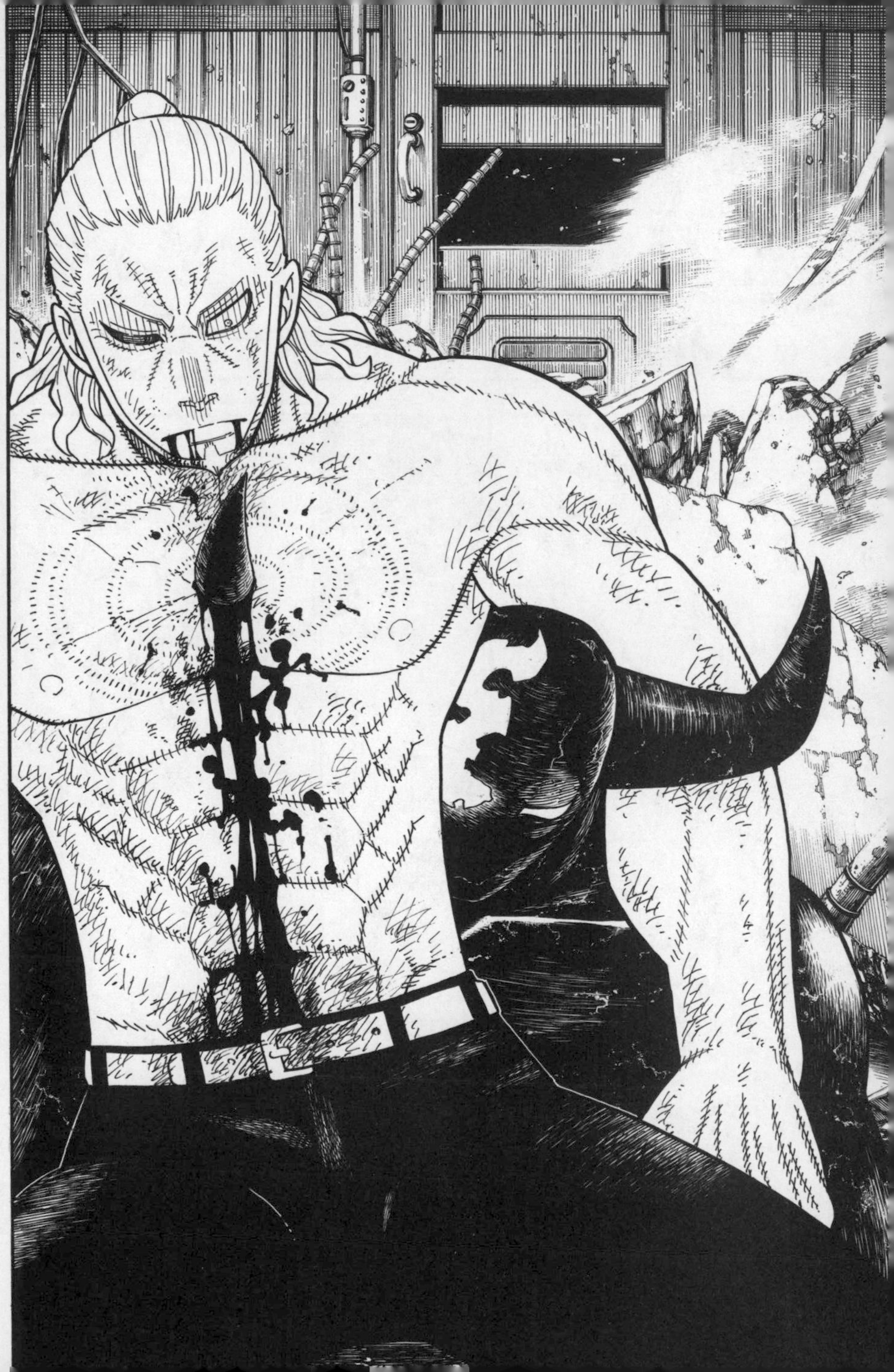

CHAPTER CXCV: SUDDEN TURN

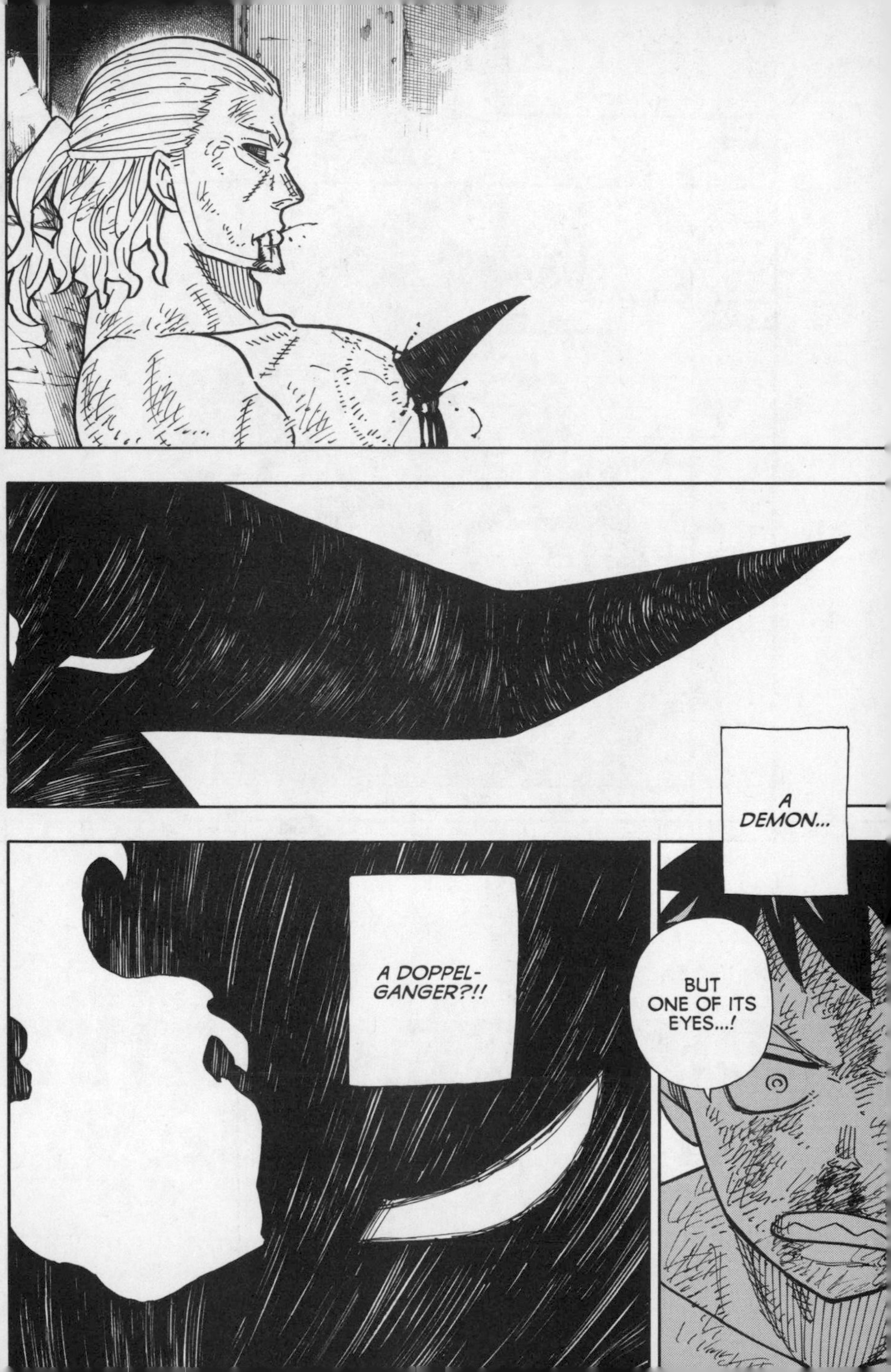
A DEMON...
BUT ONE OF ITS EYES...!
A DOPPEL-GANGER?!!

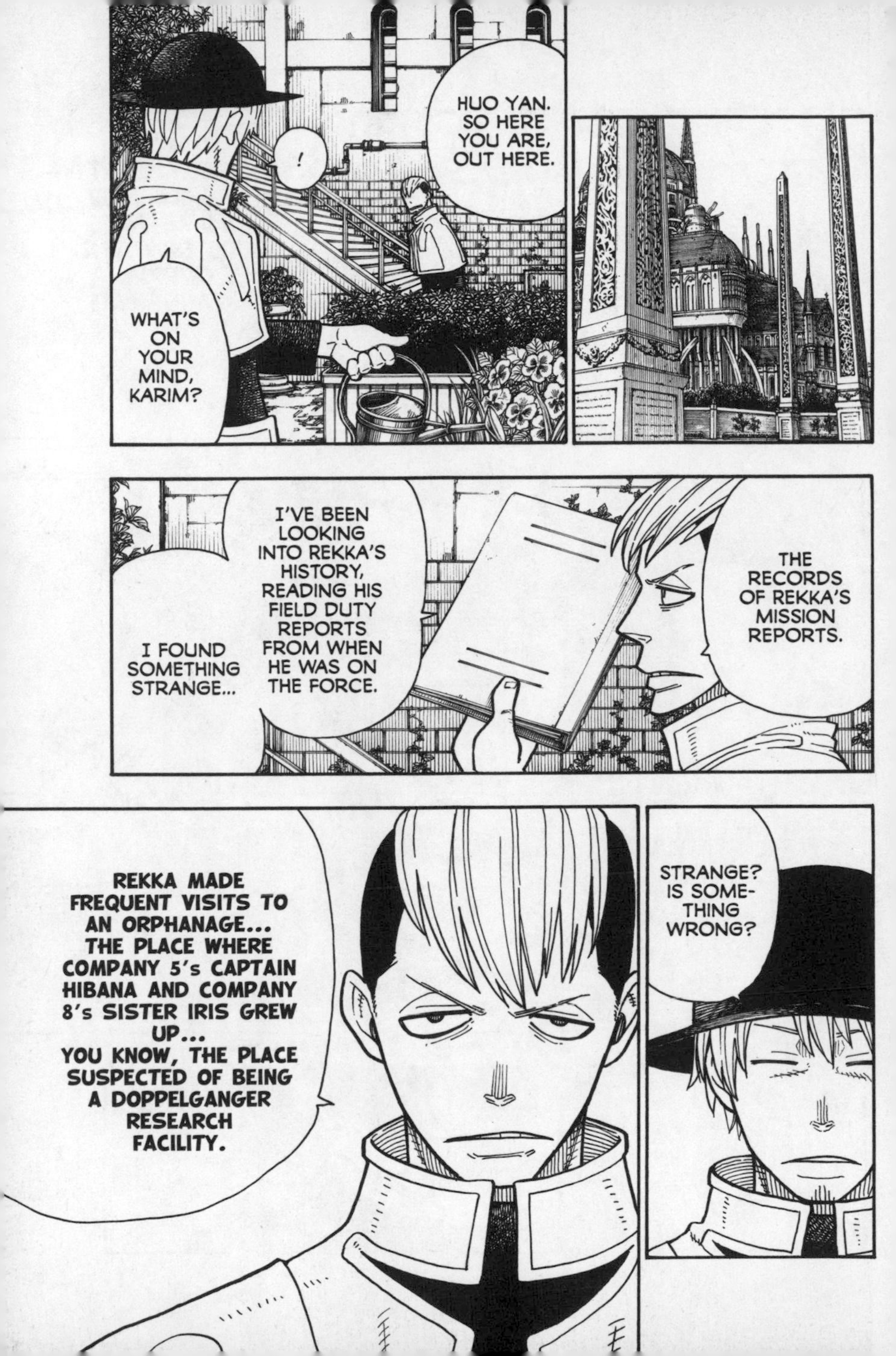
HUO YAN. SO HERE YOU ARE, OUT HERE.
!
WHAT'S ON YOUR MIND, KARIM?
THE RECORDS OF REKKA'S MISSION REPORTS.
I'VE BEEN LOOKING INTO REKKA'S HISTORY, READING HIS FIELD DUTY REPORTS FROM WHEN HE WAS ON THE FORCE.
I FOUND SOMETHING STRANGE...
STRANGE? IS SOME-THING WRONG?
REKKA MADE FREQUENT VISITS TO AN ORPHANAGE... THE PLACE WHERE COMPANY 5's CAPTAIN HIBANA AND COMPANY 8's SISTER IRIS GREW UP... YOU KNOW, THE PLACE SUSPECTED OF BEING A DOPPELGANGER RESEARCH FACILITY.

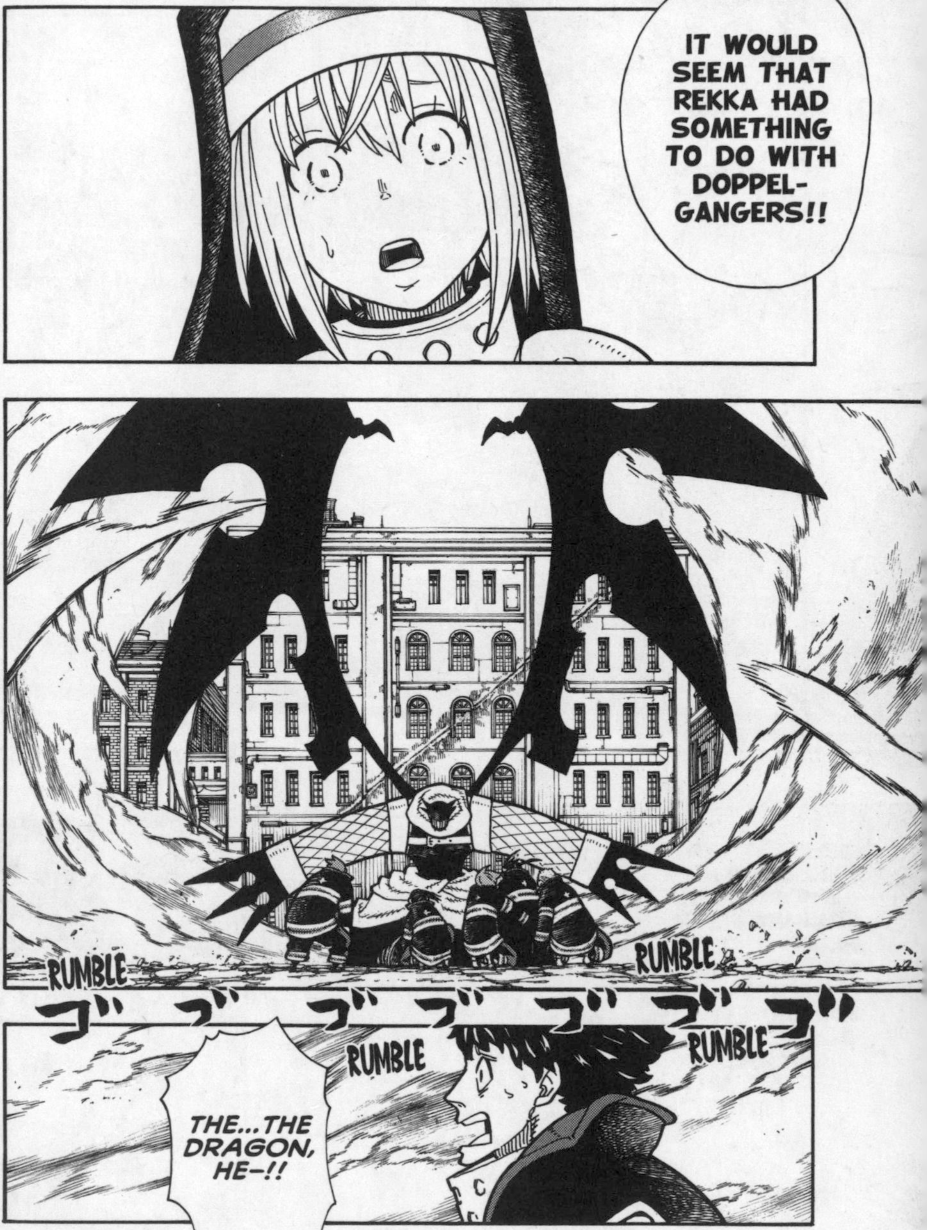
IT WOULD SEEM THAT REKKA HAD SOMETHING TO DO WITH DOPPEL-GANGERS!!
RUMBLE
RUMBLE
ゴ ゴ ゴ ゴ ゴ ゴ ゴ
RUMBLE
RUMBLE
THE...THE DRAGON, HE–!!

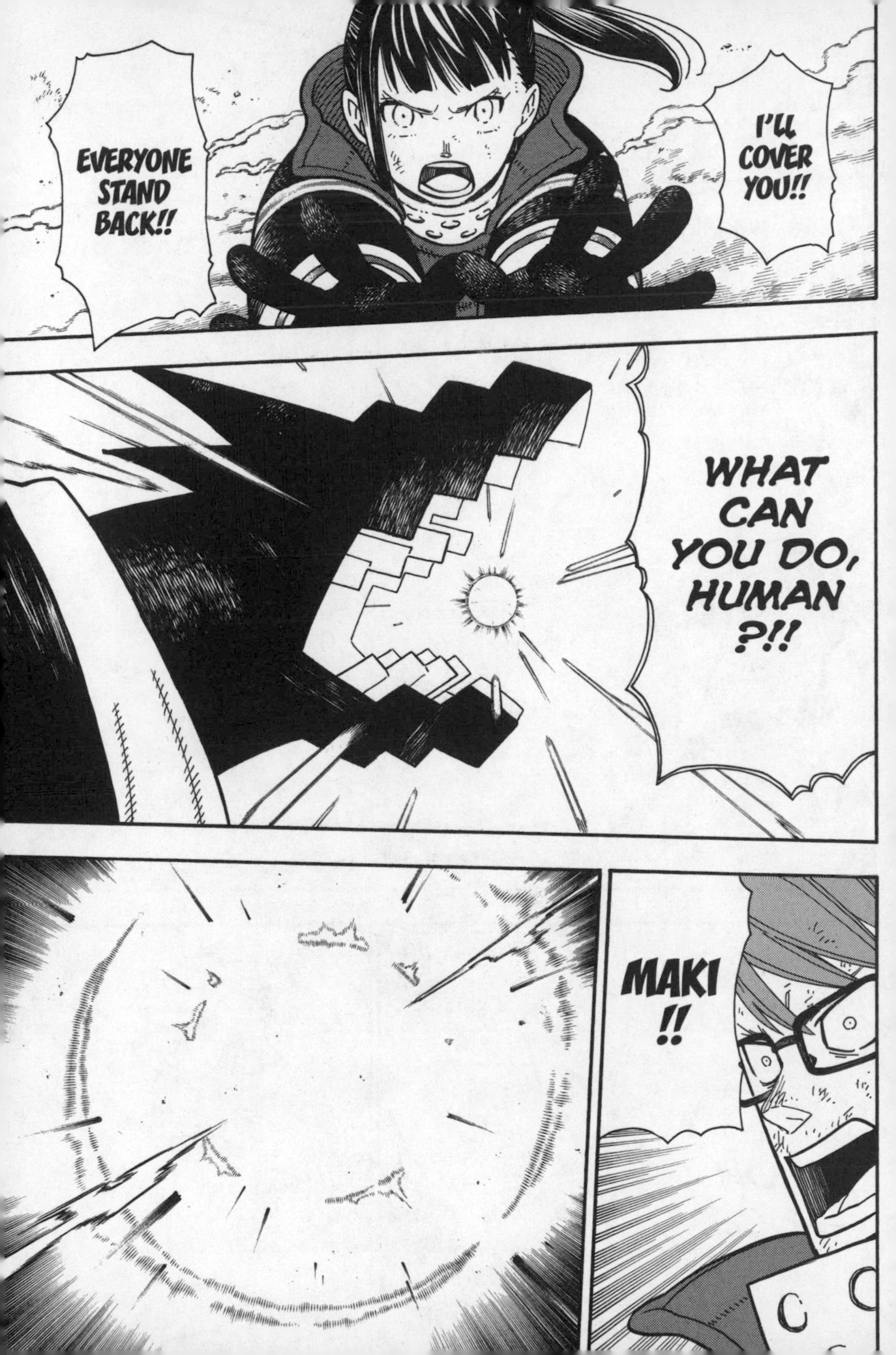
I'LL COVER YOU!!
EVERYONE STAND BACK!!
WHAT CAN YOU DO, HUMAN ?!!
MAKI !!

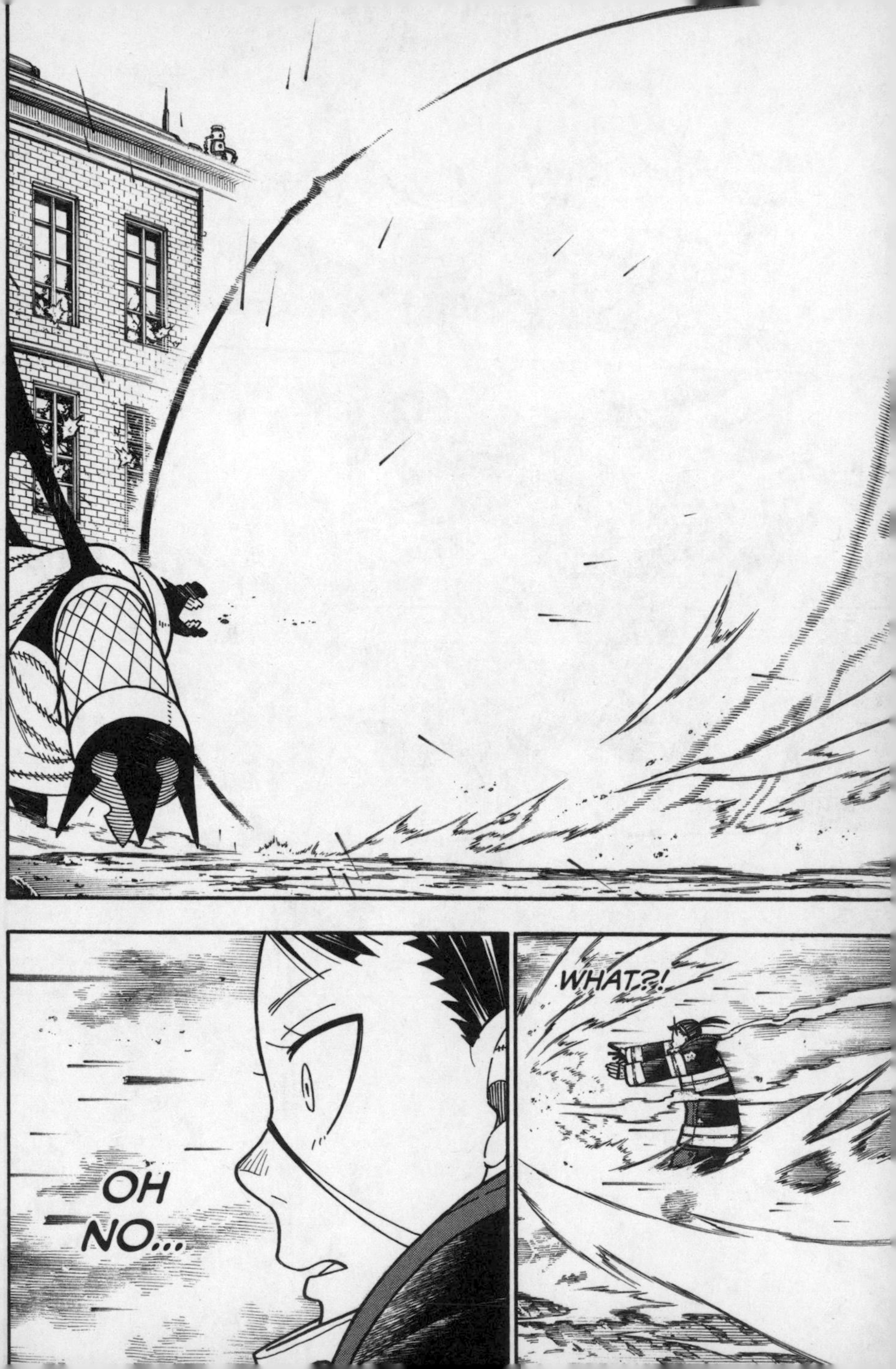
WHAT?!
OH NO...

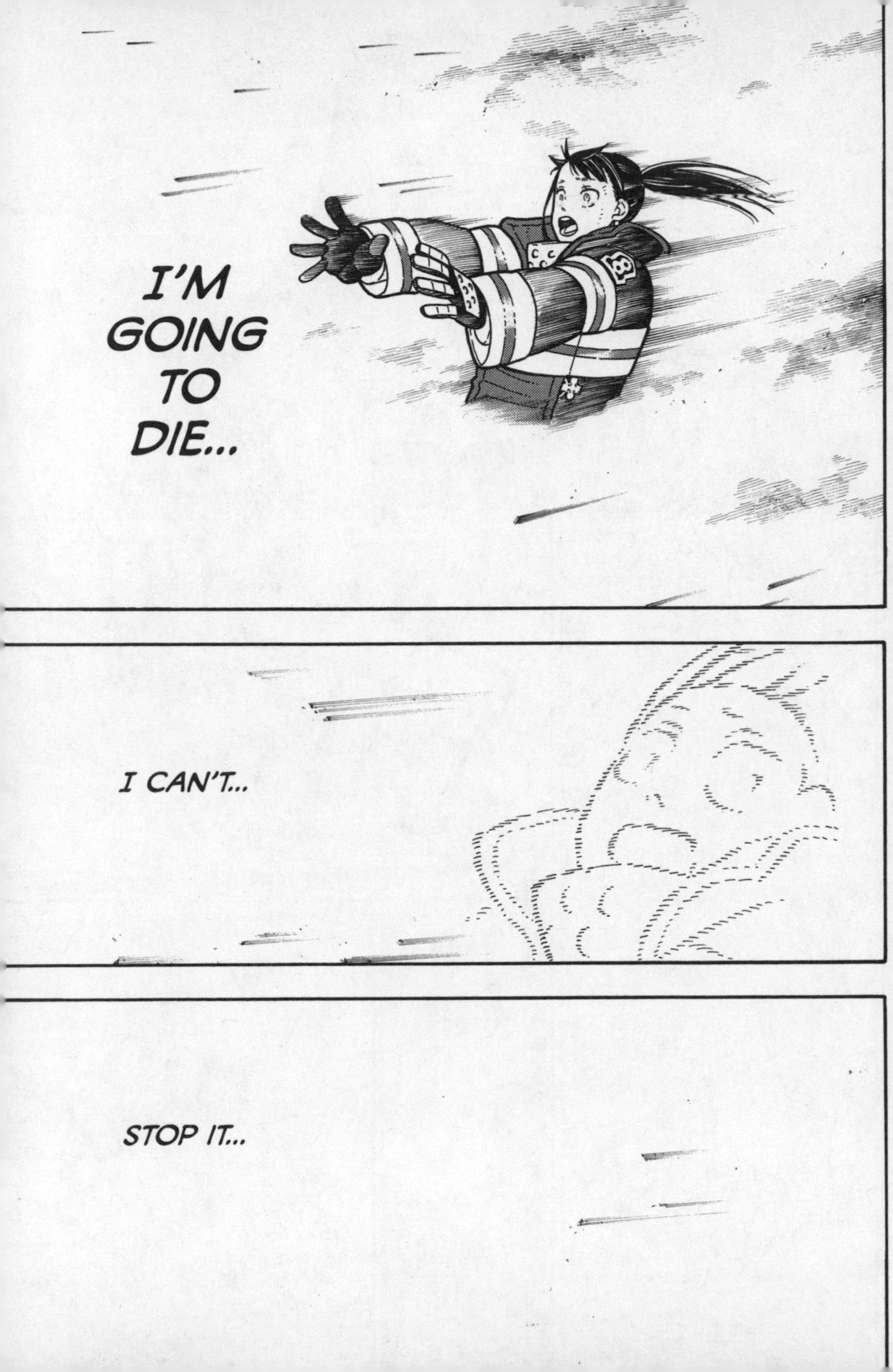
I'M GOING TO DIE...
I CAN'T...
STOP IT...

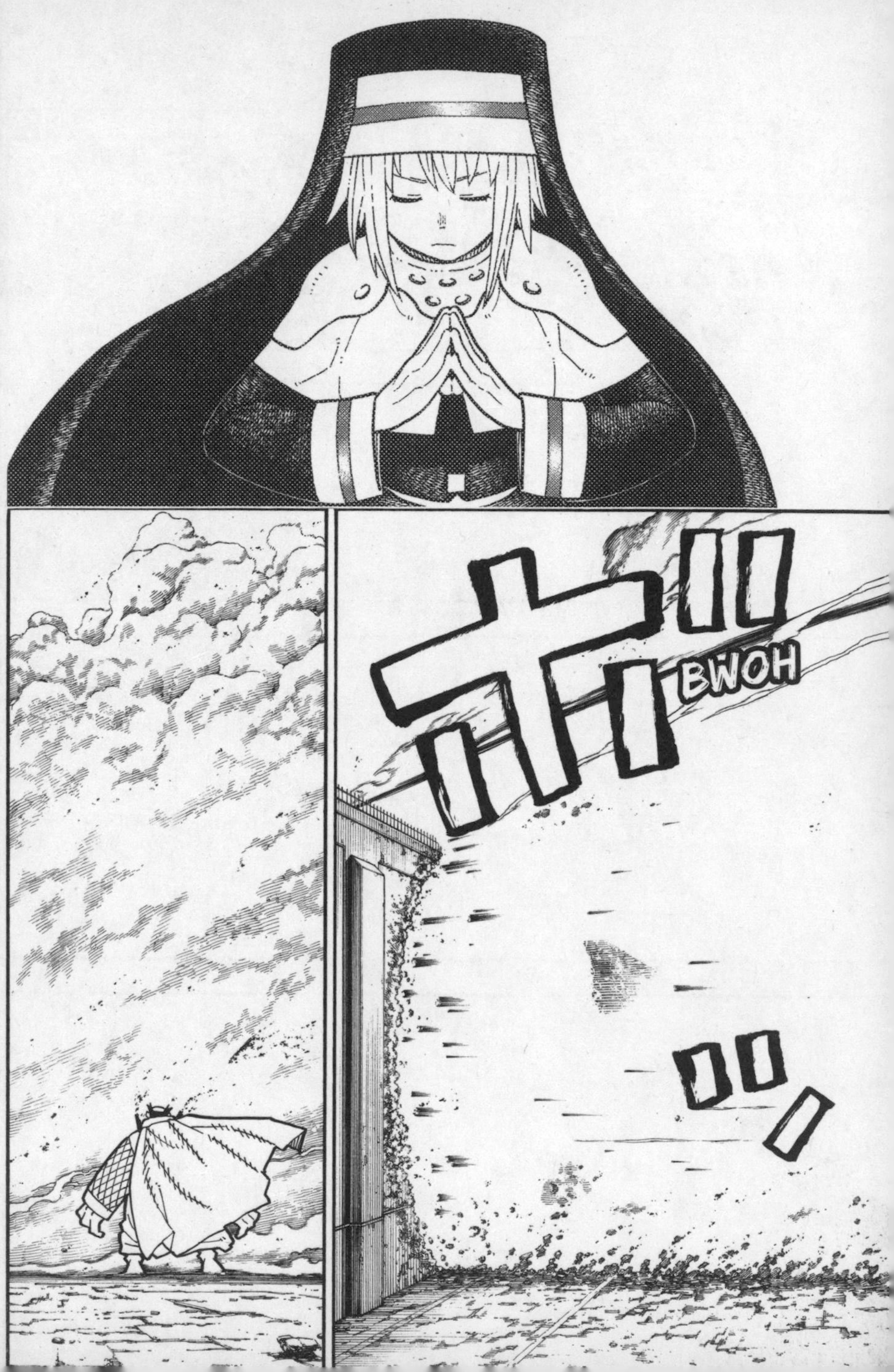
BWOH

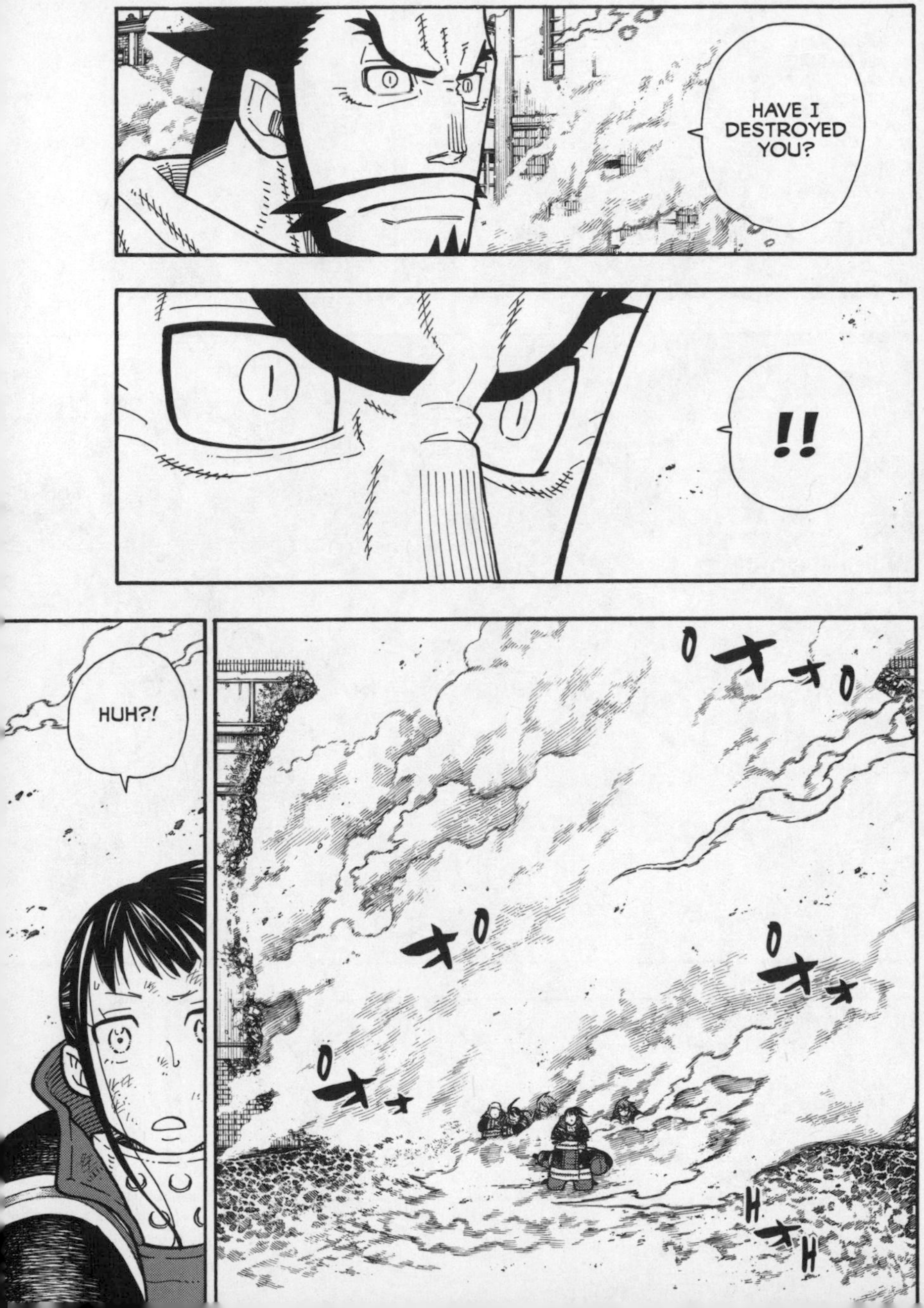
HAVE I DESTROYED YOU?
!!
HUH?!

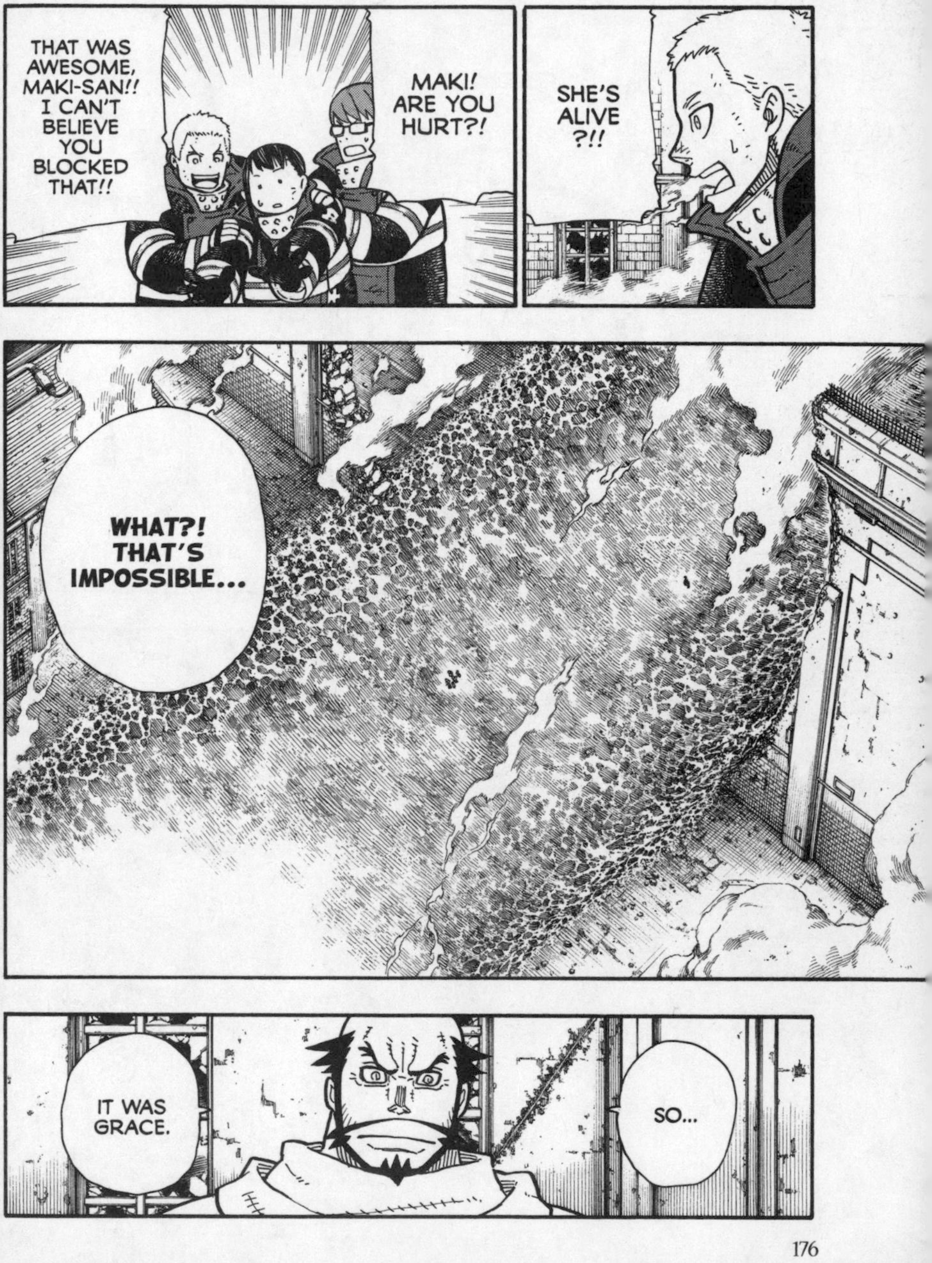
SHE'S ALIVE ?!!
MAKI! ARE YOU HURT?!
THAT WAS AWESOME, MAKI-SAN!! I CAN'T BELIEVE YOU BLOCKED THAT!!
WHAT?! THAT'S IMPOSSIBLE...
SO...
IT WAS GRACE.

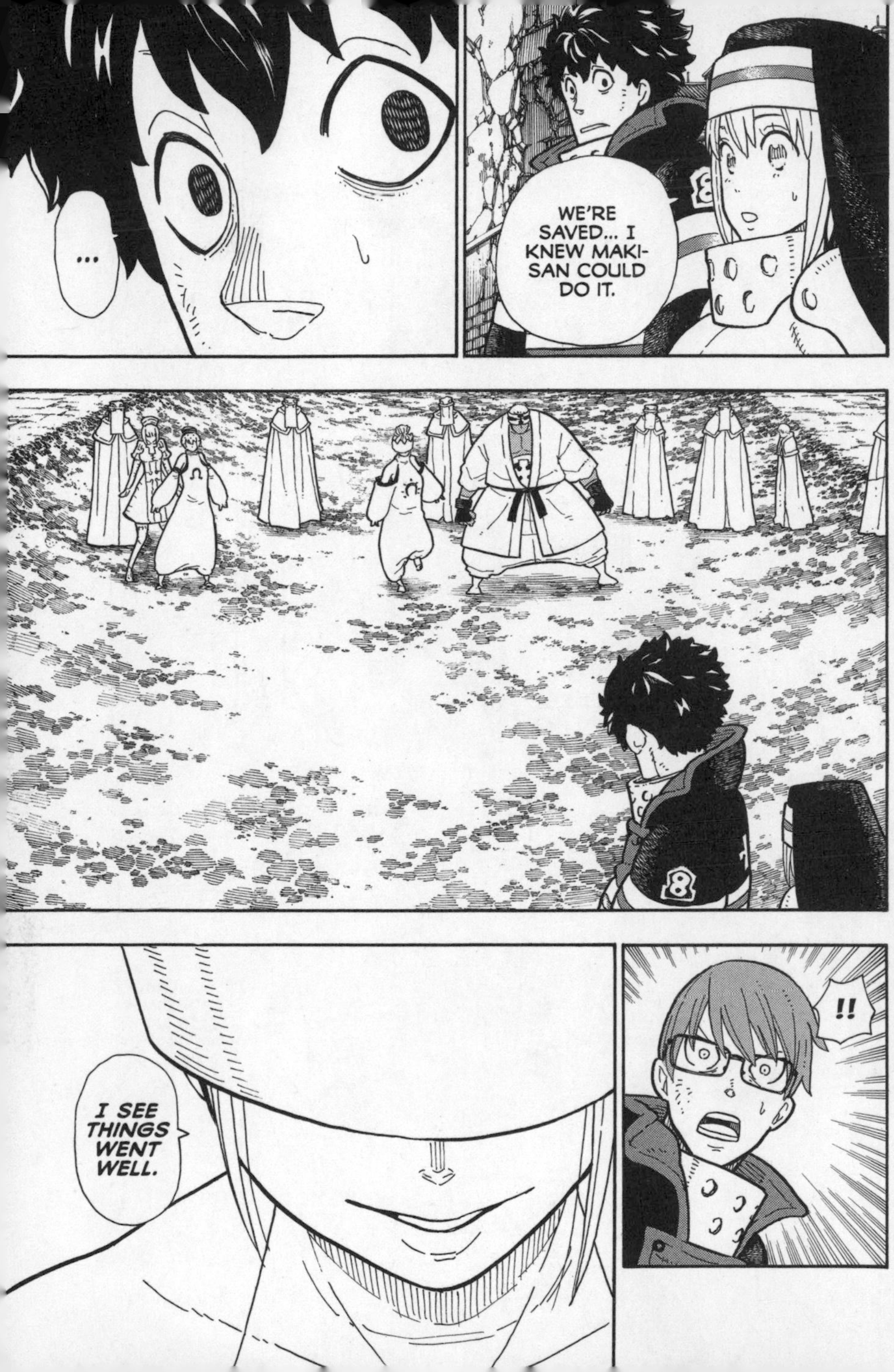
WE'RE SAVED... I KNEW MAKI-SAN COULD DO IT.
...
!!
I SEE THINGS WENT WELL.

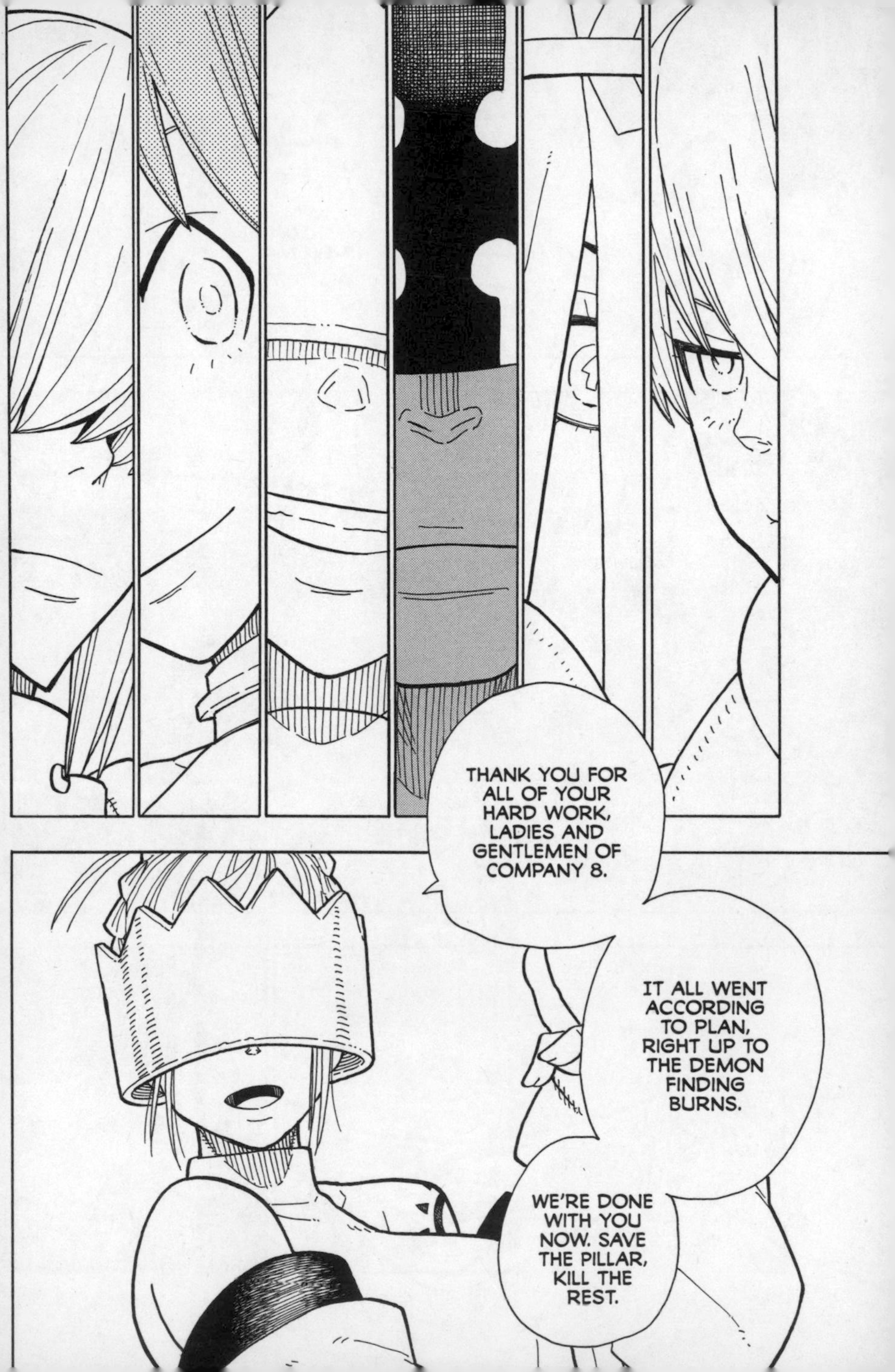
THANK YOU FOR ALL OF YOUR HARD WORK, LADIES AND GENTLEMEN OF COMPANY 8.
IT ALL WENT ACCORDING TO PLAN, RIGHT UP TO THE DEMON FINDING BURNS.
WE'RE DONE WITH YOU NOW. SAVE THE PILLAR, KILL THE REST.

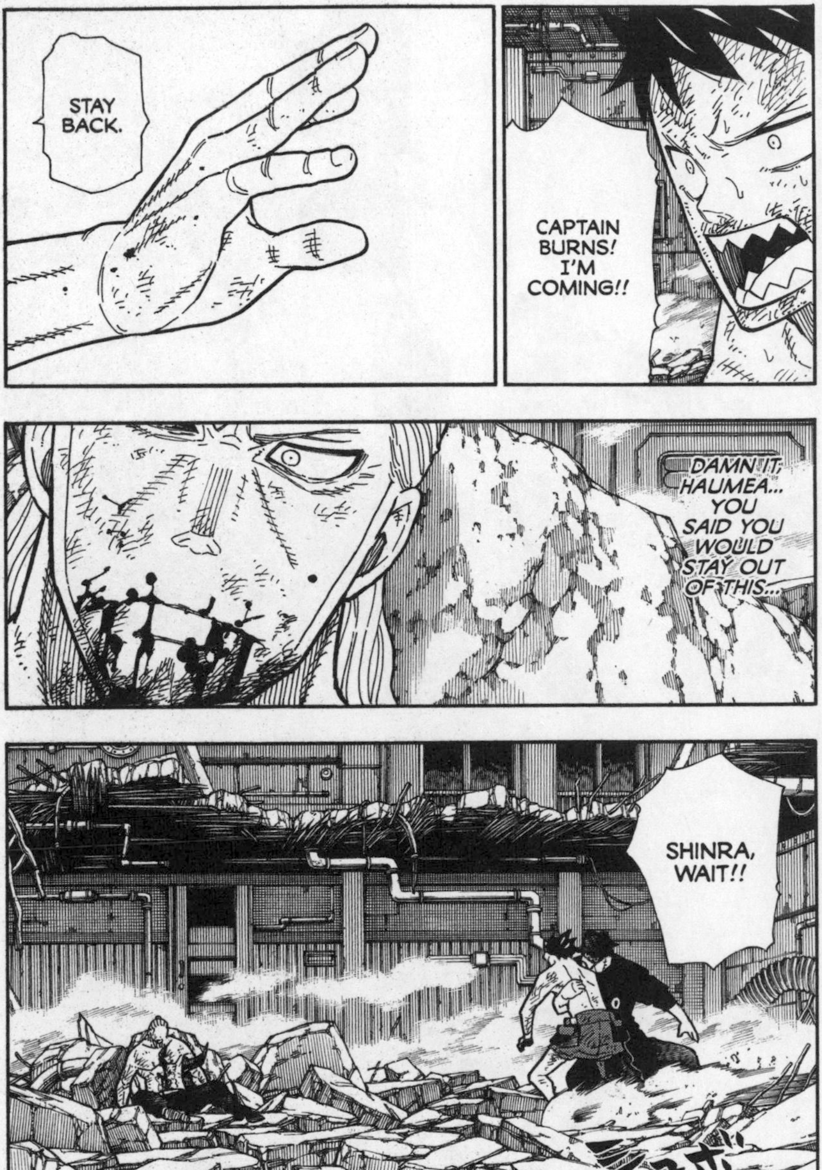
CAPTAIN BURNS! I'M COMING!!
STAY BACK.
DAMN IT, HAUMEA... YOU SAID YOU WOULD STAY OUT OF THIS...
SHINRA, WAIT!!
SWI-BWOH

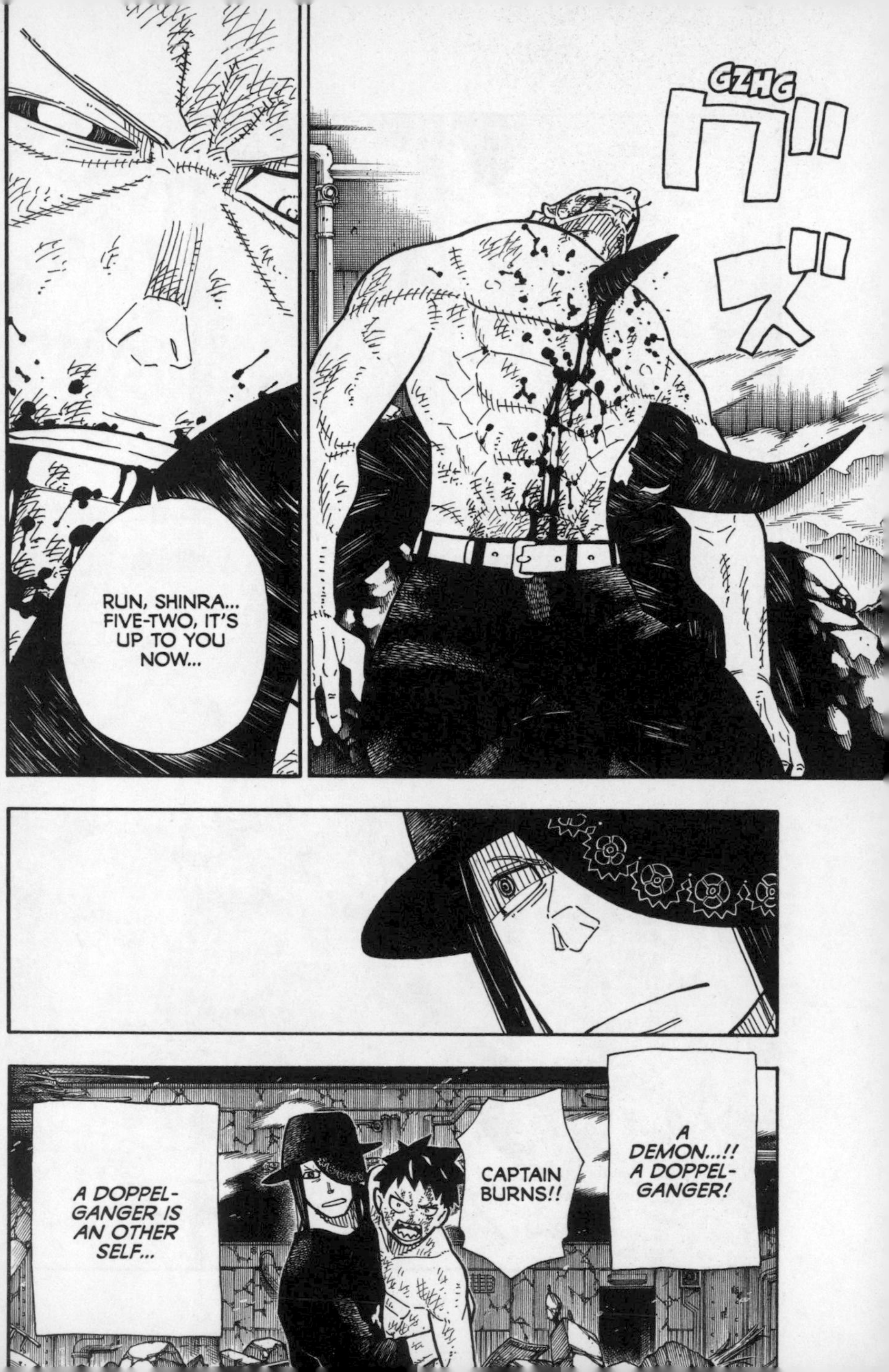
GZHG
RUN, SHINRA... FIVE-TWO, IT'S UP TO YOU NOW...
A DEMON...!! A DOPPEL-GANGER!
CAPTAIN BURNS!!
A DOPPEL-GANGER IS AN OTHER SELF...

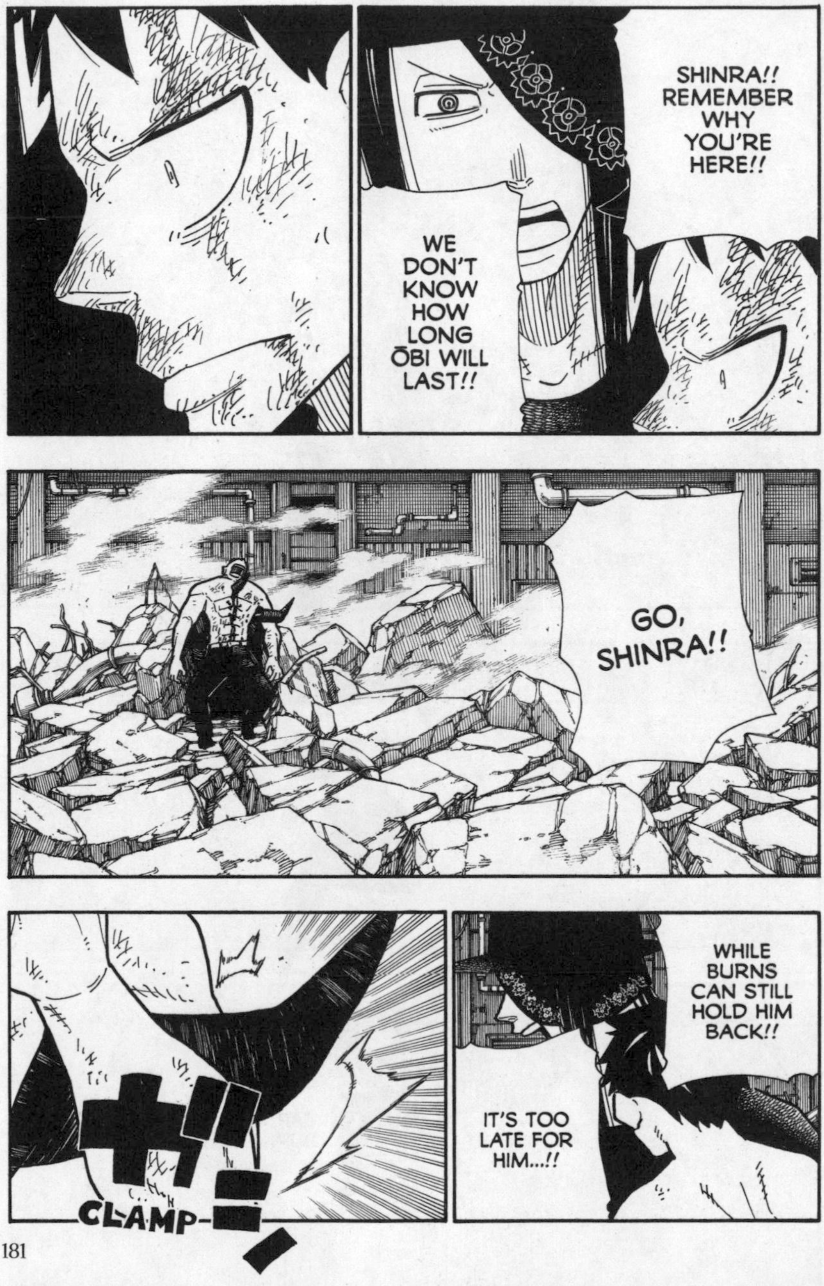
SHINRA!! REMEMBER WHY YOU'RE HERE!!
WE DON'T KNOW HOW LONG ŌBI WILL LAST!!
GO, SHINRA!!
WHILE BURNS CAN STILL HOLD HIM BACK!!
IT'S TOO LATE FOR HIM...!!
CLAMP

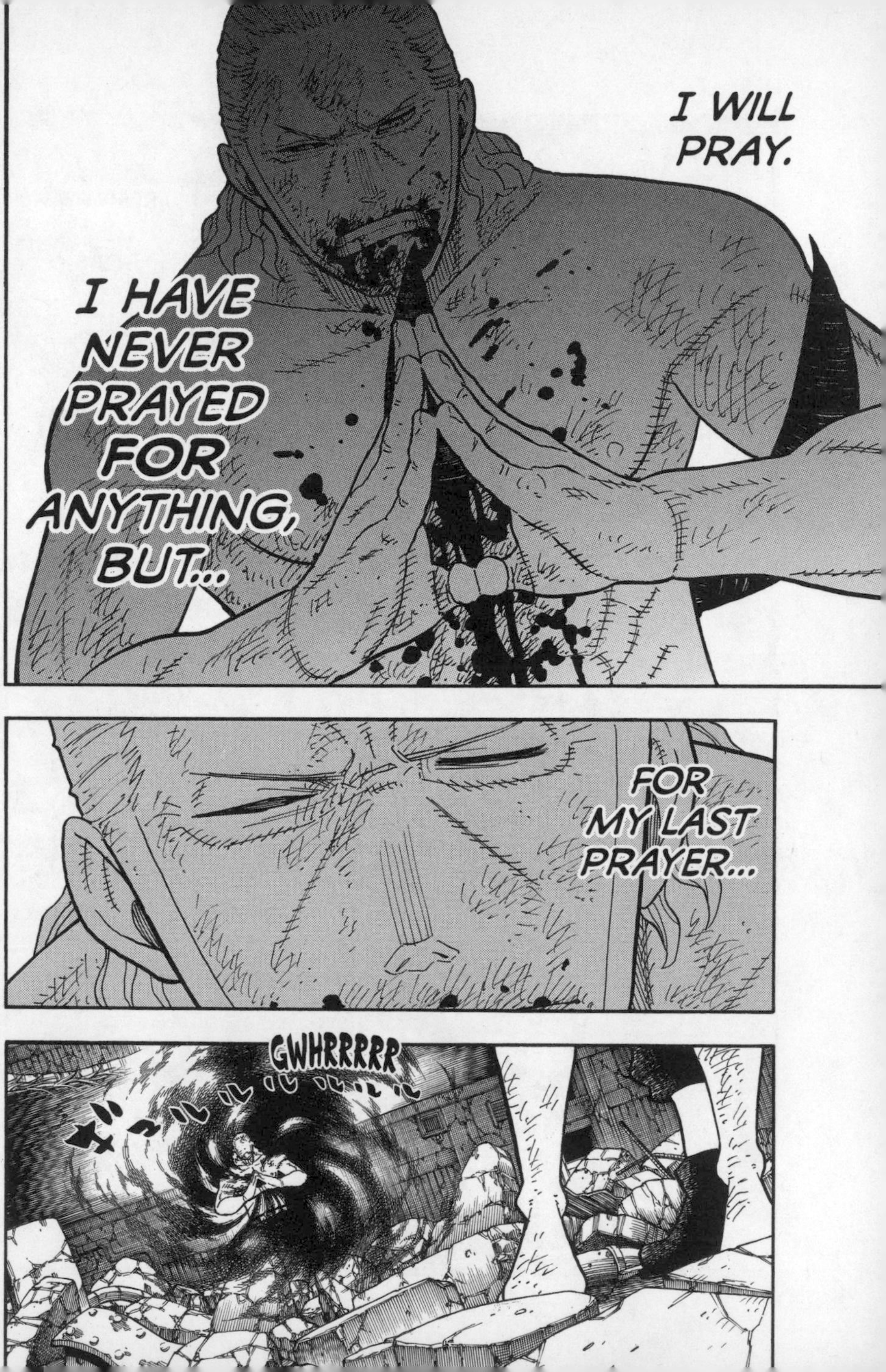
I WILL PRAY.
I HAVE NEVER PRAYED FOR ANYTHING, BUT...
FOR MY LAST PRAYER...
GWHRRRRR

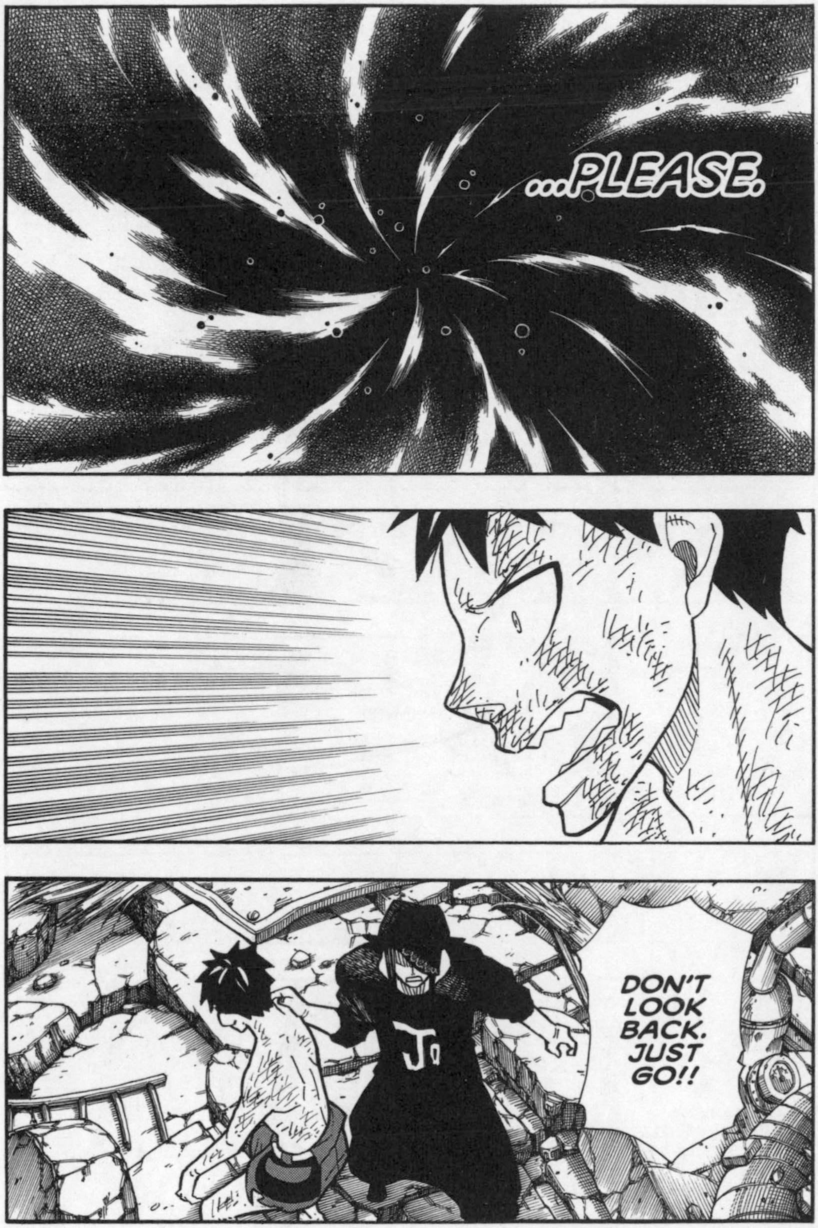
...PLEASE.
DON'T LOOK BACK. JUST GO!!

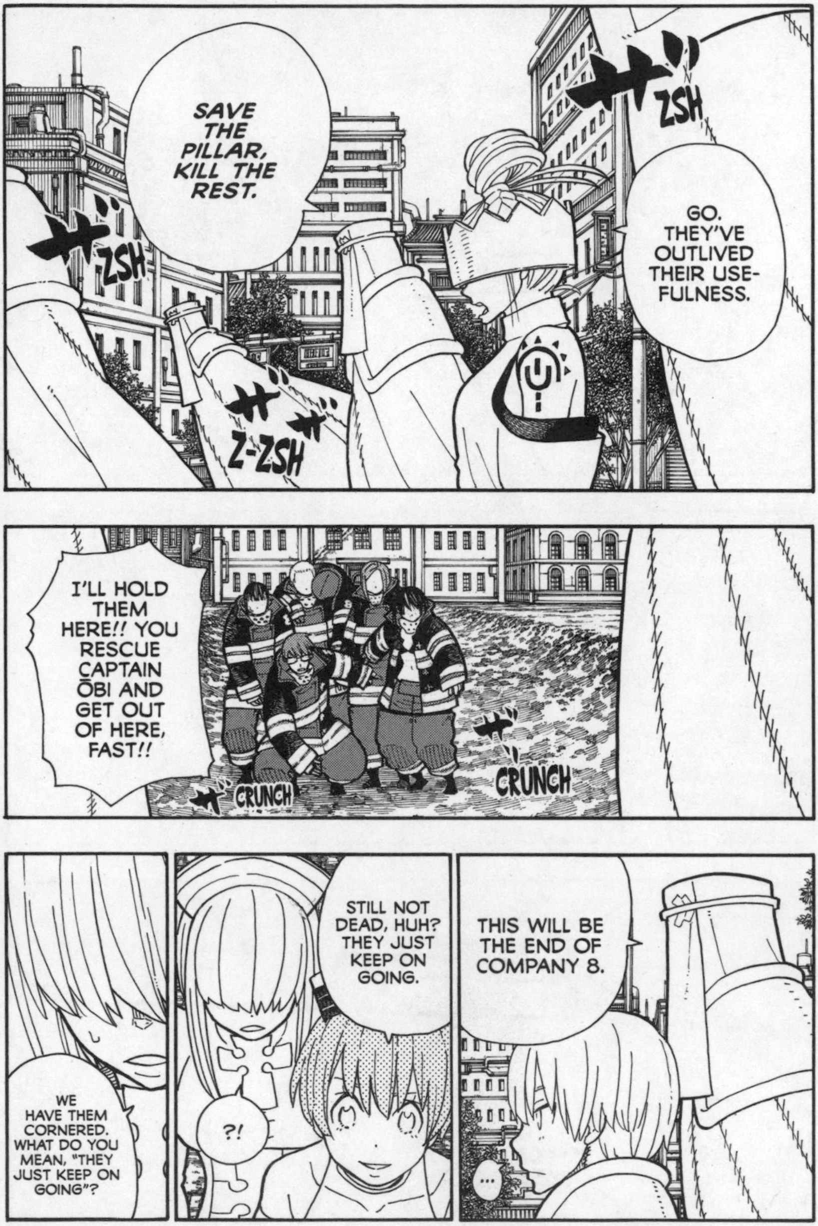
ZSH
GO. THEY'VE OUTLIVED THEIR USE-FULNESS.
SAVE THE PILLAR, KILL THE REST.
ZSH
Z-ZSH
I'LL HOLD THEM HERE!! YOU RESCUE CAPTAIN ŌBI AND GET OUT OF HERE, FAST!!
CRUNCH
CRUNCH
THIS WILL BE THE END OF COMPANY 8.
...
STILL NOT DEAD, HUH? THEY JUST KEEP ON GOING.
?!
WE HAVE THEM CORNERED. WHAT DO YOU MEAN, "THEY JUST KEEP ON GOING"?

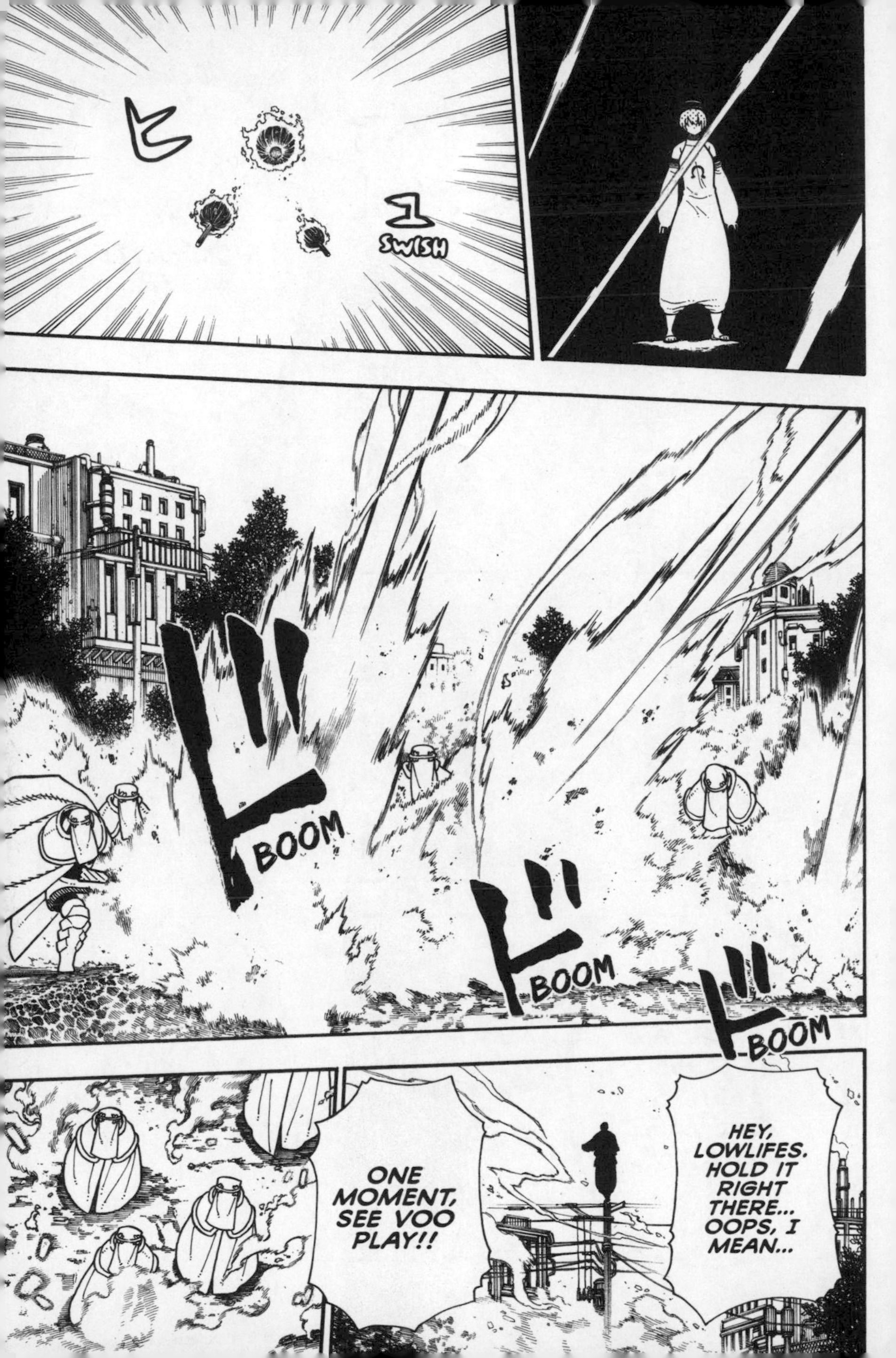
SWISH
BOOM
BOOM
BOOM
HEY, LOWLIFES. HOLD IT RIGHT THERE... OOPS, I MEAN...
ONE MOMENT, SEE VOO PLAY!!

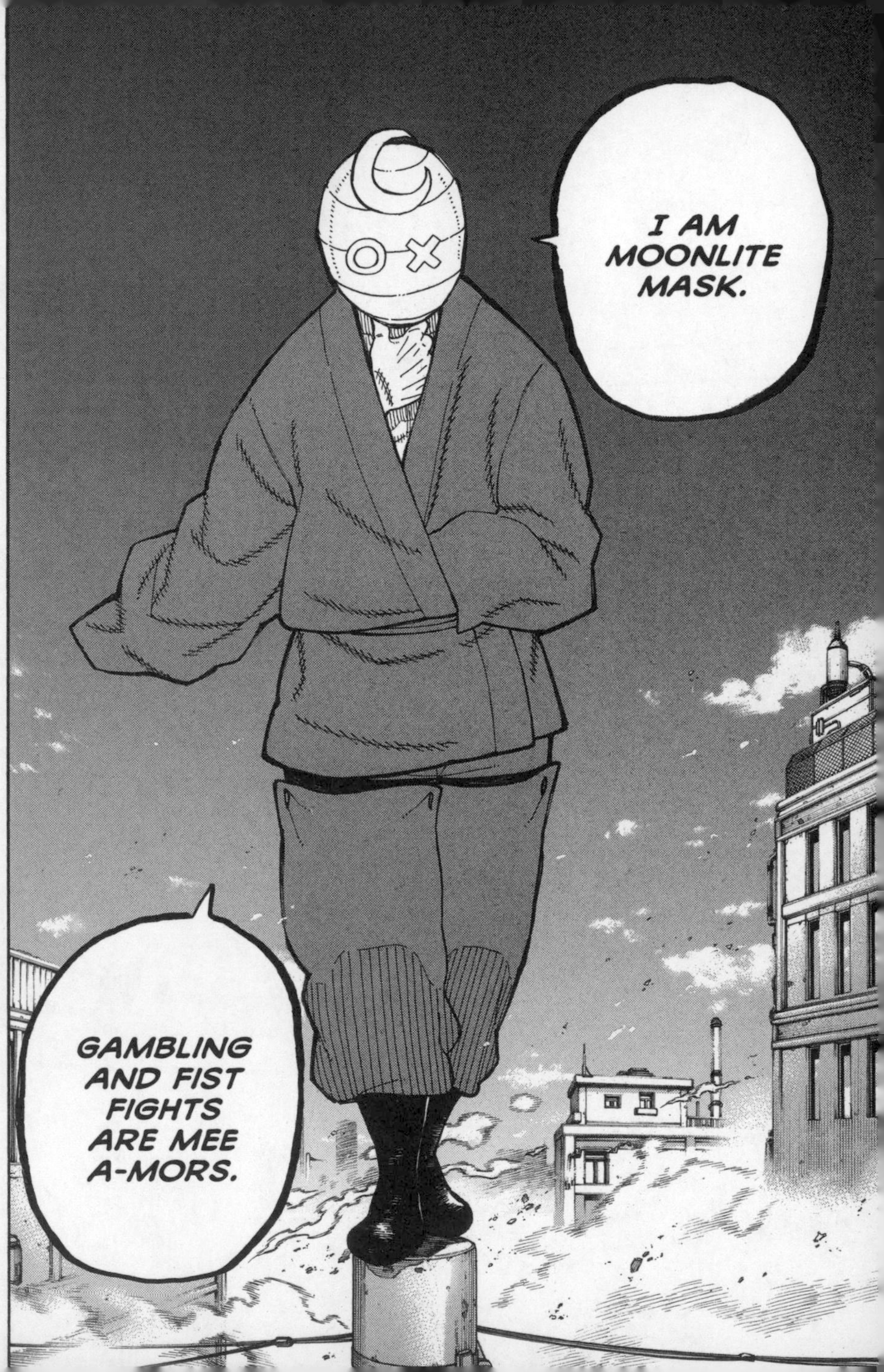
I AM MOONLITE MASK.
GAMBLING AND FIST FIGHTS ARE MEE A-MORS.

TO BE CONTINUED IN VOLUME 23!!

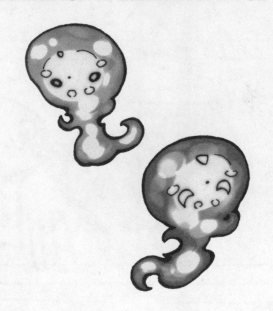

AFTERWORD MANGA ATSUSHIYA

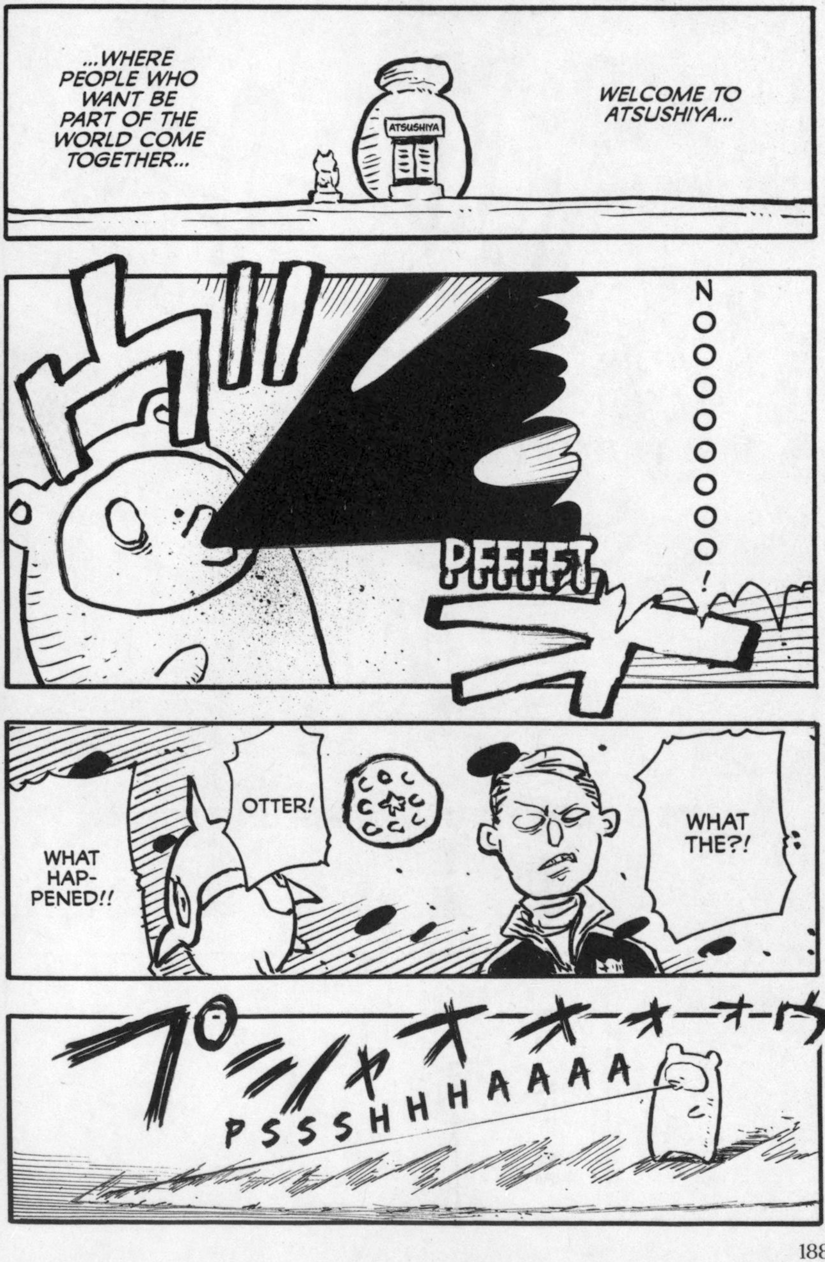
WELCOME TO ATSUSHIYA...
...WHERE PEOPLE WHO WANT BE PART OF THE WORLD COME TOGETHER...
ATSUSHIYA
NOOOOOOOOO!
PFFFFT
WHAT THE?!
OTTER!
WHAT HAP-PENED!!
PSSSHHHAAAA

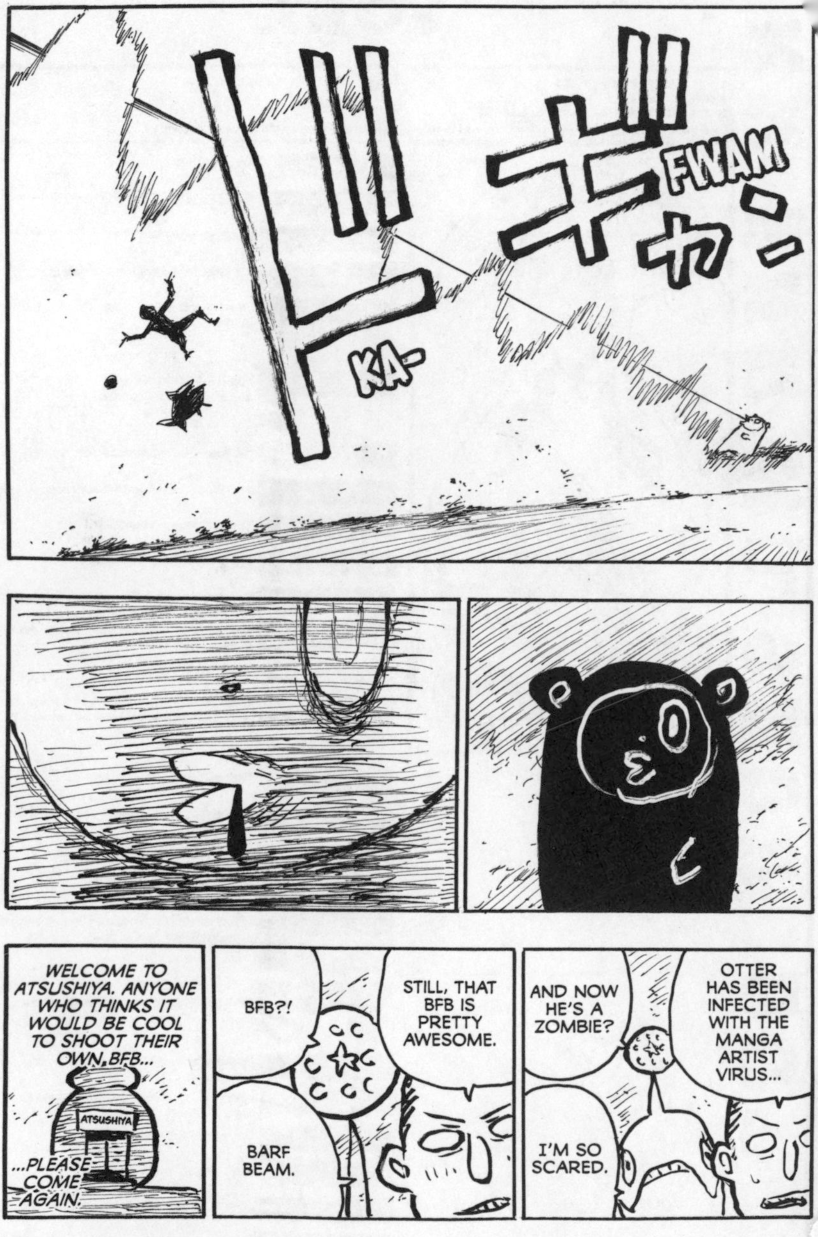
ギャー
FWAM
ド
KA-
OTTER HAS BEEN INFECTED WITH THE MANGA ARTIST VIRUS...
AND NOW HE'S A ZOMBIE?
I'M SO SCARED.
STILL, THAT BFB IS PRETTY AWESOME.
BFB?!
BARF BEAM.
WELCOME TO ATSUSHIYA. ANYONE WHO THINKS IT WOULD BE COOL TO SHOOT THEIR OWN BFB...
ATSUSHIYA
...PLEASE COME AGAIN.

YONA

AFFILIATION: THE EVANGELIST
RANK: ???
ABILITY: THIRD GENERATION PYROKINETIC
Uses heat to manipulate blood vessels and localized bodily swelling to change appearances.

Height	It depends♥
Weight	It depends♥
Age	No such thing!
Birthday	It's actually pretty rude to ask that.
Sign	I am myself a sign, so to speak. The sign of Me.
Bloodtype	You can't find your blood... sorry, that doesn't make any sense.
Nickname	Nicknamed the Wondiferous Artiste.
Self-Proclaimed	The Self-Proclaimed Wondiferous Artiste.
Favorite Foods	Those things humans eat.
Least Favorite Food	Anything with no emotion.
Favorite Music	Emotion turned into melody. It's beautiful.
Favorite Animal	Animals with high intellect. I suppose that means humans.
Favorite Color	Black, the combination of all colors. And white, the combination of all colors.
Favorite Type	We're all on the same team.
Respects	All artistes are worthy of respect.
Hates	Those who are not artistes.
Is Afraid Of	I feed off of fear. Doesn't it just make you so emotional?
Hobbies	I act according to my nature, so I don't have hobbies or any of that business.
Daily Routine	To put it in human terms, I follow my instincts.
Dream	I prefer to give dreams rather than to have them.
Shoe Size	Once again, it depends♥
Eyesight	I can see all kinds of things.
Favorite Subject	I'd love you to teach me everything.
Least Favorite Subject	Too many to name.

ENN ENN NO SHOUBOUTAI

Translation Notes:

Chivalrous with excitement, page 56

In Japanese, they have a word for "trembling with excitement," and that word is *musha-burui*, which literally means "the trembling of a warrior," presumably in anticipation of an upcoming battle or quest. Of course, Arthur is not satisfied to be a mere warrior (*musha*), because he is a knight (*kishi*), so he changes the word to the more worthy *kishi*-burui, or "trembling of a knight."

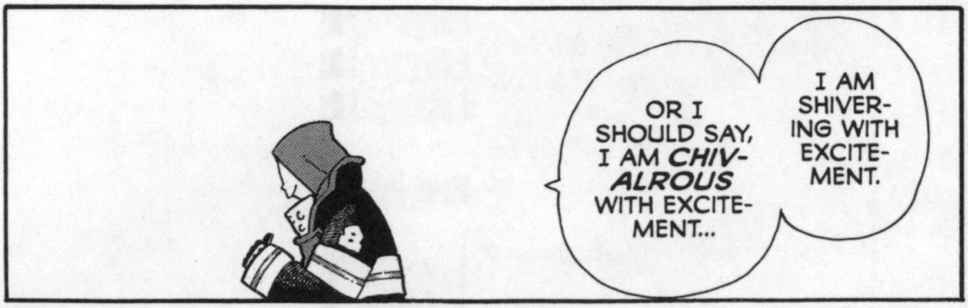
I AM SHIVERING WITH EXCITEMENT.
OR I SHOULD SAY, I AM *CHIVALROUS* WITH EXCITEMENT...

See voo play, page 185

This mysterious masked man appears to be trying to maintain his secret identity by speaking English, as opposed to Japanese, the language the others all speaking. However, the Japanese text is written with *hiragana* characters rather than the katakana characters that are more commonly used for foreign words, suggesting to the reader (or at least, the translators) that he is not confident in his pronunciation of this new vocabulary. The translators attempted to replicate this effect by misspelling non-English phrases, such as the French *s'il vous plait*, meaning "please."

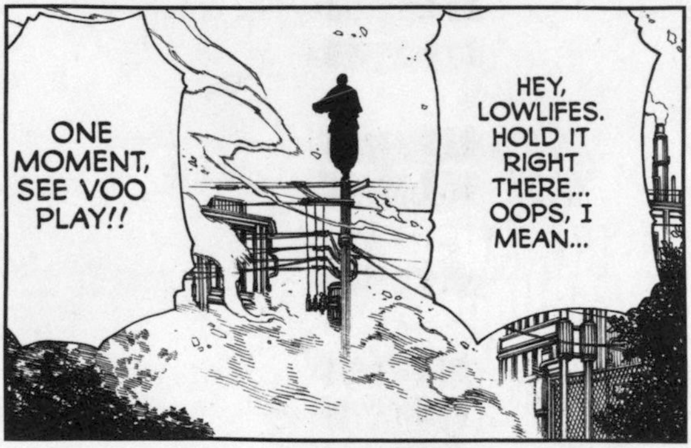
HEY, LOWLIFES. HOLD IT RIGHT THERE... OOPS, I MEAN...
ONE MOMENT, SEE VOO PLAY!!

YA

Fire Force 22
03/30/2021

A Kodansha Comics Trade Paperback Original
Fire Force 22 copyright © 2020 Atsushi Ohkubo
English translation copyright © 2021 Atsushi Ohkubo

Published in the United States by Kodansha Comics, an imprint of
Kodansha USA Publishing, LLC, New York.

Publication rights for this English edition arranged through
Kodansha Ltd., Tokyo.

First published in Japan in 2020 by Kodansha Ltd., Tokyo.

ISBN 978-1-64651-190-7

Printed in the United States of America.

www.kodanshacomics.com

9 8 7 6 5 4 3 2 1
Translation: Alethea Nibley & Athena Nibley
Lettering: AndWorld Design
Editing: Ryan Holmberg
Kodansha Comics edition cover design by Phil Balsman

Publisher: Kiichiro Sugawara

Director of publishing services: Ben Applegate
Associate director of operations: Stephen Pakula
Publishing services associated managing editor: Madison Salters
Assistant production manager: Emi Lotto, Angela Zurlo